Operations Management FOR DUMMIES®

A Wiley Brand

by Mary Ann Anderson, Dr. Edward Anderson, and Dr. Geoffrey Parker

FOR DUMMIES®

A Wiley Brand

Operations Management For Dummies®

Published by: **John Wiley & Sons, Inc.,** 111 River Street, Hoboken, NJ 07030-5774, www.wiley.com

Copyright © 2013 by John Wiley & Sons, Inc., Hoboken, New Jersey

Published simultaneously in Canada

No part of this publication may be reproduced, stored in a retrieval system or transmitted in any form or by any means, electronic, mechanical, photocopying, recording, scanning or otherwise, except as permitted under Sections 107 or 108 of the 1976 United States Copyright Act, without the prior written permission of the Publisher. Requests to the Publisher for permission should be addressed to the Permissions Department, John Wiley & Sons, Inc., 111 River Street, Hoboken, NJ 07030, (201) 748-6011, fax (201) 748-6008, or online at http://www.wiley.com/go/permissions.

Trademarks: Wiley, For Dummies, the Dummies Man logo, Dummies.com, Making Everything Easier, and related trade dress are trademarks or registered trademarks of John Wiley & Sons, Inc., and may not be used without written permission. All other trademarks are the property of their respective owners. John Wiley & Sons, Inc., is not associated with any product or vendor mentioned in this book.

For general information on our other products and services, please contact our Customer Care Department within the U.S. at 877-762-2974, outside the U.S. at 317-572-3993, or fax 317-572-4002. For technical support, please visit www.wiley.com/techsupport.

Wiley publishes in a variety of print and electronic formats and by print-on-demand. Some material included with standard print versions of this book may not be included in e-books or in print-on-demand. If this book refers to media such as a CD or DVD that is not included in the version you purchased, you may download this material at http://booksupport.wiley.com. For more information about Wiley products, visit www.wiley.com.

Library of Congress Control Number: 2013938098

ISBN 978-1-118-55106-6 (pbk); ISBN 978-1-118-55109-7 (ebk); ISBN 978-1-118-55107-3 (ebk); ISBN 978-1-118-55108-0 (ebk)

Manufactured in the United States of America

10 9 8 7 6 5 4 3 2 1

Contents at a Glance

Table of Contents

Introduction

*W*e like to think of operations management as the neurological system of a healthy business. It coordinates the behavior and system functionality of living, breathing organizations to ensure that they continue to grow and thrive in the real world. The more complex the organization, the more vital it is for its operations management to be strong and in good working order.

Successful operations management leaders tend to be the well-organized and systematic types of the world. They fuss and arrange and then ponder and tweak. They see the wrinkles and iron them out to ensure that their companies make the most of what they've got. And many people think operations managers thrive on bringing order to chaos, but this shouldn't be the case! In this book we show you how to plan operations and implement those plans so that your company's operations run smoothly — chaos-free.

Maintaining order and efficiency is a fact of life — in business, families, personal relationships, and other human systems. And operations management is essentially the science of managing resources and behavior. But unfortunately, this important field of study is often explained in a way that makes it sound like an exercise in advanced math instead of a vital part of corporate governance and strategy development.

We wrote this book to help you get a handle on the fundamentals of operations management and to make your life more comfortable when dealing with operations. Whether you'll actually be managing operations or just want to understand what goes on in operations, this book is for you. If you plan on taking an operations management course as part of your business major or MBA coursework, this book provides a foundation for your understanding. It will also be there for you when it's time to apply the concepts in real situations as you advance your career!

About This Book

Like all other *For Dummies* books, *Operations Management For Dummies* isn't a tutorial. It's a reference book that, we hope, provides you with as much information as you need on the fundamental concepts of operations management to succeed in your coursework and your entry-level tasks in the real world. Use this book as you need it. That is, don't feel pressured to read it cover to cover — although you'd no doubt be fascinated at every turn! You can jump right to the topics that are giving you nightmares, get the assurances you need, and be on your way with tips and insight that may not be available in your regular textbooks.

We've done our best to describe operations management concepts in a fun and lively way. We point out the most important theories, techniques, and ways of thinking about managing products, processes, services, supply chains, and projects without all the mind-numbing details, outdated examples, and complicated explanations that fill some other books on this topic. Here's a glimpse of the topics in this book:

- ✓ Evaluating and measuring current performance
- ✓ Designing processes to meet your objectives
- ✓ Improving your processes
- ✓ Estimating and predicting demand
- ✓ Planning and managing capacity
- ✓ Determining the right amount of inventory
- ✓ Getting the right products to the right place at the right time
- ✓ Selecting and managing suppliers
- ✓ Getting the gist of Six Sigma and lean production
- ✓ Planning and managing projects
- ✓ Scaling operations for the life cycle of your product

Read the chapters in any order, and feel free to go straight to the subjects that interest you. You don't need to bother with a bunch of stuff that you already know — although you may wonder how well you really know it. There is, after all, always room for improvement, right?

As you work your way through this book, keep in mind that sidebars and Technical Stuff icons are skippable. Reading these bits will certainly add to your understanding and appreciation of the topic, but you won't miss anything crucial if you skip over them.

Foolish Assumptions

We're well aware of the fact that you're a one-of-a-kind person with countless unique attributes, but as we wrote this book, we had to make some assumptions about our readers. Here's what we assume about you:

- ✓ You're smart, resourceful, and interested in how the world works.
- ✓ You have a new interest in operations management. You may be currently taking an introductory operations management course as part of your

business major or MBA studies and need help with some core concepts. Or you're planning to take an operations management course next semester, and you want to prepare by checking out some supplementary material.

✔ You may have just been promoted into a position of operations management from another field (that has happened to all three of the authors), and you need to learn how to manage operations fast.

✔ You may be focused on a different field of study and have an interest in what those OM folks do, or you may find yourself promoted into a management position and realize that operations are important to every field; time to get up to speed on OM principles.

✔ You've had algebra and statistics and remember enough of the basics to get by with a few gentle reminders.

Icons Used in This Book

To make this reference book easier to read and simpler to use, we include some icons to help you home in on certain types of information.

Any time you see this icon, you know the information that follows is so important that it's worth recalling after you close this book — even if you don't remember anything else you read.

This icon appears next to information that's interesting but not essential. Don't be afraid to skip these paragraphs.

This bull's-eye points out advice that can save you time when establishing and analyzing processes.

This icon is here to prevent you from making fatal mistakes in your operations management work.

Beyond the Book

In addition to the material in the print or e-book you're reading right now, this product comes with some access-anywhere goodies on the web. Check out the free Cheat Sheet at www.dummies.com/cheatsheet/operationsmanagement for helpful formulas and more.

Where to Go from Here

This isn't a novel — although you may find as many twists and turns as there are in the best whodunit. But this book is set up so you can follow the information in any given section or chapter without reading it cover to cover. It's possible for you to know what's going on even if you skip around.

The book is divided into independent parts so that you can, for instance, read all about managing risk without having to read anything about project management. Take a look at the table of contents to see what topics we cover where.

If you're brand-new to operations management, we suggest starting with Part 1. In this part you can find everything you need to know about processes. Regardless of your field or career path, this part can help you understand processes that affect everything you do.

If your interest is primarily related to quality, then you may want to start in Part III, which focuses on quality management and improvement and highlights the popular Six Sigma methodology. If you've recently been assigned to a product development team, then Part IV is likely to be your favorite; find the basics you need to get a solid start on your new job.

If you're not sure where to start, no problem — that's exactly what this book is for. Be vintage about it: Start at the beginning and read through to the end. We expect that you'll gain useful knowledge from every page that you can use to ace your operations management course and advance your career.

Part I

Getting Started with Operations Management

In this part . . .

- ✔ Get the lowdown on the fundamentals of operations management and understand why it's so essential to successful businesses.

- ✔ Learn how to document and improve your business processes in order to gain a decisive advantage over your comany's competitors.

- ✔ Figure out what you want to accomplish and then determine whether you have the processes in place to meet that goal. If your processes need improvement, find out how to improve them in a structured and systematic way.

- ✔ Discover how to overcome common process management challenges, such as shared resources, batching, and rework to keep things running as smoothly and efficiently as possible.

- ✔ Make your job as an operations manager easier by ensuring that you're designing processes that create a product in the best way possible, keeping costs low and profit margins high.

Chapter 1

Discovering the Fundamentals of Operations Management

*O*perations — a set of methods that produce and deliver products and services in pursuit of specific goals — are the heartbeat of every kind of organization, from iron foundries and hospital emergency wards to high finance and professional services. Well-designed operations enhance profitability. Poor operations, at best, equal ineffective processes and wasted resources. At worst, poor operations can drive a company out of business. Therefore, managing operations with competence is vital to meeting strategic goals and surviving financially.

In this chapter we point out what's part of operations and what isn't. We also describe key concepts in the world of operations and tell you what you can do to improve operations in a business or any other type of organization.

Defining Operations Management

When most people think of operations management, if any picture comes to mind at all, an image of a large factory billowing smoke often emerges. And, yes, factories that billow smoke are indeed performing operations, but they're only a small subset of everything that's involved with operations management. Ultimately, operations determine the cost, quality, and timing of every interaction an organization has with the people it serves.

In this section we tell you exactly what operations management is — and what it's not. Moreover, we point out why operations are such a critical part of an organization and why all departments must care about operations for an organization to be successful.

Getting beyond the smokestack

No job is so simple that it can't be done wrong.

—Message in a Chinese fortune cookie

set of
m

Operations management is the development, execution, and maintenance of effective *processes* related to activities done over and over, or to one-time major projects, to achieve specific goals of the organization.

Operations management covers much more than smokestacks or manufacturing parts and products; it also encompasses services and all sorts of projects and initiatives that groups of people undertake together. From restaurants and fast-food joints to medical services, art galleries, and law firms, operations management ensures that organizations minimize waste and optimize output and resource use for the benefit of customers as well as everyone else with skin in the game, or the *stakeholders*.

Doing something a little inefficiently one time is no big deal, but when you do something inefficiently over and over, hundreds or even millions of times per year, even little mistakes can add up to very expensive amounts of waste. Mistakes in an operation that result in defective products, even if they represent only 1 percent of total output, can alienate millions of customers. Similarly, if poorly designed operations result in habitually serving customers late, a company will eventually lose customers to better-functioning competitors.

In for-profit firms, operations management is concerned with the cost-effective operation and allocation of resources, including people, equipment, materials, and inventory — the stuff you use to provide goods or services for customers — to earn the big bucks and maximize your return on investment. Just look at the annual reports of big successful firms. Some, like ExxonMobil, take pride in their operational excellence. In the case of ExxonMobil, just 1 or 2 percentage points better energy efficiency or plant up-time can represent millions in additional profit.

In nonprofit organizations, managing resources is also vital. Here, operations management may be concerned primarily with maximizing a specific metric, such as people served while staying out of the red.

Seeing the relevance of operations management

Operations management is a fundamental part of any organization. In fact, *Forbes* magazine reported in 2011 that about three quarters of all CEOs came from an operations background. Not all these CEOs studied operations in school; only some of them did. Many majored in finance, marketing, information systems, or engineering and ended up in operations at some point in their careers.

Even if you don't want to be a CEO or ever work in operations, you'll probably have to work with operations people during your career. So consider these facts about the impact of operations on various business functions:

- **Engineering:** Engineers are notoriously great with numbers and focus. That doesn't always translate to being great with operations. Operations analysis is both quantitative and intuitive, and engineers without operations training can — and do! — waste millions of dollars when tasked to oversee operations. For maximum benefit, you need to evaluate the individual process in the context of the overall system of processes it connects to. So some operations knowledge can help engineers place their analysis of an individual process into an overall context of the operations system.

- **Finance:** Corporate finance folks exercise oversight over budgets, so having some operations knowledge can help this team make good decisions. For instance, when an operations leader asks for money to *de-bottleneck* a process (check out Chapter 3 for information on bottlenecks), knowing what this means tells you the intent is to increase the capacity of an existing operation. This almost always makes more economic sense than building a new plant. It also makes it easier to evaluate costs and benefits of the investment. Otherwise, you may suspect it's like spending money to put paint on an old jalopy.

- **Information technology (IT):** A big part of IT within some companies is to automate operations. Knowing the core principles of operations can help these folks build an operations superhighway instead of paving a cow path. Companies tend to easily accept the traditional way of doing things without question. There's a great temptation to simply automate an existing process with imbedded inefficiencies. Some knowledge of operations may help IT professionals to more effectively partner with operations management people to truly create competitive advantage by improving processes while they automate.

- **Marketing:** When the marketing folks come up with a new product idea or promotions concept, they need to talk to operations to find out whether it can be produced profitably. If the answer is no — operations managers are sometimes a grumpy lot — persuading them to find a solution may be easier if marketing can speak the language of operations and understand their concerns.

Understanding the Process of Operations

The field of operations management isn't always intuitive. Ultimately, the intent is to eliminate waste and maximize profitability. Depending on the type of organization and its specific goals, operations can be managed with a wide range of strategic approaches and techniques.

This section describes some of the major aspects of operations that often trip up people who study and work in this field.

Driving the business model

An organization's business model should influence operations strategy; likewise, operations strategy drives the business model (see Figure 1-1). The *business model* — which identifies the target market, the product or service available for sale, pricing, marketing, and overall budget — is intimately entwined with operations.

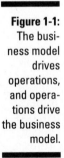

Figure 1-1:
The business model drives operations, and operations drive the business model.

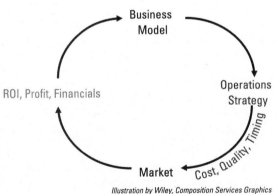

Illustration by Wiley, Composition Services Graphics

In other words, operations determine the cost, quality, and timing of the value proposition that a company delivers to its customers. Operations determine the customer experience, whether it's a service or a tangible product. If the customer experience is good, then financials also tend to be good — and there are always ways to further improve the business model (much more on continuous improvement later). If, on the other hand, operations and the customer experience are poor, then financials are also likely to be poor. This situation calls for a reevaluation of the business model, the operations strategy, or both.

In the pragmatic gray area of the real world, operations at a company may be independently good in some areas but out of alignment with the business model. For example, if the operations strategy emphasizes low cost, but the business model relies on using customization to obtain a higher markup from customers, then a company is functioning with fundamentally incompatible goals, making the "good" operations ineffective.

Recognizing the diversity of processes

Processes vary in thousands of ways for different kinds of organizations with different kinds of needs. Start-up firms need to scale up rapidly, and the restaurant business requires some artistry. Pharmaceutical companies must stay focused on strict regulations, and firms in the personal computer industry need to worry about their products' shelf life (find details on the product life cycle in Chapter 18). To manage operations effectively, you need to understand a company's processes in context of its business model and industry.

This section highlights some important characteristics of organizations that can help illustrate the nature of certain processes.

Customer interface

Processes vary quite a bit based on the amount of face time with customers they involve. Service processes that don't directly interface with customers, such as reconciling checks, are more like manufacturing processes than processes that involve interaction with customers. After all, reconciled checks, like pizzas or widgets, don't become upset if the resource processing them doesn't smile. Nor do they get confused by poor signage, waiting in line, or bad process design.

The customer interface aspect of operations also differs based on whether the customer is the end consumer, known as a *B2C relationship,* or another business, or *B2B relationship:*

- ✔ B2C firms tend to market products to a lot of customers who each purchase a small quantity of units.
- ✔ B2B firms tend to deal with a small number of customers with high quantity demands that require heavy customization and significant customer service.

In general, business customers are much less forgiving of late deliveries than end consumers.

Scale

The scale of an operation definitely impacts operations. Producing thousands of parts or serving thousands of customers per hour is quite different from handling only a few. If a company is working by the thousands, then automation may make a lot of sense because the fixed costs of automation can be spread out over many customers. A low-volume operation typically requires more flexible processes, which may rule out automation.

Customization

If a company's product or service is highly customized, then flexibility in processes is extremely important. Automation may not be practical. Producing products before a customer places an order is also impractical in many of these situations, and this may prevent a business from obtaining *economies of scale,* which refers to the fact that it becomes increasingly cheaper to produce a unit of something as unit volume grows. Customizing products usually means higher production costs per unit and higher prices for customers.

Customer priorities

Successful businesses know what matters most to their target customers: time, cost, or quality. If time is most important, you may try to produce the product before the customer orders it. If cost is the priority, maximizing economies of scale — possibly through level production runs or outsourcing (covered in Chapter 17) — is critical. An emphasis on quality may require more expensive materials and equipment to make the product.

Managing processes

Although processes vary in many ways, they also share some common characteristics that apply across a broad spectrum of operations.

Nearly all processes in operations have three major components:

- ✔ **Inventory:** This includes not only the *finished goods inventory* (products that are complete) but also jobs (products or services) that are only partly complete in your process (known as *work in progress,* or WIP).

- ✔ **Materials:** These are the items needed to make a product or provide a service.

- ✔ **Resources:** The equipment, information systems, and people in an operation that make the product or provide the service are considered resources.

Assuming that the business model is aligned with operations strategy, effectively managing inventory, materials, and resources achieves the two goals of operations management: efficiency and risk management. Here are some ways to manage these laudable goals:

- ✔ **Standardize the process and draw it out.** Before you try to modify any process, standardize it and all the operations within it. Drawing a standardized process is the first step of process management (see Chapter 2). And don't get hung up on making this perfect. Even a rough process drawing can help you spot trouble points in the process, and the drawing can be perfected later as you work to improve the process.

- ✔ **Use resources effectively.** The key to utilizing resources effectively is to find the bottleneck. The *bottleneck* is the resource that limits the capacity of a process, and it can be surprisingly hard to find. It's not necessarily the biggest machine in a process or the most expensive person you employ; it's simply that operation that is the slowest or most rate-limiting in the whole process chain.

  The best way to find the bottleneck is to determine which resource on average spends the most time working on each job (unit of product) that's completed by your process (find more on bottlenecks in Chapter 3).

  If you need more capacity, make sure to add it at the bottleneck; adding it anywhere else doesn't help and just wastes it. For non-bottleneck resources, resist the temptation to utilize them 100 percent of the time on the same job (unit of product) because this just ends up creating WIP that builds up.

- ✔ **Keep material moving.** Try to minimize the amount of time a job waits around in the process. This is especially important in face-to-face services or when a product is made to order, but using material quickly also matters in standard manufacturing. WIP is essentially tied-up cash that could be used for better purposes (such as collecting interest!). (Flip to Chapter 3 for details.)

✔ **Keep the process simple.** One mark of a simple process is an easy-to-read process flow diagram (check out Chapter 2 for advice on how to draw a process flow diagram). Complex processes are hard to schedule and manage; they accumulate lots of WIP and hide defects (see Chapter 5 for tips on simplifying processes).

✔ **Hedge against variability.** Variability in demand is a big problem for process management. If the company sells tangible product from a finished goods inventory, a company can carry extra inventory to ensure that unexpected surges of customer demand are satisfied. However, big inventories are costly. (See Chapter 6 for how to forecast demand and Chapter 8 to set inventories.) Extra capacity to make more finished goods is another tool for managing demand variability and is particularly critical in face-to-face services and make-to-order businesses. But capacity, too, can be pricey. (Find details on capacity in Chapter 7.) Finding the right balance of tools to handle demand variability can provide one of the biggest paybacks from operations management.

✔ **Don't fall in love with technology.** Avoid the misdirected comfort of assuming that just buying the fanciest information system can solve a company's slew of operational problems. The right technology and aggregate planning (see Chapter 9) can help, but these support tools are not cure-alls; they can't compensate for a basic mismatch of capacity with demand.

✔ **Manage the supply chain.** A product or service is only as good as the weakest link in the *supply chain,* the network of suppliers that provide the materials, services, and logistics that support an organization (see Chapter 10). If a company can make suppliers into actual partners in the business and integrate them tightly into product development and productivity improvement efforts, profitability follows (see Chapter 11).

✔ **Improve quality.** Figuring out what the customer actually wants and delivering it is everything in business (flip to Chapter 12). Continuously improving the quality of processes is necessary to keep up with changing customer expectations. Better quality can also reduce waste and improve profitability. Chapter 13 covers quality improvements.

✔ **Realize it's a system thing.** Operations aren't about doing one thing right. They're about doing a lot of things right — at the same time. This means using resources and materials efficiently, producing high quality goods, and maintaining a reliable supply chain while keeping things simple and managing risk. Got all that? Chapter 11 presents one especially effective way to achieve this: the lean process methodology.

Handling special situations

Operations managers must sometimes cope with a number of special situations. These range from one-off projects to outsourcing processes and may include managing immature or obsolete products. Here's some advice on managing special situations.

One-off projects

Though most of this book concentrates on *processes* (things that a company does over and over), operations managers must often deal with projects that are executed only once. However, some projects are big enough and occur often enough that reusable processes for managing them can emerge (see Chapter 14).

Planning is important for any operation, but even more so for projects. Mistakes or failures in upfront planning can't be gradually fixed through later tweaks the way they can be for routine ongoing processes. (For information on planning projects, see Chapter 15.) Another part of the problem is that, by definition, a one-time project hasn't been done before, so upfront estimates need to be created without data from past performance. This is part of the reason that so many projects are completed late, over budget, or both. (Find more on project estimation in Chapters 15 and 16.) Allowing for estimate error and planning for contingencies are critical parts of project planning.

Good project management also requires aggressive risk management. Because projects aren't repetitive processes, risks can be harder to identify and manage. Fortunately, a few good tools are available; among them are risk registers to help identify, mitigate, and track risks. (Check out Chapter 16 for more on risk.)

Outsourcing

There are a lot of good reasons to outsource, but outsourcing isn't a panacea for poorly considered business models and operations planning. Companies need to carefully identify what work to perform in-house and what to outsource. Then, after an outsourcing relationship is established, a structure to manage it effectively is vital. Be sure to figure out how to manage contracts, specifications, managerial and co-located personnel, and information-sharing structures. (Outsourcing is the focus of Chapter 17.)

Product life cycles

Operations must adapt to the product life cycle. For products at an early stage of the life cycle, companies need to put a premium on flexibility for processes. As the product or service takes off and enters its growth phase, operations become more about scalability. When a product is mature, reducing costs while maintaining quality is the main focus. And as the product declines, the challenge is to figure out how to reduce commitment to the product without alienating customers. (Find more about product life cycle issues in Chapter 18.)

Meeting the Challenges

The mountain of challenges to implementing good operations management may seem daunting, but a healthy dose of common sense and old-fashioned experience can help you chip away at them bit by bit. In this section, we describe some common operations management challenges and point out why it's important to overcome them.

Firefighting

The field of operations management is packed with adrenaline junkies and pressure hounds. But crises provide a high potential for inefficiency, mistakes, and customer disappointment. The goal of an operations manager is to create processes that respond smoothly to pressure so crises don't erupt.

Technology

Despite what many people may believe, automation and computerization aren't the best answers to every problem in the world of operations. After all, an automated bad process is still a bad process. In fact, automation may make a bad process even worse because automating often hides problems and makes some issues more difficult to solve. Fix the process first and then automate it.

Similarly, enterprise management software (EMS) systems can't improve a company's processes. As with most data systems, garbage in equates to garbage out. An EMS system, no matter how expensive it is, can't improve a bad process. So clean up the process and then bring in the information technology to help the new process along if appropriate.

Complacency

People in various parts of an organization may assume that what happens in operations is simple. Operations managers may get resistance when they try to standardize, measure, or improve processes. A common retort to process improvement efforts is, "We've always done it this way, so why change?" But if a process is costing money for the firm to complete, then it's worth trying to do it more efficiently and less expensively. If the process is sometimes done wrong, then it's costing even more — money or maybe even customers. No business can afford not to take the time to standardize, measure, and improve processes.

Metrics

For one reason or another, some organizations use performance metrics in ways that can be counterproductive to good operations. For example, *utilization,* or how busy your resources are, is often a defining metric in operations. Logically this seems to make sense, because who wouldn't want the resources working as much as they could? However, over-utilization often leads to excessive inventory.

As a metric, utilization is a good idea — but sometimes only in the abstract. For example, labor utilization at a workstation measures how many hours a company is paying its people versus how many work hours are going into the parts at the workstation. When this metric is divorced from its context, real problems can emerge. Any non-bottleneck resource that's working faster than the bottleneck is just going to create excess WIP that ties up cash, increases defects, and reduces material usage efficiency (see Chapter 3).

Say one workstation is already working faster (putting the wheels on toy cars, for example) than the next workstation (painting the toy cars in different colors) in the process. If you increase labor utilization at the wheels workstation, you're just going to increase the pile of unpainted cars. So you want to move some of the workers from wheels to painting to improve the overall productivity.

In short, any metric that's stripped from its context may be lying to you. The only important question is this: Is the change you're proposing going to make more money for the firm over the long run?

Perspective

Possibly the most important source of information for improving operations is a company's line workers and front-line staff. Curiously, these valuable people seem to be neglected in the process of designing processes and fine-tuning operations, yet they have the most accurate information about how things really work.

An operations manager may be better educated than the line workers, but no one knows the challenges and opportunities of producing a product or delivering a service better than those who actually do the work. That's why every legitimate process improvement methodology leverages the line workers' knowledge (see Chapter 13). And if a company ignores employees' suggestions on how to improve its processes, it runs the risk of demotivating the very people who make the process run.

Outsourcing

The idea that outsourcing everything and becoming a marketing company is a viable strategy is a very real challenge for operations professionals. Outsourcing can be a good way for a company to reduce cost and improve quality by leveraging the expertise of its supply chain. However, by outsourcing critical operations, a firm can lose its competitive advantage and open the market door to competitors. For more on how to decide what operations to outsource, see Chapter 17.

Chapter 2

Defining and Evaluating Processes

· ·

In This Chapter

▶ Illustrating processes using process maps

▶ Employing various metrics to measure a system's performance

· ·

A company with well-designed and perfectly functioning processes has a decisive advantage over its competitors, primarily because it uses resources to generate profits and doesn't waste them. And the job of ensuring that a company's processes are profitable belongs to — you guessed it — the operations manager.

Technically speaking, a *process* is a collection of operations that are connected by the movement of goods and information that transform various inputs into useful — and often consistent — outputs. In other words, a process is any series of actions that a company repeats over and over, ideally with the same result(s).

How well a business performs processes matters. Not much harm is done if a firm isn't effective at completing a one-time, isolated process, but inefficiencies affecting ongoing critical tasks usually add up to big problems (financial and organizational) over the long run.

The first step toward meaningful process improvements is finding out what's working and what's not. Unfortunately, few firms make the effort to even document their existing processes — let alone measure their performance! So initiatives to improve processes end up chewing through valuable resources, only to spit out new processes that fail to improve efficiency and boost the bottom line.

In this chapter we explain the value of documenting processes and show you how to do it with process flow diagrams. You can also find definitions for common terminology used in the operations management world and get a handle on metrics used to assess process performance.

Mapping Processes

A well-defined process doesn't have many special cases or deviations, so documenting or describing business processes in a clear and practical way ensures that everyone involved — employees, managers, and stakeholders — can see how specific operations relate to others and what happens at each point in a process. Clear documentation can also help with employee training and performance assessments, operational analysis, and other business functions. Operations managers usually use *process maps* (which are also called *flow diagrams, flow maps,* or *flowcharts*) to represent processes.

Figure 2-1 shows a black-box process for converting inputs to outputs. The term *black box* refers to the inability to see the transformation that's occurring within the process. The only things visible are what goes *in* and what comes *out* of the process.

Figure 2-1:
Transformation activity is hidden in a black-box process.

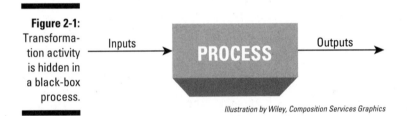

Inputs   **PROCESS**   Outputs

Illustration by Wiley, Composition Services Graphics

Process maps often include these specific symbols, as shown in Figure 2-2, for a very simple process:

✔ **Operations:** Usually represented as rectangles in a diagram, *operations* are the steps, workstations, activities, or tasks performed to produce the output. Some operations managers — as well as different flowchart diagramming programs and standards — separate operations into categories such as transformation, inspection, documentation, and transportation. In that case, different symbols, such as the circle for inspection, may be incorporated.

✔ **Flows:** Represented as the lines and arrows in a diagram, *flows* can either be goods or information. For example, in a diagram illustrating the production of scotch, the flows would relate to the movement of barley, yeast, and so on. On the other hand, in a diagram illustrating the mortgage process, the flows may represent mortgage applications, e-mailed approvals, and so on. If more than one type of material or information is used in a process, operations managers generally use a different color or a dashed line to represent the different flows.

Process flow diagrams generally run left to right, but they can some-times run from top to bottom or even right to left. And flows don't always face forward. For example, if material must return to a worksta-tion for additional processing or rework because of a defect or other reason, the flows may point backward.

✔ **Delays:** Some operations managers use upward-facing triangles to rep-resent delays; others use down triangles. Triangles mean the same thing whether they point up or down. A delay can be any of the following types of inventory:

  • **Raw material inventory (RMI):** Inventory that has not yet entered the process. No value-added activities have been performed.

  • **Work in progress (WIP):** Inventory that the process has worked on but not completed.

  • **Finished goods inventory (FGI):** Inventory that the process has completed.

  Check out Chapter 8 for more on inventory.

✔ **Resources:** Labor and capital equipment such as computers are exam-ples of resources. In Figure 2-2, the programmer needs a computer to perform Operation C. Find more information on managing resources in Chapters 3 and 4.

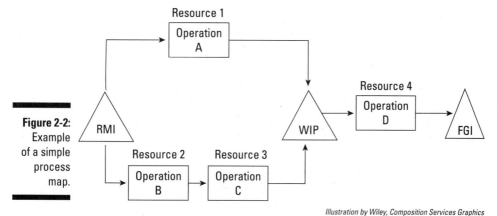

Figure 2-2: Example of a simple process map.

Illustration by Wiley, Composition Services Graphics

Regardless of which symbols you use, being consistent across process maps is important to avoid confusion.

Distinguishing between operations and delays

Operations are tasks, activities or actions that transform an input in some useful way. *Delays* are moments in the process when the input is waiting for another operation, but no further change is occurring. Often, however, people mistake operations for delays.

For example, in the production of wine, after several operations that transform the solid grapes into liquid, the winemaker leaves the resulting liquid to sit for some time in barrels to age (often for several years). A common process-mapping mistake is to represent this operation as a delay point (triangle in our process flow diagram) when, in fact, it is a critical operation. After all, the aging process is often the difference between sour grape juice and a fine adult beverage.

 When deciding whether something is an operation or a delay, ask yourself: If I removed this step from the process, would it alter my end product? If it will, then it's an operation; if not, then it's just a delay. And if it doesn't contribute to the end product, it should be removed as waste.

Not all operations add value, but delays never do. Delays just increase the time required to create a product or serve a customer. Removing delays in a process has no effect on the quality of the end product.

Identifying waste

Though delays are always non-value-added (NVA), operations can be value-added (VA), business-value-added (BVA), or NVA. If you're wondering why you'd even have NVA operations, keep in mind that NVA can describe an operation that's necessary for the current methods but doesn't add value to the product or service from a customer perspective. These are the activities that you need to identify and eliminate to improve the process.

Business-value-added operations are activities that add no value to the customer's experience but are necessary from a business perspective. An example of a BVA activity in services is an engineer who documents his time on each project to enable the department manager to determine how much of the engineer's work to bill to each project. A classic manufacturing example involves inspections for which data is used to determine whether a process is stable. Though these activities benefit the business, they're of no direct value to the customer.

An operations manager may consider BVA activities for elimination or reduction, but he must first consider their impact on the rest of the business. For example, too many inspections are generally a waste of time. But some inspections, such as those that test finished goods inventory at the end of the line, are often necessary to avoid sending defective components to the customer.

Waste is the act or instance of using or expending something carelessly, extravagantly, or to no purpose. Processes may have many types of waste, and locating and eliminating waste is crucial to improving efficiency. Here are some common sources of waste in operations:

- ✔ **Defective or substandard production** wastes resources by creating outputs that don't have sufficient quality to fulfill customer requirements. In some cases, these goods or services need to be fixed. Yet, in manufacturing, fixing defective products is often not worth the effort, so the goods must be scrapped, which means all the material and resources that created the defective product is wasted. Find more on the effects of poor quality in Chapter 4. We cover quality improvement in Chapters 12 and 13.

- ✔ **Idle time** results when resources have no material to work on. Find out how to manage this type of waste in the "Analyzing a process" sidebar at the end of the chapter.

- ✔ **Material movement** is any movement that doesn't directly change the material and support production. Some material movement is necessary in any process to get it from one operation to another. But you want to reduce this source of waste as much as possible because no value is added to the product during material movement.

  For example, moving an empty bottle on a conveyor belt to a filling spigot, then to a bottle capper, and finally to a carton is necessary movement to produce a bottle of beer. Moving that carton of beer to a holding area and then a warehouse are examples of wasteful material movement when you could have put the carton straight onto the delivery truck.

- ✔ **Movement of people and machines** that doesn't contribute directly to the value of the product or service is a waste of resources. The goal is to reduce this movement as much as possible because either employees or equipment (such as conveyor belts or robots) must perform the movement, which means they're not working on productive operations.

- ✔ **Overproduction** occurs when a company produces more items than is needed. See Chapter 3 for details on what can happen if a process overproduces. Find out how to manage the production rate so it matches customer demand in Chapter 8, and get information on production control strategies to prevent overproduction in Chapter 11.

- ✔ **Processing waste,** such as defective WIP, is effort that adds no value to the product or service but requires time and raw material. Eliminating this kind of waste is hugely important for maximizing profitability and quality.

- ✔ **Waiting** results when products or customers must wait for resources. This is represented by delays in the process map. We cover how to manage wait times in Chapter 7.

Developing a process map

Creating accurate and useful process maps requires considerable time and resources, but these maps are vital to any meaningful process evaluation and improvement effort. Here's some advice for creating an accurate process map:

- ✔ **Always ask why.** While constructing an initial process map, find out why certain actions are being done. In many cases, the answer is "We've always done it this way" or "That's the way they told me to do it." The question "why" often reveals good places to begin improvement efforts.

- ✔ **Be prepared to revise the process map.** When you first complete a process map, consider it a rough draft. You won't get everything right the first time around. In fact, the first few times you review your process map with line workers and management (which you must do!), new wrinkles in the process will inevitably turn up. You may even find disagreements among employees on how a process works and need to personally observe the operation to get it right on the map.

When developing your first version of a process map, assume nothing is trivial. Document everything, including informal communications. The piece of information shared at the coffee machine every morning may turn out to be what keeps a certain process moving.

- ✔ **Beware of resistance.** Feeling protective and even defensive is human nature, especially if someone feels that her job is at stake or otherwise threatened. Employees often view the mapping process and process-improvement projects as a way for company leaders to reduce payrolls and eliminate jobs. It is important to explain the purpose and benefits of the project before you start. The general approach could include the message that process improvement is necessary to keep the company competitive and that a company must be competitive to provide jobs. Be aware of possible resistance during the mapping process and carefully examine what's occurring at each process step to make certain that what you're being told is actually being done so that you can build an accurate map.

- ✔ **Create a hierarchy of maps.** Process maps can become very complex, and creating maps with increasing detail may be important to some businesses. Start with a high-level aggregated representation of the process in question and then break down each operation until you reach a level where meaningful analysis can take place. You want to avoid making a single map that's so complicated it's difficult to understand and communicate to stakeholders.

Determining what level of breakdown is necessary for a given process can be difficult. A high-level map that references general activities is great for communicating with upper management, who tend to be primarily concerned with where handoffs occur between groups/departments or across reporting structures. More detail is important when a process map is intended to train employees or inform middle managers, who need to see where changes occur in resource requirements.

✔ **Document everything necessary to perform each task and the output of each task.** A record that includes all resources and any information needed to complete a given task ensures consistency. Many people forget that the information an operation generates can be as important as the tangible resources.

For example, on a process-improvement project, an operation was identified as non-value-added and eliminated, but it actually produced a vital report needed later in the process. When the operations management team members completed the initial process map, they overlooked the existence and importance of this document, so when they implemented the new process, the system broke down because of the lack of information in the report.

✔ **Solicit input from all levels of the organization.** It's important to obtain input from the range of people involved in the process. Conduct interviews with those on the line doing the actual work as well as with company leaders.

We're routinely surprised by how many managers don't know exactly how work gets done in their firm. A fatal operations mistake is developing a process map with only management involvement.

✔ **Walk the process yourself.** If possible, observe the process in question. Often, information from front-line staff, line workers, and managerial data is wrong or misleading. If what you see and what you're told don't match, find out why discrepancies exist. Through direct observation and follow-up conversations, you may discover critical insight into why a process behaves the way it does.

Evaluating the Elements of a System

After you map out your process, you need a way to measure its performance, but traditional financial metrics don't often give operations managers insight into how their processes are performing. For example, return on investment (profit from the resources divided by the cost of those resources) can be misleading because it doesn't tell you how much waste is actually involved in a process.

In this section, we introduce common metrics used to determine how well a process is really performing. Many of these metrics are known by other names, so we include the alternate names when we're aware of them.

Checking productivity

Productivity provides a meaningful measure for an operations manager because it evaluates an operation at the individual process level.

Productivity measures how well a process uses its resources, typically defined as the ratio of the value of outputs to the value of inputs:

$$\text{productivity} = \frac{\text{value of outputs}}{\text{value of inputs}}$$

The outputs of a manufacturing process are the goods or services (or both) that the process creates. The inputs include materials, labor, capital equipment, computers, and energy needed to create the outputs. To be profitable, a firm's productivity must be greater than 1. In other words, the value of outputs must exceed the value of inputs.

Considering capacity

The most common metric you'll encounter is capacity. *Capacity* is how much output can be produced in a specified period of time with no losses to *yield* (percentage of parts that are "good") or *downtime* (time the resource can't operate). Common measures of capacity are products per hour or clients per day. Capacity is a measure of the most the operation can produce if it's unconstrained. In other words, if the resource always has material to work on and can work without interruption, how much can it produce in any time period? See Chapter 7 for a detailed discussion of capacity.

You can express capacity on both an operational and system level. Each operation in a process has a certain capacity, and every process has a capacity. The upper limit of a process's capacity is determined by the system's slowest operation.

Clocking cycle time

Cycle time is the minimum possible time between completion of successive units. It's simply the inverse of capacity. Cycle time = 1/capacity.

A common measure of cycle time is minutes per product produced. For example, in automobile assembly plants, cycle times are around 60 seconds per car. This doesn't mean that it takes 60 seconds to produce a car; it means that every 60 seconds, a car is completed by the process.

A typical cycle time in services is one hour per customer. Again, this doesn't mean that each customer takes one hour to get through the entire process, but that the average time between one customer completing the process and the next is one hour when the process is operating at capacity.

Like capacity, you express cycle time in terms of a single operation as well as the overall system.

Don't confuse cycle time with flow time, which we define in the section "Going with the flow time" later in this chapter.

Getting a handle on constraints

Every process has a constraint, or *bottleneck* — the resource that limits production of any process. The bottleneck is the slowest operation in the system, meaning it has the longest cycle time and lowest capacity. The bottleneck determines how much a process can produce. In other words, the capacity and cycle time of any system — no matter how fast every other operation in a process works — can't exceed that of the bottleneck. Figure 2-3 illustrates a bottleneck.

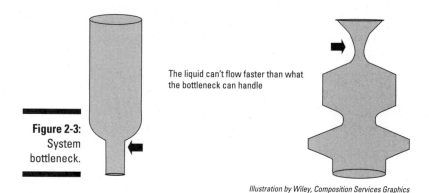

The liquid can't flow faster than what the bottleneck can handle

Figure 2-3: System bottleneck.

Illustration by Wiley, Composition Services Graphics

When you're trying to identify a bottleneck, be sure to actually observe the operation in question instead of relying on published equipment specifications, because specifications are typically calculated under optimum operating conditions and can vary significantly from what you experience.

Also, keep in mind that identifying the bottleneck can be especially tricky if a resource performs more than one operation in a process or operates in more than one process. For example, a receptionist in a doctor's office not only greets patients when they enter but also collects payments and schedules their next appointments when they leave. The receptionist is performing more than one operation in a process (a patient visit). Similarly, a bank employee who helps a customer with the loan application process and also performs a function in the process for opening new checking accounts for the same or a different customer is performing operations in two separate processes. Both of these situations require special analysis. See Chapter 4 for the how-to on analyzing a process with shared resources.

A quick and easy way to identify a potential bottleneck is to take a walk through your facility. Because the bottleneck is the slowest operation, a pileup of inventory or people waiting for the operation is often in front of the bottleneck. Use this as a guide, not as a diagnostic approach, because other factors such as overproduction (see the "Analyzing a process" sidebar at the end of the chapter) or cycle time variability at a single operation in the process can also lead to pileups.

Talking thruput and takt time

Thruput represents how much usable output an operation or a process actually produces in a specified period of time. Thruput is always less than or equal to capacity because, by definition, you can't produce more than the capacity. If thruput is less than the capacity of the bottleneck, then it equals the arrival rate of material for customers. Thruput is also sometimes referred to as *throughput,* the *thruput rate,* or *flow rate.*

Takt time has the same relation to thruput that cycle time has to capacity. Takt time is the average time between the completion of two successive flow units and is equal to the inverse of thruput.

$$\text{Takt Time} = \frac{1}{\text{Thruput}}$$

Takt time, which is sometimes referred to as *actual cycle time,* is always greater than or equal to the cycle time. In fact, comparing takt times and cycle times can often identify waste in a process when the process isn't producing what it's capable of. Identifying why there's a difference in the times and fixing the problem should increase the thruput. Visit Chapter 3 to see how to do this.

Going with the flow time

While cycle time represents the minimum possible time between the completion of two successive jobs, *flow time* is the time it takes one unit to get completely through a process from beginning to end.

Many organizations confusingly use the term *cycle time* to represent flow time, cycle time, and takt time. We know this is confusing. Understanding how your organization defines and distinguishes among these concepts is critical because the terms have no standard definition use in all sources. For clarity, we've separated the three concepts.

Another terminology trap is that some companies use *thruput time* as a synonym for *flow time* but never use it for *takt time*. For clarity, we avoid the use of *thruput time* in this book.

The best way to illustrate the difference between flow time and cycle time is to look at an assembly line producing automobiles.

- ✔ **Cycle time:** If production is occurring continuously, the cycle time is the period between the completion of one car and the next. In most automotive plants, this is somewhere around 60 seconds.

- ✔ **Flow time:** The flow time is the amount of time that any one car spends on the assembly line from start to finish. The flow time for a car is around 8 to 16 hours. This is the sum of each operation's cycle time and any time spent waiting in queues along the way (delays). (See Chapter 7 for details on how to calculate flow times and wait times.)

The *rush order flow time* represents the time it takes for one flow unit (a car, a customer, a dozen cookies) to go through the system from beginning to end without any waiting. It's simply the flow time minus the wait, and you can often calculate it as the sum of all the operation cycle times. However, if some of the operations can occur simultaneously, the picture is more complex (see Chapter 3).

The *process cycle efficiency* is the ratio of rush order flow time to the flow time. Process cycle efficiency is always less than or equal to 1; this metric reveals how much of the flow time is wasted in waiting.

Monitoring utilization

Utilization is the ratio of time that a resource spends actually working on a product or performing services over the total time available. You can calculate utilization by dividing what you get out of a resource by what you should get. For example, if you have a machine that can produce 100 parts an hour and it's only producing 75, then the utilization of the machine is 75%. Utilization is always less than or equal to 100%. Utilization is equal to thruput divided by capacity or cycle time divided by takt time.

Utilization can be the most dangerous metric of system performance. Maximizing utilization can lead to overproduction and excess inventory as well as unnecessary use of resources. You should manage a process based on actual demand or on matching the capacity of the bottleneck if demand exceeds the capacity of the bottleneck. Flip to Chapter 3 for more on overproduction and to find out how to manage bottlenecks.

Analyzing a process

Understanding how to calculate process metrics and what they mean can be difficult, especially when starting out. The best way to get a handle on process analysis is to look at an example. The following example illustrates a simple customer service process.

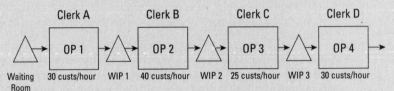

Illustration by Wiley, Composition Services Graphics

In this figure, customers arrive and sit in the waiting room until Clerk A is available to perform Operation 1 (OP 1). Customers then proceed to Operation 2 (OP 2), Operation 3 (OP 3), and Operation 4 (OP 4), which are performed by Clerk B, Clerk C, and Clerk D. A waiting area for customers exists between each operation. The capacity of each operation is noted under the operation. Note that *custs/hour* stands for customers per hour.

1. **Identify the bottleneck** by looking at the capacity or the cycle time of each operation. The bottleneck is the resource with the least capacity or the greatest cycle time. Cycle time is the inverse of the operations capacity. Here are the cycle times for each operation in the figure:

> OP 1: 1 hour/30 customers = 2 minutes/customer
>
> OP 2: 1 hour/40 customers = 1.5 minutes/customer
>
> OP 3: 1 hour/25 customers = 2.4 minutes/customer
>
> OP 4: 1 hour/30 customers = 2 minutes/customer

The bottleneck of this process is Clerk C performing OP 3 with a capacity of 25 customers per hour and a cycle time of 2.4 minutes per customer. The system can't process more than 25 customers per hour with a cycle time of 2.4 minutes because this is the capacity of the bottleneck.

2. **Find thruput and takt time** at the system level. Capacity is the maximum that a resource can produce, while the thruput is what the resource is actually producing. The cycle time is the minimum time between successive units, and the takt time is the actual time. Many factors influence the actual versus the theoretical. Operations managers must know the thruput and capacity of their systems. Great process improvement opportunities may exist where there's a difference between these two metrics.

3. **Identify the flow time and rush order flow time (ROFT)**. In this example, the shortest time that a product or customer can complete the process (the ROFT) is calculated as the sum of the cycle times, which is 7.9 minutes, so it takes at least 7.9 minutes for a customer to get through the system. You can't calculate the flow time with the available information because you have no way to know how long a customer spends waiting in each of the waiting areas. You can only observe the flow time by measuring the actual time it takes the customer or product to complete the entire process.

4. **Calculate utilization** based on what's called the *material release policy.* You must decide when an operation will work. Here are three possible policies:

Case 1: Pushing each operation to work as fast as it can: In this case, resources work as long as there's something to work on, regardless of whether other resources can keep up with the pace. In the case of manufacturing, products are produced regardless of actual demand. This policy produces the highest utilizations:

Clerk A: Assuming that a customer is always in the waiting room, Clerk A is always working with a utilization of 100%.

Clerk B: Customers proceed to WIP 1 after OP 1. Because Clerk A processes 30 customers per hour, 30 customers per hour arrive in WIP 1. Clerk B at OP 2 is able to process all the customers that arrive because her capacity is 40 customers per hour. Clerk B's utilization is 30/40, or 75%.

Clerk C: After OP 2, the customers advance to WIP 2 and wait for Clerk C at OP 3. Although Clerk B can process 40 customers per hour, she's limited by what Clerk A processed and only delivers 30 customers per hour to WIP 2. Although 30 customers arrive, Clerk C is the bottleneck, processing 25 customers per hour and having a 100% utilization.

As you probably notice, customers arrive faster in WIP 2 than Clerk C can process. This results in a continuously growing WIP 2. If this sparks your curiosity about what happens to the system in this scenario, flip to Chapter 7 to find out.

Clerk D: After Clerk C, the bottleneck, completes his task, customers go to WIP 3 to wait for Clerk D at OP 4. Customers arrive at WIP 3 at the rate of 25 customers per hour. Clerk D can process customers at the rate of 30 customers per hour and has a utilization of 25/30, which is 83.3%.

Case 2: Releasing materials or customers into your process at the speed of your bottleneck: If you're lucky enough to enjoy demand that's greater than or equal to your capacity, and you want to avoid the overproduction, then you release customers (material) only at the speed of your bottleneck. Here are your utilizations:

Clerk A: This clerk works at the speed of the bottleneck, which is 25 customers per hour. His utilization is 25/30, or 83.3%.

Clerk B: 25 customers per hour arrive in WIP 1, and Clerk B's utilization is 25/40, or 62.5%.

Clerk C: Because this clerk is the bottleneck and customers are being processed at his speed, his utilization is 100% (25/25).

Clerk D: As in Case 1, customers arrive at the rate of 25 per hour, and Clerk D has the capacity to process 30 customers per hour. Clerk D's capacity is 83.3%.

Case 3: Processing customers as they arrive: If your capacity is greater than your current demand, then you process customers as they arrive. If only 20 customers arrive per hour, here are the utilizations of each clerk:

Clerk A: 20/30 or 66.7%

Clerk B: 20/40 or 50%

Clerk C: 20/25 or 80%

Clerk D: 20/30 or 66.7%

The following table illustrates the dangers of managing based on utilization. Is the high utilization in Case 1 useful? Probably not. If demand is greater than or equal to the capacity of the

(continued)

(continued)

bottleneck, then you want to introduce material into your process only at the rate that the bottleneck can process it. The high utilizations of Clerks A and B only lead to a buildup of inventory in WIP 2 in front of Clerk C, the bottleneck. But if your demand is less than your capacity, you want to release material at the rate of demand, as in Case 3. Although doing so results in the lowest utilizations, it also prevents unnecessary buildup of inventory. For a closer look at the links among utilization, demand, capacity, and inventory, see Chapters 6, 7, and 8, which cover demand forecasting, capacity planning, and inventory management, respectively.

Comparison of Utilization Rates

Clerk	Case 1	Case 2	Case 3
Clerk A	100%	83.3%	66.7%
Clerk B	75%	62.5%	50%
Clerk C	100%	100%	80%
Clerk D	83.3%	83.3%	66.7%

Accounting for variability

When measuring your process, be aware that *variability* always exists in any process. Variability can influence your metrics and may lead you to make incorrect conclusions. Here are some different types of variability:

- **Individual variability:** When an employee performs an operation, variation exists in how fast he performs the task each time. Aside from the physical ability of an individual to complete a task, factors such as time of day and day of the week can affect how fast the employee processes each unit. Take measurements at different times to capture this variation. (Check out Chapter 12 for details on process variability.)

- **Material variability:** People often overlook the effect of the non-labor inputs in a process. The quality of material inputs may influence how long a particular operation takes if an operation needs to adjust its processing to accommodate varying input conditions. For example, the cycle time of a sanding operation varies based on the roughness of the material.

- **Product mix:** If different products are created utilizing the same process or if customers with different requirements are served, you must take into account the product/customer mix if the different products have different cycle times. Identifying the true constraint becomes increasingly difficult if products have significantly different cycle times.

- **Staff variability:** People doing the same task vary in how quickly they can complete the work, and this type of variability is usually greater than individual variation. If different people are assigned to perform the same task, be sure to measure the cycle time of each person — or gather a representative sample.

Chapter 3

Designing Processes
to Meet Goals

*B*efore you can begin designing smart processes, you need to know what you want to accomplish. We're talking about establishing goals. Defining meaningful goals for a process requires knowing what really matters to your customers and having a clear sense of the anticipated demand for the process outcome (see Chapter 6). With these prerequisites in the bag, you can design a process to meet your goals and expectations.

In this chapter we show you how to design a process that reduces flow time and maximizes capacity. We also point out how to use line balancing and flexible resources to improve process performance. The key to improving a process is to follow a structured process improvement plan instead of trying to wing it. Without this structured plan you'll find yourself lost, wasting valuable time and resources. Keep your eye on the ball; the intent here is continuous improvement. Always look for ways to improve your processes because there is always room for improvement.

Getting Started with Process Improvement

Companies spend a lot of time and resources on process improvement projects that fail to produce the desired results. A primary reason that many projects fall short of expectations is because they fail to follow a structured approach. Documenting where a process has been and where it needs to go provides a road map — with directions — that can save an enormous amount of time and resources that may otherwise be wasted on dead ends and cul-de-sacs. How novel, right?

Follow these steps when undertaking an improvement project:

1. **Map your process (see Chapter 2 for info on how to do this).**

2. **Determine your current process metrics (also described in Chapter 2).**

3. **Determine whether you have enough capacity to meet your demand requirements.**

4. **Decide what process metrics you need to improve and set goals for each.**

5. **Use the process improvement techniques presented in this chapter to design changes that will accomplish your desired goals.**

6. **Draw the new process map, implement the design changes, and observe the new process.**

7. **Reassess your process metrics and goals.**

8. **Repeat Steps 1 through 7 for continuous improvement.**

Start by creating a "what we do now" process flow. Many companies skip this step because it's time-consuming, but having a visual of the current system can reveal valuable information. For instance, a visual of the status quo highlights cross-departmental interaction points, which can give you insights into matters involving delay and waste. A baseline process map can also facilitate buy-in for the improvement effort throughout the organization.

Planning Operations

There are countless ways to design a process. What constitutes a good or bad design depends on what your objectives are. Some general rules of thumb can help you maximize your process design and achieve your goals.

In this section we look at the effects of the placement of activities in the process. Serial processes have operations that must occur one after the other; parallel processes can occur simultaneously.

Considering a serial process

In a system with a serial process design, activities occur one after the other; no activities occur simultaneously. Figure 3-1 shows a typical serial process in which activities take place one at a time in a defined sequence. A resource performs an operation and places the output in a waiting area until the next operation is ready to receive it as an input. We refer to the part or customer in this section as the flow unit.

In this serial process, the resource performing OP1 has the smallest capacity and is the bottleneck with a capacity of one flow unit per day. The time it takes one flow unit to get through the system is two days (one day for OP1 and a half day each for OP2 and OP3). Because this calculation does not include any wait times, it's really a rush order flow time and not the actual flow time. But for simplicity, we call this variable the flow time. (See Chapter 2 for flow time definitions and flip to Chapter 7 to find out how to calculate average wait times.)

Figure 3-1:
Example
of a serial
process.

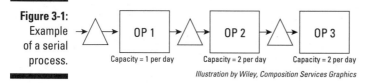

Capacity = 1 per day   Capacity = 2 per day   Capacity = 2 per day

Illustration by Wiley, Composition Services Graphics

A major problem with a serial process is that the flow time can be very long; after all, the flow unit must go through the system one step at a time. It may be possible to reduce flow time if you can identify where in the process operations can happen simultaneously. An example of this opportunity is in a medical clinic where a customer can see the doctor at the same time that office staff processes paperwork for insurance. Operations that happen at the same time are said to be in *parallel*.

Placing operations in parallel

Placing two or more operations *in parallel,* a term that indicates operations perform their functions at the same time, can either reduce flow time (see Chapter 2) or increase capacity (see Chapter 7), depending on whether the parallel operations perform different functions *(unlike operations)* or perform the same function on different parts *(like operations)*.

Placing unlike operations in parallel reduces the flow time but doesn't impact capacity. Placing like operations in parallel increases the operation's capacity — and the system capacity if the operation is the bottleneck — but doesn't affect the flow time.

Unlike operations

Multiple operations that perform different processes on the same flow unit at the same time are referred to as *unlike operations*. For example, a cashier at a fast-food restaurant can take your money at the same time the fry cook is preparing your order.

Figure 3-2 shows the serial process in Figure 3-1 transformed by placing OP1 and OP2 in parallel.

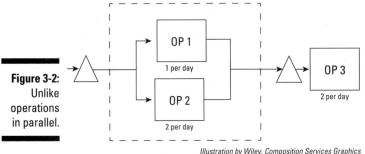

Figure 3-2:
Unlike operations in parallel.

Illustration by Wiley, Composition Services Graphics

In Figure 3-2, OP1 and OP2 are completed at the same time, but both operations must be completed before the flow unit can proceed to OP3. The capacity of the bottleneck stays the same, so the system capacity remains one per day, but the flow time is reduced.

When unlike operations are parallel and both must be completed before the flow unit can proceed, the flow time for the pair is the greater of the two. In other words, the slowest one is the pace setter. The flow time in Figure 3-2 decreases by the 0.5 days of OP2 because this operation begins and ends inside the time it takes to complete OP1; total flow time for the process is now 1.5 days.

You can place unlike operations in parallel for the same flow unit only if they can work on the flow unit at the same time. For example, operations that attach each of four different doors and the hood of a car in assembly can be placed in parallel. But you can't attach a door to a car in assembly at the same time the flow unit (the car) is going through the paint booth unless you also desire to paint the equipment and operators.

Like operations

When like operations are in parallel, more than one of the same type of resource is performing the identical operation but on different flow units. In a restaurant, for example, several servers take orders from different customers. In this case, the servers are functioning in parallel.

Adding like operations in parallel to a system usually requires adding equipment or an employee to the process. Because the bottleneck determines system capacity, if your goal is to increase capacity, you only want to add resources to the bottleneck operation because adding them to another operation won't change capacity.

Figure 3-3 shows what a process looks like when another resource is added at OP1. A flow unit is now positioned at each of the OP1 stations. Because OP1 was the bottleneck, the system capacity is increased. You now have two resources, each producing one per day, making the new capacity two per day.

OP1 now has the same capacity as OP2 and OP3. You've effectively balanced the production line! (More on this later.) Now, all operations can be considered a bottleneck; to improve capacity any further, you need to take action on all three of the bottlenecks.

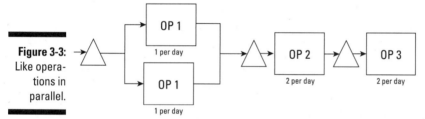

Figure 3-3: Like operations in parallel.

Illustration by Wiley, Composition Services Graphics

Although you increased the system capacity, the flow time — the time needed to get one unit through the entire process — holds steady. Even though you have two resources performing OP1, they're doing so on different flow units, and each flow unit still takes one day at OP1. Therefore, the flow time remains the same at two days.

Improving Processes According to a Goal

Any given business has a variety of objectives that are related to different parts of the business. Designing your processes to operate effectively can help you meet those objectives. In this section, we examine how one process can be arranged in many configurations to produce a different outcome. Starting with a simple serial configuration, we then look at ways to improve the process based on an objective to reduce the flow time. We make different adjustments to increase capacity, and show you one more variation to improve both flow time and capacity. We also look at the effect of each version of the process on its utilization of the workers.

Figure 3-4 illustrates the simple service process of obtaining a passport at a post office. We use this example to show the required steps to either reduce the flow time, increase capacity, or accomplish both goals. In the analysis that follows, we make the following assumptions:

- ✔ There's a waiting period (WIP) between each operation.
- ✔ Customers arrive at the post office and enter the process at the speed of the process bottleneck.
- ✔ There's no variability in customer arrival rates and operation cycle times.

In this example process, a customer enters the post office and is greeted by a clerk who reviews the individual's application. Another clerk checks all of the customer's documents for completeness and hands the documents to another who enters the information into the computer.

The customer then proceeds to an employee who takes his fingerprints (not part of a real passport process but included here to emphasize the process structure issues) and then to another who takes his picture. Next, the application is prepared for mailing, and the customer pays a clerk before leaving.

This system has a capacity of 60 passports per hour, and the bottleneck in this process is the clerk who enters customer information into the computer. The rush order flow time for any customer without wait times is 225 seconds (sum of all of the cycle times).

If you're thinking that this kind of efficiency at your local post office is but a pipe dream, you're probably not alone. But if you're the operations manager of this post office, you may be concerned with the utilization of your resources. Assuming that you're lucky enough to have unlimited demand and smart enough to only let customers in the door at the rate your bottleneck can process them, then you avoid the temptation to push too many customers into your process (find more on this in the "Managing Bottlenecks" later in this chapter).

In our example, customers arrive at the speed of the bottleneck, which is one every 60 seconds. Here's the utilization for the resource at each operation:

Review application:	15/60 = 25%
Check documents:	30/60 = 50%
Enter info into computer:	60/60 = 100%
Fingerprint:	40/60 = 66.7%
Take picture:	20/60 = 33.3%
Prepare for mailing:	20/60 = 33.3%
Collect payment:	40/60 = 66.7%

Another metric that may be important to you is *average labor utilization.* As the name states, this metric is the sum of all worker utilizations divided by the number of workers. The post office example includes seven employees (one worker assigned to each station), so the average labor utilization is 225/420 or 53.6%.

Figure 3-4: Passport application process.

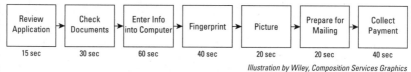

Illustration by Wiley, Composition Services Graphics

There are many different process configurations for even this simple system. How you design your process depends on what you want to accomplish.

Reducing customer flow time

If your goal is to reduce customer rush order flow time in the process, you need to start by removing any non-value-added time from each of the operations. Every second removed from any operation reduces the flow time. After that is done, flow time can be further reduced by placing unlike operations in parallel as described in the section "Placing operations in parallel" earlier in this chapter.

Figure 3-5 shows the process in Figure 3-4 when the "Enter info into the computer" operation is placed in parallel with the "fingerprinting and picture taking" operations. This can only be done because the customer is not needed to interact with the clerk who enters the information. In this case, the customer goes one direction, and the paperwork goes another. The customer then meets back up with his paperwork before proceeding to the clerk who prepares all of the documents for mailing.

Figure 3-5: Reducing customer flow time.

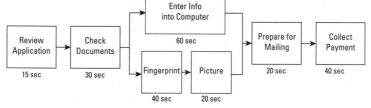

Illustration by Wiley, Composition Services Graphics

In this new configuration, the bottleneck (entering the information into the computer) still needs to be addressed; that's why process capacity remains the same. However, flow time has been reduced by 60 seconds because the time the customer spent waiting for the clerk to enter information into the computer is eliminated now that it happens at the same time a different clerk takes fingerprints and a picture. The new flow time is 165 seconds.

Flow time is an important metric for a customer, so if improving customer service is on your wish list, then you may seriously consider this design. The improvement involves no additional expense because the number of resources stays the same. This means you can improve customer service for free!

By the way, the utilizations for each resource also remain the same because customers still enter the system at the rate of one per minute.

Increasing system capacity

To increase the process's capacity, you must address the speed of the bottleneck. The first step is to analyze all actions related to the bottleneck and removing all non-value added operations. (See the "Managing Bottlenecks" section later in this chapter for more ideas.) Then you want to break down the bottleneck's task into specific actions and assign some of the actions to other resources, if possible, to improve the bottleneck's pace.

To further increase the bottleneck's capacity, you need to add another resource to the bottleneck operation, placing it in parallel with the original.

Figure 3-6 shows the new process. Note that you added another employee, which brings the staff head count to eight. What is the new system capacity?

Figure 3-6: Increasing capacity by adding a resource to the bottleneck.

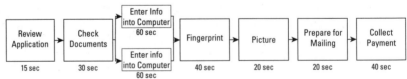

Illustration by Wiley, Composition Services Graphics

To find out, first calculate the new capacity of the original bottleneck. You now have two workers with each processing one customer every minute; that's 60 customers per hour per worker. The new capacity at this operation is 120 customers per hour.

But this isn't the new system capacity. You now have a new bottleneck —
actually, two bottlenecks. The resources at fingerprint and collect payment
are the new bottlenecks in this system because they both have a cycle time
of 40 seconds per customer, making the new system capacity

$$\text{System Capacity} = \frac{1\,\text{Customer}}{40\,\text{Seconds}} \text{ x } \frac{3{,}600\,\text{Seconds}}{1\,\text{Hour}} = 90\,\text{Customers per Hour}$$

Although this version of the process significantly increases capacity, flow
time remains the same at 225 seconds. Despite having two workers entering
information, each flow unit still takes 60 seconds at this operation.

Assuming that you have demand of 90 customers per hour (1 customer
arrives every 40 seconds), here are the new utilizations:

Review application:	15/40 = 37.5%
Check documents:	30/40 = 75%
Enter info (clerk 1):	60/80 = 75%
Enter info (clerk 2):	60/80 = 75%
Fingerprint:	40/40 = 100%
Take picture:	20/40 = 50%
Prepare for mailing:	20/40 = 50%
Collect payment:	40/40 = 100%

You may be wondering how the utilization of the clerks entering information
was calculated. There are two ways to look at this:

- ✔ **Clerks as separate units:** Customers come into the process at the rate of
  one every 40 seconds. They proceed through the process and arrive in
  the WIP in front of the clerks entering the information. The first available
  clerk processes the customer. Theoretically, each clerk processes every
  other customer, so from an individual clerk's perspective, the arrival
  rate is one every 80 seconds, making the utilization of each clerk 75%.

- ✔ **Clerks as a single unit:** If you calculate utilization by looking at the
  clerks as one unit and it takes 60 seconds to process a customer
  and one arrives every 40 seconds, total congestion is 60/40 or 150%.
  Because you have two workers, the utilization of each is 150/2 or
  75%. (See Chapter 7 for details on analyzing operations with multiple
  resources at an operation.)

The average labor utilization in this configuration with eight employees is
225/320 or 70.3%. This reveals that this configuration, to some extent, better
balances the worker utilizations.

Adding capacity usually means adding costs — possibly in the form of
hiring additional employees, purchasing additional equipment, and even
acquiring additional space. In the post office example in this section,

implementing this configuration increases expenses by one employee as well as an additional computer, and you may need to change the facility layout to accommodate the new flow.

Balancing the line

Moving assembly lines require a balanced line because an assembly line can only move at the speed of the bottleneck. If it moves any faster, the bottleneck cannot complete its operation. To avoid idle time at the other stations, the process design must ensure that the processing time for all of the operations comes as close as possible to the bottleneck's cycle time.

Balancing the line also has many advantages in service operations — namely, it allows you to spread work across resources so that every employee has approximately the same volume of work. Dividing the work such as by breaking a long operation into smaller tasks can lead to reduced cycle times thus increasing your system capacity. Line balancing also prevents some employees from "doing all the work" while others are idle. This can have a remarkable effect on worker morale.

In the post office example, adding an additional resource at the original bottleneck creates two new bottlenecks. If demand remains greater than capacity, then you must find a way to increase capacity at both bottleneck operations. One way to do this is to look for ways to equalize work content across your resources through *line balancing.*

If you combine the fingerprint operation with the picture-taking function and also combine the mailing prep operation with payment collection, then the processing time becomes 60 seconds for each combination, the same as the original bottleneck.

If you combine these operations, you have two clerks that you can place in parallel to perform the combined operations. Figure 3-7 shows this process with two clerks performing each of the three new operations.

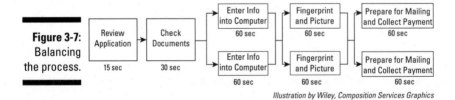

Figure 3-7:
Balancing
the process.

Illustration by Wiley, Composition Services Graphics

The process now has three operations that take 60 seconds to complete. With two employees assigned to each, the new capacity is two customers per minute, and the new process cycle time is 30 seconds.

These adjustments balance the line, except the review application operation. The new process capacity is 120 customers per hour, but it does not change the time it takes for a customer to get through the system. It still takes 225 seconds.

If demand is 120 customers per hour, then here are the worker utilizations:

Review application:	15/30 = 50%
Check documents:	30/30 = 100%
Enter info (clerk 1):	60/60 = 100%
Enter info (clerk 2):	60/60 = 100%
Fingerprint/picture:	60/60 = 100%
Fingerprint/picture:	60/60 = 100%
Mailing/payment:	60/60 = 100%
Mailing/payment:	60/60 = 100%

The average labor utilization with eight employees is 750/8 = 93.75%.

Implementing this configuration will most likely require that you alter your facility layout. You not only have two computers in this configuration, but this version also requires an additional camera as well as equipment to take fingerprints. The additional expense of the eighth employee is also a factor.

Utilizing flexible resources

Another possible configuration for a process is to cross train workers to perform more than one task in a process. Figure 3-8 shows the case where all of the workers in the post office example can perform every operation in the process.

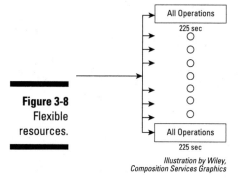

Figure 3-8
Flexible
resources.

Illustration by Wiley,
Composition Services Graphics

With eight workers, the process capacity is 128 customers per hour (8 customers every 225 seconds). The flow time remains 225 seconds and the utilization for every worker is 100% if the demand exists.

This process requires additional equipment and space because every station needs a computer, a camera, and fingerprinting supplies. That eighth employee also needs to be paid. In addition, all employees need to be trained to perform each function. Depending on the complexity of the different functions, this option may be cost prohibitive for some systems.

Table 3-1 summarizes the effect that each process configuration has on system performance. The right process configuration for a specific situation depends wholly on the objectives you want to achieve and any constraints you have on resources.

Table 3-1	**Comparison of Process Configurations**			
Process	*Action*	*Flow Time*	*System Capacity*	*Average Labor Utilization*
Base case		225 seconds	60 per hour	53.6%
Reducing customer flow time	Place unlike activities in parallel	165 seconds	60 per hour	53.6%
Increasing system capacity	Add another resource to the bottleneck	225 seconds	90 per hour (bottleneck as moved)	70.3%
Balancing the line	Make each operation have about the same cycle time	225 seconds	120 per hour	93.8%
Utilizing flexible resources	All employees perform all the operations on the same flow unit	225 seconds	130 per hour	100%

Improving a process that has excess capacity

Though every businessperson's dream is to have unlimited demand for her product or service, many businesses have more than enough capacity; customer demand is the actual bottleneck. In this case, an internal bottleneck no longer exists. Until you can increase the demand, there are some concrete things you can do to reduce your process expenses. These savings can then be used on activities to increase demand.

Line balancing can reduce resource requirements. By combining operations until each new resulting station has a processing time as close to the bottleneck as possible, the process can be staffed with fewer employees or completed with less equipment. Figure 3-9 shows the example process with combined operations.

Figure 3-9:
Balancing
the process
to meet
demand.

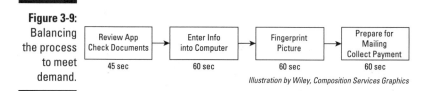

Review App Check Documents	Enter Info into Computer	Fingerprint Picture	Prepare for Mailing Collect Payment
45 sec	60 sec	60 sec	60 sec

Illustration by Wiley, Composition Services Graphics

With one employee assigned to each operation, the system capacity is 60 customers per hour; the new process requires only four employees. The flow time for any customer remains 225 seconds, and our average utilization is 93.75% if demand is equal to the capacity.

Implementing a flexible process with four employees enables you to increase system capacity to 64 customers per hour (4 customers every 225 seconds).

The key to minimizing expenses is to design process so that the maximum cycle time is as close to demand as possible. In this case, with just one full-time employee, the process capacity would be 16 customers per hours. As you add employees and maintain a flexible configuration, you increase capacity by 16 per hour with each employee. Of course you can always add part-time employees if you know your demand patterns over the course of the day so you can schedule the resources to work when needed.

Keep in mind that variability in the real world — variability in processing time, customer arrival rates, equipment breakdowns, and other types of unpredictable fluctuations in a given process — affects the clean calculations of this example and the different configurations we describe. This chapter is intended to simply point out the theoretical results of different adjustments you can make to a process design to meet specific business objectives. We introduce variability in Chapter 7.

Managing Bottlenecks

If you're lucky enough to be in a situation where demand for your product or service exceeds your ability to make the products or deliver the service, then you want to find ways to increase your production so you can sell more. Effective management of your *bottleneck*, or constraint — resources that limit a process's output — is a key to productivity and profitability.

In this section, we point out how overproduction can conceal the true process bottleneck and provide tips on how to get the most out of an existing bottleneck.

Getting tripped up by overproduction

Overproduction occurs when you allow each operation to work as fast as it can without regard to the ability of other operations in the process to keep up. If you're in a state of overproduction, inventory can build up anywhere in the process before the bottleneck where successive operations have different cycle times. Figure 3-10 represents such a situation.

Figure 3-10:
Hidden
bottleneck.

Illustration by Wiley, Composition Services Graphics

For example, assume that you're releasing material into the process at the rate of the first operation. OP1, in Figure 3-10 processes a part every 2 minutes and places it in WIP 1, where it waits for OP2. However, OP2 requires 4 minutes to process each part. Since OP2 only has a capacity of 15 parts per hour and OP1 is processing 30 per hour, WIP1 grows by 15 parts per hour (30 – 15). Imagine the scene after an 8-hour shift.

If you think you can easily spot the bottleneck by finding the operation with the most inventory in front of it, then you may be making a big mistake. Here's why: OP2 feeds parts to OP3 at the rate of 15 units per minute, and OP3 processes them at the same rate. With no variability in the cycle times of these operations, inventory shouldn't accumulate in WIP2. The output of OP3 waits in WIP3 for the true bottleneck — the resource(s) at OP4. Because OP4 can process only 12 of the 15 parts it receives per hour, 3 parts per hour accumulate in WIP3 — significantly fewer than the 15 parts per hour that accumulate in WIP1.

This situation applies to services as well. Instead of parts waiting for an operation, customers would be waiting in line. See Chapter 7 to see what happens to the time a customer must wait as the number of customers in line increases.

Overproduction at OP1 can lead a less experienced operations manager to mistakenly conclude that the resource at OP2 is the bottleneck because it appears to be the operation that's holding up production. In reality, the bottleneck is at OP4 because it's the slowest operation.

If you're wondering why a firm would allow a process to overproduce, there could be many causes. For example, look to a common accounting practice that leads companies to make this mistake. When costing products, accountants often calculate the cost per piece at each operation by dividing the total expense for the operation by the number of units it produces. By producing more units, the operation can seem to be improving and cost less per item.

If the line manager's performance is only evaluated by the artificial cost per piece or utilization of the resources, then overproduction becomes a desired situation. But if a combination of different, more bottom-line friendly metrics are used to measure the performance of the process and its manager, such as the cost to actually produce a piece compared to the cost of producing it with a perfectly efficient process, then a different outcome is likely. Other factors may also cause a firm to overproduce, such as inaccurate forecasts of demand or the desire to build inventory in anticipation of future demand.

Employees tend to perform to the metric on which you evaluate them, so be sure to consider the priorities and outcomes you may facilitate when setting up an evaluation system.

Increasing process capacity

Increasing capacity of an overall process relies on increasing the capacity of the bottleneck. The system's capacity can't exceed the capacity of the bottleneck, so increasing the capacity of OP4 in Figure 3-10 is the priority. If improvement resources are limited, focus on OP4 first.

As you improve any bottleneck resource, you may move the bottleneck to another resource. It is vital that you continually monitor the effects of your process changes to identify when the bottleneck does indeed change. After it does, you want to change your focus to the new bottleneck.

Here are some ways for you to increase capacity at the bottleneck:

- **Add resources at the bottleneck operation.** You can increase the number of resources that are performing the operation without adding head count if you can assign an employee from another operation to help perform the bottleneck operation during unutilized time.

- **Always have a part for the bottleneck to process.** Be sure to monitor the WIP in front of the bottleneck and that it always has a part to process. This involves managing the resources feeding the bottleneck to ensure that nothing is slowing them down, such as equipment failures. If scheduling overtime, you must also make sure that the bottleneck has enough parts to process during the overtime period. Overtime can be expensive, especially if the bottleneck resource is idle during this time because it runs out of material.

✔ **Assure that the bottleneck works only on quality parts.** Don't waste the bottleneck's time on bad parts. If you need quality checks in the process, place them before the bottleneck operation. This increases the thruput of the process.

✔ **Examine your production schedule.** If a process is used to make several different products that use varying amounts of the bottleneck's time, then an analysis of the production schedule can create a product mix that minimizes overall demand on the bottleneck.

✔ **Increase the time the operation is working.** Keep the bottleneck resource working. Always have someone assigned to the operation, including during scheduled breaks and lunch periods, and use overtime if necessary. Though doing so won't technically reduce the cycle time, it will allow the bottleneck to produce when other operations are idle. The more time the bottleneck works, the more parts the system produces.

✔ **Minimize downtime.** Avoid scheduled and unscheduled downtime. If the bottleneck equipment suffers a breakdown during scheduled operations, dispatch repair personnel immediately to get the bottleneck up and running as quickly as possible. This may involve keeping replacement parts on hand and easily accessible. Perform preventive maintenance on equipment during non-operating hours when possible. In addition, do what you can to reduce changeover times from one product to the next, because this time takes away from actual production time.

✔ **Perform process improvement on the bottleneck resource.** A good place to start is to document everything the resource does. Then eliminate all non-value-added activities and look for ways to reduce the time it takes to do value-added activities by getting rid of all the waste in the operation. This results in a shorter cycle time. Process improvement is almost always focused on eliminating waste.

✔ **Reassign some of the bottleneck's work.** If possible, break the operation down into smaller activities and reassign some to other resources. Doing so results in a shorter cycle time and increased capacity.

Chapter 4

Dealing with Shared Resources, Batches, and Rework

*E*ven the simplest processes can be difficult to analyze and manage, but some common situations make analysis even more challenging. For example, resources are often shared in a process or even across processes, and you must account for everything a resource does when calculating the resource's work time.

In many processes, operations produce more than one item at a time or an operation produces several items before they progress to the next operation. For example, you don't bake one cookie in the oven at a time; a batch of cookies bake together on one pan in the oven. In fact, you might place multiple pans of cookies in the oven at the same time. This is called *batching*. In a batching situation, a single resource is producing or serving more than one unit at the same time.

Another challenge of performance assessment involves process disruptions. Many things can happen to disrupt the smooth flow of parts through a process. One of the biggest is the production of poor quality products that require extra processing (rework). This throws all the process metrics into a tailspin.

In this chapter, we address these situations. If your knowledge of basic process analysis is rusty, you can always refer to Chapters 2 and 3.

Sharing Resources

In many organizations, *resources* (people, capital equipment, computers, and so on) perform more than one *operation* (a single activity or task) in a process or are shared across processes. For example, a receptionist in a doctor's office not only greets patients but also collects payment and schedules future appointments. Similarly, a product designer may design more than one type of merchandise in a given time period for different brands. Analyzing these situations requires special care because they affect process performance metrics.

Assigning a resource to more than one operation

Assigning a resource to more than one operation in a process can be a smart way to help *balance the line* so that each person or machine has approximately the same work content. *Work content* is the total time a resource spends working on one *flow unit*, or one part that goes through the entire process. This structure can increase resource utilization without creating an overproduction dilemma, which we describe in Chapter 3. But when assigning resources to multiple operations, you want to be sure to avoid resource conflicts.

In this section, we help you identify bottlenecks and avoid conflicts when a resource works on multiple operations.

When calculating a resource's *cycle time* — the time a resource takes to process one flow unit — you must account for everything that each resource does in the process. Often, this includes multiple operations. Considering each resource's total work time is important when identifying bottlenecks.

Figure 4-1 shows a situation in which individual clerks perform multiple operations:

- ✔ Clerk 1 performs OP1 and OP5; his cycle time is 18 minutes (6 + 12).

- ✔ Clerk 2 performs OP2 and OP4; her cycle time is 15 minutes (10 + 5).

- ✔ Clerks 3 and 4 both perform OP3, and each has a cycle time of 20 minutes.

- ✔ Clerk 5 performs OP6 with a cycle time of 15 minutes.

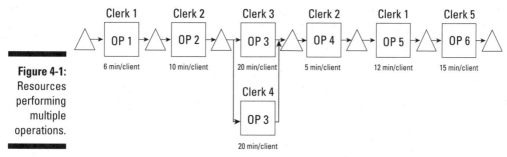

Illustration by Wiley, Composition Services Graphics

Figure 4-1: Resources performing multiple operations.

If you analyze the process without noticing that operations share resources, you may conclude that the bottleneck is Clerk 5 performing OP6 with a cycle time of 15 minutes. Or maybe you'd peg Clerks 3 and 4 at OP3 as the bottleneck; but they don't represent the smallest capacity or the longest cycle time (bottleneck metrics) because the cycle time for the resources at OP3 is really 10 minutes (20 ÷ 2) — you have two resources in parallel (see Chapter 3 for details on parallel resources). The actual bottleneck of the process is Clerk 1 because he performs both OP1 and OP5 and has the longest cycle time of 18 minutes.

When assigning resources, you need to verify that, given current demand, you aren't creating any resource conflicts. *Resource conflicts* arise when a resource must do two or more operations on different *flow units* (individual people or parts going through the system) at the same time. For example, a receptionist at a doctor's office can't check in one patient at the same time he is scheduling a future appointment for another; this is a resource conflict.

In Figure 4-1, a resource conflict would exist if Clerk 1 has to perform OP1 on a new customer at the same time he needs to perform OP5 on a different customer. Because of the potential for resource conflicts, sharing resources often increases the time a flow unit spends in the process.

Allocating resources to more than one process

A single resource may be assigned to perform one or more operations in more than one process. When this happens, analyzing the performance of a particular process becomes tricky. Here are some important questions to ask when you're evaluating a process that uses a resource that also works on other processes:

✔ **Is the resource a bottleneck in any of the individual processes in which it performs?** If the resource is the bottleneck in an individual process even if the resource was dedicated exclusively to that individual process, then you have a serious issue. The resource is limiting production in a process, so any additional activities it performs in other processes further limits the capacity of that first process.

✔ **How much total work content does the resource perform across all the processes?** The resource may not be the bottleneck in any individual process but may actually be a bottleneck given its activities across all processes in which it performs. If this occurs, then the resource may make one process wait while it performs an activity in another process.

✔ **Do you need to adjust your material release policy?** If a resource becomes a bottleneck because of its shared activities, then you may need to adjust the *material release policy* (how fast parts are introduced into the process) of all processes the resource works in to reflect the new bottleneck. Scheduling is critical when resources are shared among processes. You must schedule the processes in a way that doesn't create resource conflicts.

Find details on sharing resources across processes in Chapter 15.

Batching Parts and Setting Up Operations

Sometimes an operation can process multiple parts or customers at the same time; this is known as *batching*. For example, an oven in a bakery or a kiln in a manufacturing plant can process more than one flow unit during a single operation cycle. Depending on the size of each batch, this capability can actually create problems in a process if other operations have different *capacities,* or can't process as many units during a cycle.

Another type of batching that creates process design challenges involves using a resource to produce multiple types of units. This situation applies mostly to manufacturing, make-to-stock processes (see Chapter 5). For example, a television manufacturer may make two or more TV models on the same production line. Switching from one model to another requires what's called a *setup time*.

In this section, we tell you how to choose optimal batch sizes, with or without setup times.

Working with batches

Before you can determine what the ideal batch sizes are for a process, you need to know a few basic terms:

- **Operation batch size:** This is the number of parts that an operation processes during one cycle. A single period of a bakery oven cooking multiple cookies is an example of an operation processing more than one part during a cycle. The volume of units processed by any one operation in the process may be different, and every operation doesn't necessarily need to process the maximum number of units it can.

- **Process batch size:** A *batch process* produces multiple types of flow units in successive groups or batches. For example, an automotive manufacturing facility produces different-colored cars on the same production line. Each color is manufactured in a batch of cars.

  Therefore, a *batch size* or *process batch size* is the number of flow units that are processed between resource setups in a batch process. In an auto manufacturing facility, 100 red cars may be produced before the process switches to blue cars. The number of flow units produced in a batch is often referred to as the *production batch size*.

  Setups are downtimes during which the resource can't work on flow units because the machine is being modified to process a different type part — as in a model or color change. Every time an auto plant switches from red cars to blue, the facility must shut down to change the paint color. The downtime is the *setup time*. Setups are also commonly known as *changeovers*. Chapter 11 covers how to reduce setup times.

- **Transfer batch size:** This is the number of flow units that move from operation to operation at any time. The transfer batch size will likely be less than or equal to the process batch size. In some cases, the transfer batch size will be equal to 1, as in an automated assembly line, where parts move on as they're processed.

An important difference exists between a transfer batch and a process batch. A transfer batch doesn't require a setup. It is strictly the number of parts or customers that move to the next operation together. A process batch, however, requires some amount of downtime for an operation to switch from producing one type of unit to a different one. A process batch can include one or more transfer batches.

Maximizing operation batch size

In a process, some operations can process multiple flow units at a time and others can't, so it's important to analyze the operation batch size to maximize the total system's capacity. To accommodate other operations in a process, a particular operation's batch size may be lower than its maximum possible output.

By definition, no setup time is required between operation batches. In this analysis, we assume that the operation batch size is the same as the transfer batch size, meaning that the units processed in any one cycle of an operation move on to the next operation as a batch at the same time.

Here are the general steps for determining optimal batch size to maximize process capacity:

1. **Determine the capacity of each resource for different batch sizes.**

   Calculate the capacity for several batch sizes, including the minimum and maximum allowable size.

2. **Determine whether the bottleneck changes from one resource to another.**

   The bottleneck may shift if some resources have the same cycle time regardless of batch size and others have changing cycle times based on batch size.

   The operation's cycle time is for a batch of parts, not just a single unit.

3. **Determine the batch size that causes the bottleneck to change.**

   In general, this occurs when the capacity of the original bottleneck equals that of the new bottleneck.

For example, look at Figure 4-2, which illustrates a bakery's process for making cakes. First note the capacity of each resource for various batch sizes:

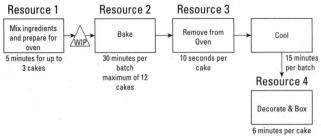

Figure 4-2:
Optimizing
batch size.

Illustration by Wiley, Composition Services Graphics

Resource 1 mixes the ingredients and prepares the pans for the oven. This resource can mix up to 3 cakes in 5 minutes, but he doesn't necessarily need to make 3 at a time. Making only 1 or 2 still takes him 5 minutes.

After preparing the cakes for the oven, Resource 1 places them in a holding area (WIP), where they wait for the oven to become available.

Resource 2 (the oven) takes 30 minutes to bake a batch of cakes, no matter how many cakes are in the oven. The oven can hold 12 pans (maximum operation batch size is 12), and all the cakes must be put in the oven at the same time.

After the 30-minute bake time, Resource 3 removes the cakes from the oven and places them on cooling racks. Doing so takes her 10 seconds per cake. Resource 3 isn't the bottleneck in this process because she needs only 2 minutes to process the maximum batch size of 12.

Each cake must cool at least 15 minutes before moving on to Resource 4, who removes each cake from the cooling rack, takes it out of the pan, brushes a glaze over the warm cake, and boxes it — at a pace of 6 minutes per cake. Cooling is an operation and not a WIP because Resource 4 can't decorate a hot cake.

The batch size in this process can range from 1 to 12 cakes, the capacity of the oven. The chosen batch size determines the process capacity and flow time. Figure 4-3 summarizes the effect of batch size on the cycle time and capacity of each resource in this example process, as well as the rush order flow time for a particular batch size.

	1 Cake	3 Cakes	5 Cakes	6 Cakes	9 Cakes	12 Cakes
Cycle Time (mins/batch)						
Resource 1	5	5	10	10	15	20
Resource 2	30	30	30	30	30	30
Resource 4	6	18	30	36	54	72
Capacity (batches/hour)						
Resource 1	12	12	6	6	4	3
Resource 2	2	2	2	2	2	2
Resource 4	10	3.33	2	1.67	1.11	0.83
Capacity (cakes/hour)						
Resource 1	12	36	30	36	36	36
Resource 2	2	6	10	12	18	24
Resource 4	10	10	10	10	10	10
Rush Order Flow Time (mins/batch)	56 mins 10 secs	68 mins 30 secs	85 mins 50 secs	92 mins	115 mins 30 secs	139 mins

Figure 4-3 Effect of batch size on process metrics.

Comparing the capacity of each resource as batch size increases, the oven (Resource 2) remains the bottleneck until batch size reaches 5 cakes. At this size, Resource 4 also becomes a bottleneck, and Resource 2 and 4 have a capacity of 10 cakes per hour. When the batch size exceeds 5, Resource 4 becomes the sole bottleneck — cakes will back up before Resource 4's station because cakes arrive faster than she can process them. Figure 4-4 illustrates the effect of batch size on resource capacity in this process.

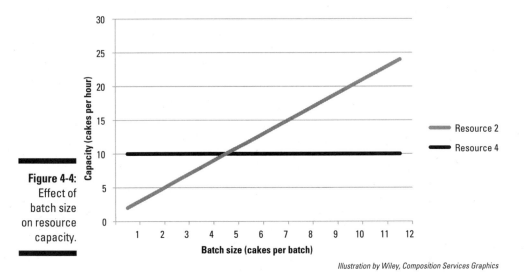

Figure 4-4:
Effect of
batch size
on resource
capacity.

Figure 4-4 reveals that the optimal batch size is 5 cakes; this is where both Resources 2 and 4 have the same capacity.

When choosing the batch size, metrics other than system capacity may influence your decision. For example, in Figure 4-3, the rush order flow time increases as batch size increases. If a smaller flow time is important to your customers, then you may want to reduce the batch size. Likewise, quality expectations can also influence batch size. In the cake example, if the batch size is 5, then the last cake will wait an additional 24 minutes beyond the 15-minute cool time before Resource 4 can decorate it (because the 4 cakes ahead of it each take 6 minutes to decorate). If this additional time allows the cake to cool too much for the glaze to spread, then you may have to reduce the batch size.

Optimizing transfer batch size

The *transfer batch size* refers to the number of units that move as a group from operation to operation. On a process map, the transfer action is represented as an operation even though it doesn't add value to the end product because the step is necessary for the parts to move through the process. See Chapter 2 for more on non-value-added activities and process waste.

Figure 4-5 shows a process that utilizes transfer batches. The process consists of three operators and one driver. The driver performs both of the transfer operations.

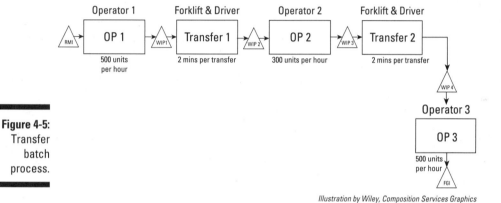

Figure 4-5:
Transfer
batch
process.

Illustration by Wiley, Composition Services Graphics

In this process map, each operation has its own waiting station for work in process (WIP). Each operation uses WIP as an input and outputs WIP to a different location. For example, OP1 processes parts into WIP1, and OP2 pulls parts to work on from WIP2. When WIP1 reaches the transfer batch size, it moves and becomes WIP2.

The following steps are useful when establishing transfer batch sizes:

1. **Determine the bottleneck of the process, assuming a transfer batch size of one.**

   Initially, don't worry about the resources used for transporting the batches from operation to operation. The amount of time these resources are utilized depends on the number of trips they have to make. As the batch size increases, they make fewer trips. In the example in Figure 4-5, Operator 2 is the bottleneck and has a capacity of 300 units per hour.

2. **Decide on your *material release policy*, or how fast you allow parts to enter the process.**

   If you're lucky and demand exceeds capacity, you'll operate at the speed of the bottleneck to prevent overproduction (see Chapter 3). If demand is less than capacity, you'll operate at the rate of demand. Refer to

Chapter 7 for situations such as seasonal demand, when you may want to produce more than current demand indicates. In the example shown in Figure 4-5, assume that demand is greater than capacity and that parts enter the process at the rate of 300 units per hour.

3. **Figure out the capacity (trips per hour) of your transportation resources.**

In the example, moving a batch of parts from operation to operation takes 2 minutes. This means that the driver can make 30 trips per hour. Because there's only one driver, he must divide his time between two transfer points. The number of transfers at each point doesn't necessarily need to be the same. Note that, to keep this simple, we're ignoring any time it takes for the driver to move between the two transfer points.

4. **Determine the minimum batch size that the transportation resources can accommodate.**

Assuming that you maintain the same transfer batch size throughout the process, the driver can make up to 15 (30 ÷ 2) transfers per hour at each transfer point. Because 300 parts are released into the system per hour, the minimum batch size that the driver can process is 20 parts (300 ÷ 15). A smaller batch size requires more transfers and exceeds the capacity of the driver.

5. **Set the batch size to meet your operational objectives.**

When choosing batch sizes, you must consider many factors, such as operator work patterns, desired inventory levels, the time it takes to get through the process, facility layout, and traffic patterns within your facility.

Not all the transfer batches in a process have to be the same size.

Resource utilization

Small batch sizes tend to smooth the workload of an operation. In Figure 4-5, if 15 batches of 20 units enter the system every hour — meaning that a batch arrives at OP1 every 4 minutes (60 minutes ÷ 15 batches) — then Operator 1 works for 2.4 minutes (60 ÷ 500, or 0.12 minutes/unit, · 20 units) to process the batch. He then waits for 1.6 minutes for the next batch to arrive to him. This means Operator 1 works for 2.4 minutes out of every 4 minutes, or 60% of the time.

On the other hand, large batch sizes generate longer continuous active periods followed by longer continuous inactive periods. If the batch size in Figure 4-5, is 300 per hour and all the units arrive at the same time,

Operator 1 works for 36 minutes (300 · .12) to process all the parts and is then inactive for the rest of the hour, until the next batch of 300 units arrives to him. The operator's utilization remains at 60%, but he now has larger blocks of working time and downtime.

Flow time

Small batch sizes reduce the time for a batch of parts to get through a system. For example, OP1 and OP3 in Figure 4-5 each requires 2.4 minutes to process 20 parts; OP2 can process a part every 0.2 minutes, taking 4 minutes to process 20 parts. Summing the time the batch spends at each operation and adding 4 minutes for the two transfers, a batch of 20 units takes 12.8 minutes to process from start to finish, not including any wait times if they exist.

Conversely, large batch sizes increase the time a batch spends in the process. Staying with the example in Figure 4-5, a batch of 300 parts goes through the process in 136 minutes: 36 minutes + 2 minutes + 60 minutes + 2 minutes + 36 minutes.

Facility traffic

Small batch sizes usually create more traffic in a facility because more transfers occur. In some situations, this may be dangerous and undesirable.

Inventory storage

Small batch sizes result in less wait time for an individual part, which results in less WIP inventory. Flip to Chapter 7 to see how flow times and inventory are related.

Optimizing batch size with operation setups

Company resources are often used to produce more than one type of product. Examples include a manufacturing facility that produces different models of automobiles or a facility that makes sweaters of different sizes and colors. Product versatility allows an organization to get the most out of its resources. However, changing over from one product to another takes time and labor. To minimize setups and the costs associated with them, many processes produce multiple types of flow units in batches.

Figure 4-6 shows a machine that produces two types of products and the setup that's required before switching to the next part.

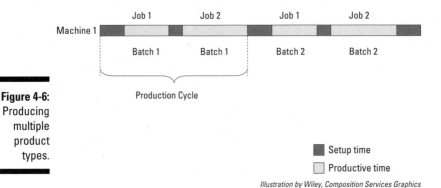

Figure 4-6: Producing multiple product types.

The figure shows that the machine doesn't produce parts during the setup between batches of parts. This downtime reduces the resource's capacity. The batch size affects the resource's maximum *thruput* (what is actually produced) and utilization. The larger the batch size, the higher the resource's thruput and utilization.

In general, you can calculate the maximum thruput as

$$\text{Max Thruput} = \frac{\text{Batch Size}}{\text{Setup Time} + (\text{Batch Size} \cdot \text{CT})}$$

Watch the time units you use in this equation. Setup time and cycle time (CT) must have the same units.

The equation for maximum utilization is

$$\text{Max Utilization} = \frac{\text{Batch Size} \cdot \text{CT}}{\text{Setup Time} + (\text{Batch Size} \cdot \text{CT})}$$

Suppose that the capacity of a resource is 60 units per hour, and the setup time between batches is 10 minutes. With a batch size of 10, the hour starts with the 10 minutes of setup time followed by the production of 10 units, which takes 10 minutes. This pattern is repeated over and over. During one hour, the pattern is repeated 3 times, and the resource produces 30 parts per hour. This means that the utilization of the resource is 50% because it has the capacity to produce 60 per hour.

If you increase the batch size to 20, then 10 minutes for setup is followed by 20 minutes of production. This cycle takes 30 minutes and repeats 2 times an hour. A total of 2 batches or 40 parts are produced per hour, resulting in a utilization of 66.7%.

By increasing the batch size even further to 50, you enable the resource to produce 50 parts in 50 minutes; it is then inactive for 10 minutes for setup. Thruput is 50 parts per hour, and utilization is 83.3%

Table 4-1 summarizes what happens to the metrics as batch size increases.

Table 4-1	Thruput and Utilization As Batch Size Increases	
Batch Size	**Thruput (Parts per Hour)**	**Utilization (%)**
10	30	50
30	45	75
50	50	83.3
70	52.5	87.5
90	54	90

When you choose a batch size, your first priority is to ensure that your process thruput meets your product demand. When you reach your thruput goal, you want to reduce inventory levels and flow time by selecting the smallest batch size that meets the required thruput.

Figure 4-7 shows a simple process in which each operation has its own setup and cycle times. Selecting the process batch size requires you to analyze the process using different batch sizes and choosing the one that meets the performance objectives for your process.

Process with Setups

Figure 4-7:
Process
with setup
times.

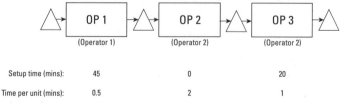

Illustration by Wiley, Composition Services Graphics

The first step is to determine the bottleneck and process thruput for several batch sizes. Using the equation for maximum thruput, Table 4-2 summarizes the thruput of the operators for different batch sizes.

Table 4-2	Summary of Thruput for Different Batch Sizes		
Max Thruput (Units/Hour)	Batch Size = 10	Batch Size = 30	Batch Size = 60
Operator 1	12	30	48
Operator 2	30	30	30
Operator 3	20	36	45
Process	12	30	30

Figure 4-8 shows the relationship of batch size to thruput for each resource. Operator 2's thruput is independent of batch size and is capped at 30 units per hour. To maximize thruput, choose the minimum batch size that results in all resources having a thruput of at least 30 units per hour. In this case you should set the batch size at 30.

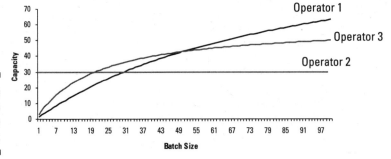

Figure 4-8:
Relationship
of batch size
to thruput.

Illustration by Wiley, Composition Services Graphics

Reducing setup times can increase an operation's thruput. If Operator 1's setup time can be reduced to 30 minutes, then the operation's thruput with a batch size of 30 would increase to 40 units per hour. The batch size can be reduced to 20 units and still maintain a thruput of 30 units per hour. Chapter 11 points out how to reduce setup times.

Managing Process Disruptions

Few things are more disruptive to a process than poor quality. Poor quality has a negative impact on all your process metrics. In Chapters 12 and 13, we show you how to define, measure, and improve process quality; until then, you need to know how to manage your process given the current quality levels.

Poor quality wastes resources in three ways:

- ✔ By producing the bad part in the first place
- ✔ By having to "fix" the bad part (often called *rework*)
- ✔ By having to find bad parts before they progress in the process or, in the worst case, before they're sold to a customer

When you find defects in a product, you can either fix what's wrong or scrap the product. If you discard the product, you waste the time and materials that went into the product. If you attempt to fix the defect, you must use resources on the rework that could be used making additional products.

You can handle rework in two ways: You can establish a separate process to handle the defective products or place them back in the main process that created them and correct the defect.

Putting rework back in the process that created it

Sometimes, when a defective product is discovered, it's repaired/fixed by the resource that created it and then placed back into the process where the defect occurred.

Figure 4-9 shows a process in which defective products are reworked in the main flow.

In this process, a customer enters the system, and a receptionist greets him. He then waits for one of the three accountants. After an accountant completes his tax return, one of the two auditors checks it for accuracy. If the return is correct, the customer pays the receptionist, who prepared his bill while the return was being processed and audited. Figure 4-9 shows the cycle times for each operation.

If returns aren't defective, then the accountants and the receptionist have a cycle time of 8 minutes and a capacity of 7.5 clients per hour. The system bottleneck (slowest resource) is the auditors, who have a cycle time of 9 minutes, giving them a capacity to process 6.67 customers per hour. If you're puzzled by how we calculated the metrics, check out Chapters 2 and 3.

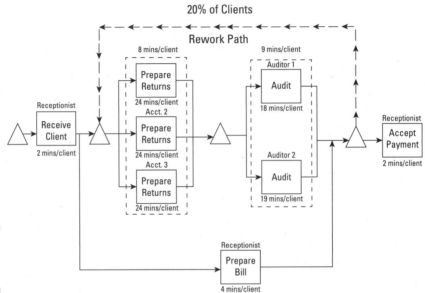

Figure 4-9:
Managing rework.

Illustration by Wiley, Composition Services Graphics

If the auditors discover that 20% of the returns have a mistake, then the return goes back to an accountant (not necessarily the one who initially worked on the return). The accountant spends an additional 24 minutes correcting the return, and the auditor must spend an additional 4 minutes rechecking it for accuracy. We assume that the return is correct the first time through the rework cycle.

To analyze this process when rework is involved, the first thing you must do is calculate the new cycle times for the accountants and the auditors. To do this, you want to calculate the cycle time for a part that requires rework and the cycle time of a good part. You can then take a weighted average to obtain a new average cycle time.

You can use the following equations:

Cycle Time for a part requiring rework = Original Cycle Time + Rework Time

New Average Cycle Time =

% of parts requiring rework · Cycle Time for a part requiring

rework + (1 − % requiring rework) · Cycle Time of good part

In the example, the accountant spends a total of 24 minutes on a good return and 48 minutes on a return requiring rework (24 minutes the first time plus an additional 24 minutes to fix the return). With 20% of the returns requiring rework, the new average cycle time is 28.8. With three accountants, the cycle time of the activity is 9.6 minutes.

Similarly, an auditor spends 18 minutes on a good return and 22 minutes (18 minutes plus 4 minutes for rework) on a return requiring rework, giving a new average cycle time of 18.8 minutes. With two auditors, the cycle time of the activity is 9.4 minutes.

 A danger of the rework cycle is that the bottleneck of the process may change. If your bottleneck changes without your realizing it, you'll try to optimize the wrong resource and won't see any process improvement as a result of your efforts.

In this example, the accountants are now the bottleneck, and the process now has a capacity of 6.25 clients per hour. Because of the rework, the process capacity is reduced by 0.42 clients per hour, or 3.36 per 8-hour day. Assuming a 5-day work week, this means that, over the 6 weeks before April 15, which is the peak time for income tax filing, the firm would lose capacity of more than 100 clients. That adds up to a lot of money lost over a short period of time.

Pulling rework out of the main process

Placing a defective part back into the main process is often hard, if not impossible. For example, consider an automobile assembly line. Moving a defective auto and placing it back on the line for repair would be extremely disruptive and costly.

Usually, a company uses resources other than the main line resources to correct quality problems. This creates a lot of waste for the organization. You need not only additional resources but also additional space and equipment to process the defective part.

In the example involving tax returns, placing defective returns back into the process is easy, but you could also handle them off the main process flow. You could hire additional personnel dedicated to handle rework or assign one of the main line accountants and auditors to perform rework as well as main process operations. The latter option would mean using resources across multiple processes, which may create a problem of its own (see the earlier "Sharing Resources" section for details on this scenario).

Chapter 5

Designing Your Process to Match Your Product or Service

. . . .

In This Chapter

▶ Classifying processes and balancing costs

▶ Creating successful customer interfaces and back-office operations

▶ Deciding between making to stock and making to order

▶ Using certain design techniques for specific products

. . . .

*W*hen you're designing processes to create a product or deliver your services, a good relationship between process and product makes your job as an operations manager easier. In other words, every aspect of a manufacturing process depends on the product you're trying to create, and process design is a fundamental aspect of product development. Your product, whether it's a widget or a service, drives process design, and your processes ultimately determine your costs and profit margins.

In this chapter, we classify processes along four dimensions and describe a concrete method for evaluating the costs associated with process design choices. We also explore the anatomy of manufacturing and service operations with a focus on how to design and exploit a process to get the most productivity out of it. We conclude with a description of the design for (DFX) terms that operations management leaders use regularly.

Considering Costs, Standardization, Volume, and Flexibility

Processes fall into four different categories based on the nature of their function. Some processes relate primarily to a product's cost structure; others address the company's product standardization needs, output volume, or production flexibility. In this section, we look at processes that focus on these types of business considerations and provide general guidelines on how to best select a process to meet the requirements of your product.

Before you dive into classifying a process, consider the nature of the product it's intended to produce. After all, creating a unique item, such as an interstate highway bridge, is wildly different from producing a million bottles of contact-lens solution or thousands of socks in two different colors. Here are common process classifications, arranged according to fixed costs (lowest to highest):

✔ **Projects:** These generally result in an output of one. Examples include constructing a building or catering a party. Although the result of a project is one deliverable, the process of creating the item can be duplicated with modifications for other projects. Flip to Chapter 14 for details on projects.

✔ **Job shops:** This type of process produces small batches of many different products. Each batch is usually customized to a specific customer order, and each product may require different steps and processing times. Examples of job shop products include a bakery that specializes in baking and decorating wedding cakes, each one customized for a bride, or a programmer that creates customized websites for his clients.

✔ **Batch shops:** These produce periodic batches of the same product. Batch shops can produce different products, but typically all the products they produce follow the same process flow. A facility producing shirts of different sizes and colors or a bakery preparing different flavors of cakes or types of cookies are examples of batch shops. These processes make one type of shirt or cookie in a batch and then switch to a different type, but all types follow the same flow.

Batch shops usually require some *setup time* — time required to prepare resources to produce a different type of product. Chapter 4 provides a detailed analysis of how to manage a batch shop process.

✔ **Flow lines:** This type of process consists of essentially independent stations that produce the same or very similar parts. Each part follows the same process throughout the process. Output on a flow line is dictated by the *bottleneck,* or the slowest operation. For more on bottlenecks, see Chapters 2 and 3. The flow line is similar to the assembly line but the parts don't move at a constant rate dictated by the line speed.

The terms *flow lines* and *batch shop process* are often erroneously used interchangeably.

✔ **Assembly lines:** These produce discrete parts flowing at controlled rates through a well-defined process. The line moves the parts to the resources, and each resource must complete its task before the line moves on. This requires a balanced line, meaning that each operation completes its task in a similar amount of time. The line moves at the speed of the slowest operation, or bottleneck. Automobile production is the classic example of an assembly line. Check out Chapters 2 and 3 for more on bottlenecks and balancing a process.

✔ **Continuous flow processes:** As the name implies, these processes produce items continuously, usually in a highly automated process. Examples include chemical plants, refineries, and electric generation facilities. A continuous flow process may have to run 24/7 because starting and stopping it is often difficult.

Figures 5-1 and 5-2 illustrate where each process falls on the standardization, volume, and flexibility matrix for both products and services. Figure 5-1 shows how different products vary along these metrics, and Figure 5-2 shows how services differ on the dimensions.

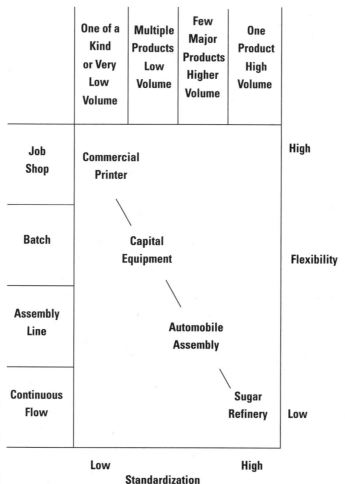

Figure 5-1:
The product process matrix.

Illustration by Wiley, Composition Services Graphics

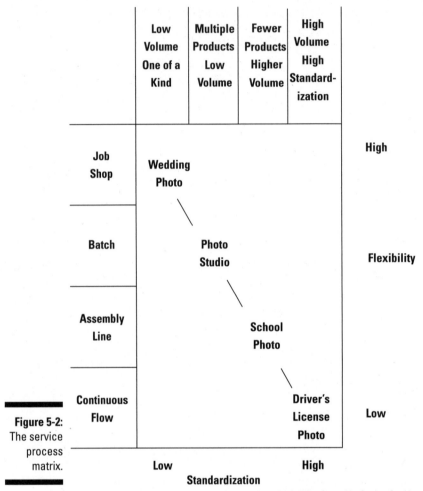

Balancing operating costs

Each process has its own operating cost structure that determines two important factors:

- ✔ Cost of the units produced at various volumes of production
- ✔ Minimum production volume at which the process becomes profitable

Operating costs are either fixed or variable:

- ✔ **Fixed costs (FC) are independent of unit volume produced.** Examples include rent, mortgage payments, property taxes, insurance, capital equipment, and certain administrative and overhead expenses.

- ✔ **Variable costs (VC) are dependent on unit volume produced, meaning they vary directly with volume.** Examples include power to run equipment, material and labor (because these costs change depending on how much of them you use), and a wide range of other considerations, such as quantity discounts when purchasing material.

An automated process usually has a higher investment in fixed cost assets like sophisticated machinery than a small manual process, which is more likely to have a higher proportion of a variable cost like labor. But the division between fixed and variable costs can be fuzzy sometimes. For example, union contracts often require that a certain employment level be maintained. In this case, you can't consider labor costs as variable. Similarly, some maintenance must be performed routinely on equipment, regardless of volume produced. So the operations manager must designate operating costs as fixed or variable according to the operations' circumstances and often according to company accounting practices.

Finding the right balance between fixed and variable costs can be difficult. Automating a process to reduce the number of employees you need to pay for manual labor requires significant upfront investment and usually reduces the amount of customization you can offer on the product. A variable cost structure requires more labor, but well-trained people power is better at accommodating customization.

When making fixed versus variable process design decisions, you need to know how to calculate the impact of these choices on the bottom line.

The total cost (TC) associated with a given volume of output is equal to the sum of the fixed cost (FC) and the variable cost per unit (VC) times volume produced (Q):

$$TC = FC + (VC \cdot Q)$$

Assuming you sell everything you produce for a fixed price per unit (R), total revenue (TR) is equal to $R \cdot Q$. Figure 5-3 illustrates the relationship among volume, costs, and revenue. The difference between the TR and TC curves represents the profit (or loss) of the process.

Total profit (TP) is simply your total revenue minus your total costs:

$$TP = TR - TC = (R \cdot Q) - \left[FC + (VC \cdot Q) \right]$$

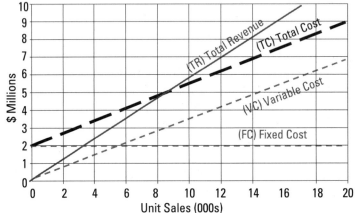

Figure 5-3:
Relationship
of cost to
volume.

Your cost structure determines your break-even point (BEP), or break-even production quantity. This is the production volume at which your total revenue and total costs are the same. Every unit you produce above this BEP results in a profit.

$$TR = TC$$
$$R \cdot Q = FC + (VC \cdot Q)$$

Solve for Q to determine your break-even point:

$$R \cdot Q - (VC \cdot Q) = FC$$
$$Q(R - VC) = FC$$
$$Q = \frac{FC}{R - VC}$$

So the break-even quantity Q is determined by dividing the fixed costs FC by the marginal profit generated by one unit of production (R – VC).

How do you use this equation to guide your process decisions?

The first thing you may notice is that your BEP — the quantity Q — increases with your fixed costs. If you're uncertain about your expected sales volume, you probably want to choose a process that limits the amount of money you must invest in fixed costs. This means trying to secure short-term rental agreements rather than purchasing facilities and capital equipment. You may also want to utilize manual labor rather than automating the process with expensive machinery.

On the other hand, by transferring the fixed cost to a variable cost, you may reduce the contribution margin of each unit sold. The *contribution margin* is the price you sell the product for minus the variable cost per unit (R – VC). If you have a high variable cost per unit, you receive less profit per unit sold after you reach your BEP. You may want to consider making an investment in fixed assets to automate your process if you expect higher volumes.

You want to evaluate the BEP using several scenarios for fixed and variable costs so you can determine how sensitive your Q is to varying costs assumptions.

Consider a firm that must make a decision on purchasing equipment for producing highlander kilts. The firm has four options, each with different fixed and variable costs. Assuming that the firm plans to sell the kilts for $30 each, Figure 5-3 shows the combinations, the resulting BEP, and the expected profit at different sales levels.

Figure 5-4:
Comparison of fixed and variable cost scenarios.

Case	FC $	VC $/Unit	BEP	Marginal Profit/Unit	Profit at 200 Units	Profit at 500 Units	Profit at 668 Units	Profit at 1,000 Units	Profit at 2,000 Units
1	15,000	5	600	25	−10,000	−2,500	1,700	10,000	35,000
2	10,000	10	500	20	−6,000	0	3,360	10,000	30,000
3	5,000	12	278	18	−1,400	4,000	7,024	13,000	31,000
4	1,000	18	84	12	1,400	5,000	7,016	11,000	23,000

Illustration by Wiley, Composition Services Graphics

What case you choose depends on how sure you are of your expected demand and your organization's *risk tolerance* (how willing you are to gamble on high demand). Case 4 guarantees a profit at any sales level above 84 units, and you exceed the profits of any of the alternatives until sales exceed 668 units. Case 3 results in a greater profit after sales exceed 668 units. Figure 5-4 shows that as sales expectations grow, you want to invest in more FC and reduce your VC per unit. Case 1 is the most profitable if your demand exceeds 1,000 units.

Blurring the lines: Making standardized stuff customizable

At first sight, standardization and customization may appear to be an either/or decision. If you want to produce customized products for your customer, you may assume that you need to give up the benefits of standardization, such as economies of scale and reduced inventory (see Chapter 8 for details on standardization using component commonality). However, with proper product and process design, you can produce customized products and still take advantage of the benefits related to standardization.

For example, consider a fast-food hamburger chain that promises customized sandwiches for each customer. It uses the same basic processes that other chains use, but it uses a postponement strategy — a process that uses common components and delays assembly until the customer order is received (known as *made to order,* which we describe later in the chapter). If you're wondering how a postponement strategy works and benefits the business, see Chapter 8.

With proper process design, you may also be able to increase the variety of the deliverables you produce, at little additional cost, which may also increase your customer satisfaction. You just need to consider such flexibility when you design your facility layout and purchase equipment.

Improving Face-to-Face and Back-Office Operations

For many people, the term *operations* conjures images of factories and smokestacks or some other kind of manufacturing scenario. But successful businesses in the service industry also rely on efficient processes for creating customer deliverables.

There are big differences between manufacturing-based companies and service-based businesses. For starters, hotels, airlines, restaurants, theaters, and other service-based organizations can't store finished products when their capacity exceeds demand; manufacturers can. This makes the management of demand variability quite different for the two types of businesses.

But, strictly speaking, there's no such thing as a total manufacturing or service-only organization. Any business contains elements of both. For example, an automobile company must not only produce a vehicle using manufacturing operations but also provide customer service to its network of dealers and to the end customer. Banking is generally considered a service industry, but most of the functions a bank performs resemble those performed for automobile manufacturing.

Instead of classifying operations as manufacturing or service, we'd like you to view them as processes that have a direct interface with a customer *(face-to-face operations)* or processes that occur out of sight of the customer *(back-office operations)*. Every business has several processes that fall under each category. How you design an operation depends on its particular function; each has its own set of design rules.

Throughout this book, we point out the fundamental differences that exist in primarily manufacturing and mainly service organizations. Here, we're simply pointing out that manufacturing companies have many service elements and, likewise, service companies have many processes that resemble manufacturing operations.

Strengthening the customer interface

Any process that requires direct contact with the customer needs special attention. These face-to-face interactions reveal blemishes along with beauty marks to the customer. Examples of interface points include a customer entering a bank for service, a patient coming into a doctor's office for an appointment, or a patron sitting down at a restaurant table. In all these situations, customers directly interface with your resources (employees and facilities).

When designing face-to-face processes, you want to establish simple traffic patterns to make it easy for customers to get through the process, and you want to maintain a customer-friendly atmosphere.

Here are some guidelines for designing a customer interface:

- ✓ **Establish an easy service flow.** How many times have you stood in a line, only to discover you were in the wrong line? Confusing processes are infuriating to customers, so you want to avoid them. Design a process that's visible and clear from the customer's perspective.

   One way to establish a clear process is to have these components:

     • One point of entry

     • Well-marked steps

     • Personnel available to direct customers as needed

✔ **Minimize handoffs of customers.** How many times have you been at a store and gone from employee to employee, trying to find someone to answer your question or solve your problem? When designing the customer interface, clear this hurdle to customer satisfaction by creating a step in the process that makes it easy for customers to be served at their convenience or a resource that can provide a quick and clear path through the process. Implementing this may require the use of *flexible resources* (resources that can perform multiple tasks in a process). See Chapter 3 for details on using flexible resources.

✔ **Minimize the movement of the customer through your process.** The last thing you want is a customer roaming throughout your facility because she doesn't know where to go. This increases the customer's flow time and runs the risk that the customer may not end up at the next correct process step or, worse, may be exposed to those back-office processes that weren't designed for customer eyes.

✔ **Maximize the customer's comfort.** If you must make your customers wait, make sure they do so in comfort. When designing your facility, be sure to balance service and waiting areas; make sure your waiting areas are comfortable. For more ideas on how to make a favorable impression on customers while they wait, turn to Chapter 7.

✔ **Keep customers in view.** Designing a process in which your customer is always visible allows employees to make sure that the process is running as it should be and that customers aren't deviating from the desired path. Visibility also aids in security and, especially in retail operations, deters theft.

✔ **Capitalize on your space.** You generally want to place your facilities where customer traffic is high, so that potential customers can see and easily enter your facility. Because of this, most face-to-face customer interaction occurs in locations where the facility cost per square foot is high relative to less congested areas. You want high traffic or sales volume to compensate for the cost of the location. Design processes to minimize space while maintaining these directives.

✔ **Separate back-office processes from front-office processes.** Make every effort to separate your face-to-face processes from the processes that, although they must occur to satisfy the customer, the customer isn't directly involved in. Back-office processes include a restaurant kitchen, the loan approval process at a bank, and inventory storage spaces at big box stores. However, some companies expose traditional back-office processes as part of their business strategy, such as those restaurants that have open kitchens so the customer can observe the cooking or warehouse retailers that keep all inventory visible in an effort to keep costs down.

Facility layout design is critical because the design may be duplicated in many facilities. Think about your favorite fast food joint. When entering, it's often difficult to distinguish one facility from another across town or in a different state. The process and facility design of a chain restaurant is duplicated many times, so an inefficiency is magnified many times in each location.

Improving efficiencies behind the scenes

For the most part, anything that the customer doesn't have to be directly involved in should be optimized only for business efficiency. When a customer takes a check to the bank for deposit, he's unconcerned about how the money gets credited to his account — only that it does.

When designing back-office operations, you want a smooth flow of material through the process, and you want the process to be easy to control and monitor.

Design these processes with these guidelines:

- ✔ **Utilize a sequential flow pattern in the process.** You want the material to flow through the process in sequence, from station to station. Facilities, especially in manufacturing, often utilize a U-shaped design. The process begins and ends at the front of the facility. This arrangement allows a manager to observe the process over a small, confined space, making it easy to control. This design also facilitates good communication among workers because they're typically in close proximity to one another.

- ✔ **Minimize backtracking of work in the process.** Sending parts back in the process can create confusion because tracing the part in the process may become difficult; it can also impede the movement of other parts in the process. If material needs to backtrack, then maintain separate inboxes for the first-time material and returned material, or implement a marking system to distinguish the two.

- ✔ **Implement a predictable process.** If possible, all parts should progress through the process in the same steps. Aim to remove any decisions on the operator's part. If the process has decision points, then every part meeting the same criteria should go through the same predictable path.

- ✔ **Reduce material movement.** Material movement is a non-value-added activity that takes time and can lead to parts getting lost or ending up at the wrong locations. In addition, unnecessary movement can create safety concerns, especially in cases where equipment is required to move parts from place to place.

✔ **Emphasize bottleneck management.** A *bottleneck* is the operation that limits a system's overall capacity (see Chapter 2). Design processes to maximize utilization of the bottleneck. Details on how to best exploit a bottleneck are in Chapter 3.

✔ **Minimize inventory.** Inventory takes up space in your process, and you can reduce the size of your facility by reducing it. Some inventory is necessary to allow smooth operations, but too much can interfere with the smooth flow of material through the process (find more about inventory in Chapter 8).

✔ **Create an open environment.** An open environment allows everyone to see what's going on in the process and simplifies the job of managing. It exposes problems in the process because there's nowhere to hide. This applies to manufacturing operations and office environments. An open environment can also increase communication among employees because everyone can see the state of the operation.

✔ **Maintain flexibility.** A facility design should be flexible to allow for new conditions. If possible, you should be able to reconfigure the design to accommodate the introduction of new products or a change in the mix of products produced or processed at the facility.

The processes that take place out of the sight of the customer are prime for taking advantage of economies of scale. In a bank, centralizing such things as the loan decision process is common, and in fast food restaurants, employees form the hamburger patties and cut the potatoes into French fries at a central location that supplies several restaurants.

Fulfilling Customer Demand: Making to Stock or Making to Order

How do you supply products to your customer? The product-customer interface typically follows one of two patterns: make to stock or make to order. In this section, we look at both.

Making to stock

In a *make-to-stock* (MTS) process, you produce products and place them in a *finished goods inventory* (FGI) until you receive a customer order. Most consumer goods manufacturers use this process. MTS works best in environments where customers want their product on demand or where the time it takes to produce the product (the *lead time*) is greater than the time the customer is willing to wait.

In an MTS process, the firm must forecast what it believes customer demand will be (see Chapter 6 for info on how to forecast). The company produces a certain volume of product based on the demand forecast. Ready-to-sell products wait in an FGI for the customer to buy.

You can probably appreciate the benefits of MTS. Think of a grocery store shelf. When you need milk, the last thing you want to do is go to the grocery store and find out that you need to order the milk and wait for Farmer Joe to milk the cow. Often, long lead times necessitate making products to a forecast.

One downfall of the MTS process is that you have limited ability to make customized products and, if your product has a limited shelf life such as fresh fruits and vegetables, you run the risk of spoilage. In the case of consumer electronics, you run the risk of obsolete inventory. The MTS manufacturer must decide what to produce, often well before customer demand is known, because of long production lead times. You can use certain techniques to reduce lead times and increase your ability to make customized products — flip to Chapters 8 and 11 to find out how.

Making to order

A *make-to-order* (MTO) process can be your best dream or your worst nightmare. In an MTO process, you only produce something when you have a customer order. MTO allows you to avoid all the risk associated with a bad forecast and to avoid being left holding FGI that no one wants to buy. You can provide a customized product — exactly what the customer wants. However, you must produce these products within a lead time acceptable to the customer. If you can't deliver, the customer may cancel the order and/or never return to your company for future orders.

A variation of MTO is *assemble to order* (ATO). The postponement strategy used to minimize inventory (described in Chapter 8) is an example of ATO. In an ATO strategy, assembly of the final product is delayed as long as possible. This allows a firm to wait until a customer order is received but reduces the lead time because some of the process is already completed.

MTO only works if you have a good handle on what your actual lead times are and if you know the customer expectations for an acceptable lead time. In most cases, you give the customer a target delivery date for the product. If you miss this date, you risk alienating your customer and hurting your company's reputation. MTO requires a well-oiled production process because you have no stock of inventory to hide any mistakes.

Many service processes can only operate using MTO. For example, you can't process a mortgage loan application until a customer requests a loan. You can't have an FGI of approved loan applications waiting for the customer. Chapter 7 goes into detail on how to build and manage capacity in these service operations.

A tale of two companies: Making either method work

Fortunately, most companies can be successful using either the MTS or the MTO process. They just have to design a process to take advantage of the positives and be prepared to negate the negatives of each.

Take two competing personal computer (PC) manufacturers. One utilizes MTS, while the other emerged in the market utilizing MTO. Both experienced success in the PC computer revolution.

The first company remained with the traditional model of MTS. It manufactured a few models of computers and sold them through major retailers. By utilizing a superior forecasting model, it was able to supply its sales outlets with the products customers were demanding. It designed its production process to mass-produce the models and took advantage of commonality and postponement to minimize inventory (see Chapter 8).

The competitor introduced an MTO process, producing a computer only when it received an order. This company could customize computers 100 percent. It was only able to accomplish this because of outstanding knowledge of its production lead times and a process that took minimal time to make a computer. The company used such techniques as implementing a batch size of 1 (see Chapter 3) and developing a responsive supply chain that could respond to unpredictable customer demand (see Chapter 10).

In addition, the MTO strategy only worked because of the modularity of the components that make up a computer. *Modularity,* or the ability to swap one component for another, allowed the manufacturer to use different components, such as the hard drive in the same interface, so hard drives of different sizes could be easily popped in during assembly.

The market had room for both strategies. The two different strategies were possible because the target customer for each company was slightly different. MTS customers wanted a computer that met their basic requirements; they didn't care about what was under the hood. They also wanted technical assistance and/or home installation. The MTO company appealed to more sophisticated buyers who understood the differences in RAM space and computer chip speed and wanted an ability to customize what they thought was the ultimate machine. In addition, they needed limited customer support and didn't mind waiting a few days to receive their computer.

Any production strategy can work if you integrate product design, process design, and intimate knowledge of customer expectations and requirements at a competitive price point.

Designing for X: Designing Products with Operations in Mind

A large part of a product's cost to manufacture is determined by the product design itself. The design determines how many components make up the product and dictates how these components must work together to provide the product's necessary functionality. This section describes the design techniques that successful firms use when developing products.

Long ago, product designers developed new products without any input from manufacturing engineers. This "throw it over the wall" approach often resulted in designs that were difficult to manufacture and that incurred higher-than-necessary production costs.

Most firms now participate in concurrent engineering, which brings product design and process design personnel together early in the design phase. This allows manufacturing to have input into the design and to make suggestions on how best to design a product that minimizes production costs. This meeting of the product and process design minds is commonly referred to as *design for manufacturing* (DFM).

The DFM revolution has led to the *design for* revolution. Following on the heels of DFM, every aspect of the product is considered in the design, and this generates a sea of DFXs — you fill in the X. Here are some examples:

- **Design for assembly (DFA):** This is similar to DFM and focuses solely on how to design for ease of assembly and for reduced assembly time. Accomplish this by designing a product with few parts and by making the interface among the components simple, such as designing snap-together parts rather than parts that have to be bolted together.

✔ **Design for logistics (DFL):** This involves designing a product for ease of transporting from manufacturing to the customer. With rising transportation costs, the importance of DFL is only increasing. Utilizing DFL, companies design and package products to minimize the space required to ship.

✔ **Design for sustainability:** Companies now design products with the product's end of life in mind. Environmental concerns are forcing designers to consider how a product can be reused or recycled. Examples include designing an ink cartridge that can be easily refilled and incorporating biodegradable materials into the product.

✔ **Design for service:** Throughout their life cycle, many products need to be serviced or repaired. Depending on how components are placed in the design, they can be easy or difficult to access when service is needed.

✔ **Design for reliability/quality (DFR, DFQ):** Quality doesn't just happen, and it's not solely the responsibility of manufacturing. DFQ recognizes that quality starts in the product's design. For details on quality, check out Chapters 12 and 13.

Part II
Managing Variability and Risk

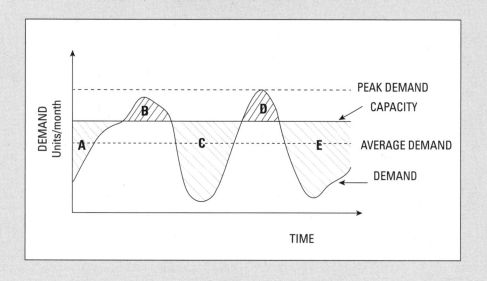

Check out this book's Cheat Sheet at www.dummies.com/extras/operations management for a compilation of the most useful mathematical formulas related to operations management.

In this part . . .

✔ Find out how to forecast demand for your product or service as accurately as possible so that you don't waste resources or leave your customers hanging.

✔ Get advice on long-term capacity planning that will help to maximize profits and accomplish other company goals.

✔ Discover how to balance inventory with customer demand and detemine which inventory management system is right for your business.

✔ Understand the importance of planning in operations management and get a look at the tools you can use to plan operations from the top down.

✔ Learn how to maintain a strong supply chain, so that you can deliver quality goods and services to your customers whenever they need them.

Chapter 6

Forecasting Demand

. . . .

In This Chapter

▶ Getting acquainted with the fundamental rules of forecasting

▶ Predicting demand using various methods

▶ Finding and measuring forecasting error

. . . .

*H*ow wonderful life would be, especially in the world of operations management, if it were possible to gaze into a crystal ball and accurately predict future events and consumer behavior. Unfortunately, that kind of foresight just isn't available. The next best thing is a well-developed forecast.

In business, a *forecast* refers to an estimate or prediction of what is likely to happen in the future. The key words here are *estimate* and *prediction.* Without the elusive crystal ball, forecasts, to some degree, are always inaccurate. At best, forecasting is an imprecise science, but not having a forecast to guide decisions about inventory, capacity, and production levels can be fatal to a business.

One of the biggest determinants of financial success is how accurately you can predict demand. If you forecast your demand too high, you may waste resources producing more products than customers will purchase. If you forecast demand too low, you may leave customers disappointed because they can't purchase your product.

This chapter is all about forecasting demand. We start by introducing the general rules of forecasting and describing the basic types of forecasting models, and then we detail the most popular methods for measuring the error of a forecast.

Getting Savvy about Forecasts

Point forecasts, or single-number predictions of demand, are generally always incorrect. That's why you need not only an *expected value* (what you think demand will be) but also a measure of your method's *forecasting error* (see the section "Acknowledging the Error of Your Ways" later in this chapter).

Here are the fundamental tenets of forecasting:

- ✔ **Aggregated forecasts are more accurate than disaggregated forecasts.** Forecasting the demand for a product at a national level is more accurate than forecasting it at each individual retail outlet. The variation of demand at each sales point is smoothed when aggregated with other locations, providing a more accurate prediction. You can achieve a similar improvement by forecasting the aggregate demand for all the variations of a product combined instead of forecasting a single variation.

- ✔ **Be prepared to change your forecasting model, but don't overreact to random changes.** Demand patterns can and do change, and when actual changes occur, you may need to change your forecasting technique. Measuring your forecasting error can alert you when changes occur; however, you need to verify that a sustainable change has actually occurred and that what you observed isn't a random variation. (For more on forecasting error, see the section "Acknowledging the Error of Your Ways" later in the chapter.)

- ✔ **Don't substitute forecasts for known information.** Many companies can become blinded by their forecast and ignore what's actually occurring in the business environment. If something changes, such as a weather occurrence, or more data becomes available, such as a sales order, be prepared to adjust your forecast to incorporate the new information.

- ✔ **If a simple technique yields acceptable accuracy, don't use a more advanced technique.** Use the simplest forecasting model that provides the desired accuracy. For example, don't use a model for seasonality unless it gives you noticeably greater accuracy than a simple exponential smoothing model (we describe forecasting models in the next section).

- ✔ **Select a forecasting technique that makes good use of the available data.** The time-series forecasting methods discussed later in the chapter rely on having not only a large quantity of data but also relevant and accurate data. If you don't have confidence in the amount or quality of the data, you may want to choose a qualitative method to forecast until data becomes available. For example, consider basing your forecasts on potential market size and adjusting based on experience. Applying sophisticated forecasting models to faulty data won't improve the underlying quality of the data or the forecast.

- ✔ **Short-term forecasts are more reliable than long-term forecasts.** The forecast *horizon,* or how long into the future the forecast predicts, has a direct impact on accuracy. In other words, predicting the sales for this month is easier than predicting the sales for a year from now. Many things can happen between now and next year, such as new competitors entering the market, customer preferences changing, or new technology causing shifts in demand. These changes become tougher to predict as the forecast horizon increases.

✔ **There is no single best forecasting technique.** The important point is to compare different forecasting models and choose the one that best meets the needs of your situation and matches the data you have available.

It's important to note that, although disaggregate forecasts can be less accurate than aggregate forecasts, disaggregate forecasts are critical to production planning (see Chapter 9). For example, if a firm produces different models of TVs, production planning at the manufacturing floor level requires a detailed number of how many of each model to produce. By postponing a commitment to the details, the firm can make a more accurate disaggregate forecast (short-term forecasts are more accurate than long-term forecasts). Reducing flow times allows a firm to delay the decision on what exact models to produce, which improves its forecasts.

Building a Forecast to Predict Demand

You have many ways to build a business forecast, and this section describes a few different basic techniques. But before you can even begin building a forecast, you must get a handle on your demand patterns.

Forecasting demand — not sales — is the name of the game. If you forecast future sales based on past sales, you may miss significant demand for your product. Sales data doesn't account for the fact that some potential customers may not have been able to purchase your product in the past because it wasn't available. It also doesn't account for a changing market size.

Recognizing demand variation

Demand isn't always consistent; demand can vary for many reasons. Recognizing why demand varies helps you increase your forecast's accuracy. Specifically, watch for these factors that may trigger variations in your demand:

✔ **Cycles** are wavelike occurrences that repeat over longer periods of time. They're usually tied to economic conditions or the business cycle. Big-ticket items such as automobiles often display this type of pattern.

✔ **Irregular variations** are changes that result from a one-time event. They're not representative of normal conditions. A celebrity using a product in public that spurs fans to go out and purchase in mass and the sale of water bottles before a major weather event are examples of irregular variations.

✔ **Random variations** occur without any known reason or explanation. They're the unforeseeable and unexpected changes in demand.

✔ **Seasonal factors** are regular variations that occur over and over and are related to some particular event. Products and services with significant seasonal demand include air conditioners and snow shovels (which vary by time of year) and back-to-school clothing and supplies (which vary according to certain events). Some industries have "seasonal" demand patterns that occur more frequently, such as the weekly increase in customers on Fridays and Saturdays at restaurants. Seasonal factors can sometimes be self-induced, as in end-of-quarter or end-of-year sales or promotions to help a firm make sales quotas.

✔ **Trends** are a long-term upward or downward movement in demand. When products experience a growth or decline in the market, trends tend to emerge. Examples include the growth of organic products in the supermarket and the decline in sales of paper books in favor of the electronic variety.

Looking to the past to predict the future

The most popular forecasting model for established products and services monitors demand over time, making predictions based on what's happened in the past. This method requires past data for current metrics. Two basic techniques —the *moving average* and *exponential smoothing* — provide this kind of forecast, and you can modify the basic techniques to account for trends and seasonal fluctuations that often exist in demand patterns.

Tracking the average

The *moving average* method uses an average of a consistent number (n) of past occurrences to predict the future value. You update the average each time you observe a new occurrence. Calculate the moving average forecast with this equation:

$$MA_n = \frac{A_1 + A_2 + \cdots + A_n}{n}$$

Compute the moving average forecast MA_n by summing the most recent past n actual observations (A_n, A_n, ... A_n) and dividing by the number of observations summed (n).

To give a three-month moving average example, assuming that demand over the last three months has been 1,225, 1,365, and 1,415 units, your forecast for next month (month 4) would be 1,335 units.

As each new actual observation becomes available, update the forecast by adding the newest observation and dropping the oldest. Updating the previous example, if demand in month four is actually 1,455, then the forecast for month five using a three-month average is (1,365 + 1,415 + 1,455) ÷ 3 = 1,412.

An important decision is how many past observations to use in the moving average. The previous example uses three observations and is often referred to as an *MA(3) forecast* because it's a moving average with three terms. Figure 6-1 shows the demand pattern for a product with its MA(3) and MA(5) forecasts.

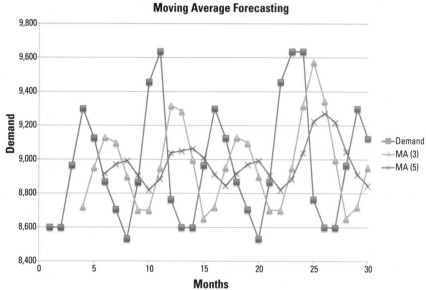

Moving Average Forecasting

Figure 6-1:
Comparison
of moving
average
forecasts.

Illustration by Wiley, Composition Services Graphics

In Figure 6-1, the MA(3) more closely follows the actual demand than the MA(5). This figure also shows that a moving average forecast follows behind the actual data series; the greater the number of observations *(n)* used in the forecast, the farther behind the actual demand the forecast will be.

In general, a forecast with a small number of observations allows quick adjustments to recent change in demand and allows you to be more responsive to these changes. However, if you're subject to random demand variations that you don't want to react to, then choosing a larger number of observations will smooth the forecast and limit the impact of random changes.

A major disadvantage of a moving average forecast is that it weighs each observation equally, no matter how far in the past it occurred. This type of forecast also fails to account for any difference that exists between what was forecast to occur and what actually did. You can address these issues by using a different approach; the exponential smoothing average is a weighted average with exponentially declining weights on past observations.

Smoothing exponentially

Exponential smoothing addresses the major issues with moving average forecasting by accounting for the error in a forecast. In exponential smoothing, each new forecast (F_t) is simply the sum of the previous forecast (F_{t-1}) plus a percentage (α) of the difference between the previous forecast and what actually happened (A_{t-1}). α is often referred to as the *smoothing constant* and is always a value between 0 and 1.

This difference between what actually occurred and what was forecasted to occur is the *forecast error*. We talk more about forecast errors in the "Acknowledging the Error of Your Ways" section later in this chapter.

The general equation for the next forecast is

$$F_t = F_{t-1} + \alpha\left(A_{t-1} - F_{t-1}\right)$$

Figure 6-2 shows demand for the product that was referenced in Figure 6-1 as forecasted with a smoothing constant of 0.2 and 0.7. At time 25, the forecast for the $\alpha = 0.2$ series (F_{25}) is 9,120 and the actual observation (A_{25}) is 8,764. The forecast for time 26 $(F_{26}) = 9,120 + (0.2)(8,764 - 9,120) = 9,049$.

Figure 6-2 shows that the forecast always lags the actual data and that the larger the α is, the more responsive the forecast is to changes in demand. On the other hand, a larger α also makes you more prone to overreacting to random changes in demand.

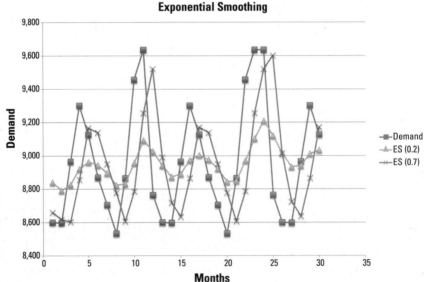

Figure 6-2: Comparison of exponential smoothing forecasts.

TIP

In general, you want to choose a small α for items with stable demand and a larger α for products with new or changing demand.

Both moving average and exponential smoothing forecasting reveal the effects of changing n and α. When choosing the best technique and parameter value for your forecast, you can set up a spreadsheet with past demand values and calculate what your forecast would have been given different parameter values. Comparing the results of this forecast and what actually happened, you can determine the value that gives you the best forecast. The accuracy, however, relies on your demand pattern holding steady based on the past.

Accounting for trend

Many products experience an upward or downward trend in demand over time. Accurately forecasting demand requires you to recognize when this occurs. If you don't, your forecast won't keep up (or down) with the trend.

A popular technique for forecasting demand when a trend exists is *trend-adjusted exponential smoothing.* The forecast (F_{t-1}) consists of a smoothed forecast (S_t) and a trend factor (T_t).

To calculate a trend-adjusted forecast, use this formula: $F_{t+1} = S_t + T_t$

Calculate S_t as

$$S_t = F_t + \alpha(A_t - F_t)$$

And solve for T_t:

$$T_t = T_{t-1} + \beta(F_t - F_{t-1} - T_{t-1})$$

You must choose two smoothing constants α for the average and a β for the trend. Be sure to use the same procedure as discussed in the preceding "Smoothing exponentially" section for choosing a β. You want to use different combinations of both α and β because there may be some interaction between the two. The optimal β can vary based on the chosen value of α.

Figure 6-3 shows the forecast for demand with an α of 0.3 and a β equal to 0.4. For example, at time 10, the forecast (F_{10}) is 137.1 but actual demand (A_{10}) turns out to be 151. From this, the smoothed forecast (S_{10}) is 137.1 + (0.3)(151 − 137.1) = 141.3. You then need to find the trend at time 10 (T_{10}). The trend at time 9 (T_9) was 6.0, and the forecast at time 9 (F_9) was 130.7. The trend at time 10 (T_{10}) is 6.0 + (0.4)(137.1 − 130.7 − 6.0) = 6.2. From that, you can find that the forecast at time 11 (F_{11}) is 141.3 + 6.2=147.5.

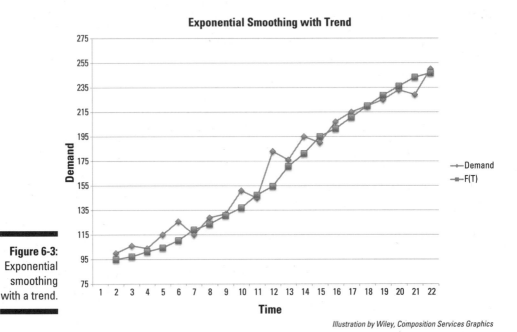

Figure 6-3:
Exponential
smoothing
with a trend.

Facing seasonality

Seasonality is the upward or downward movements in demand that are associated with recurring events, such as weather and holidays. The time period for a season can be long or short. For example, sales at movie theaters are generally higher in the summer and around Christmas. Another example of seasonal effects — the use of the term *seasonal* can be a bit confusing — is the increased number of customers in movie theaters on Friday and Saturday.

When accounting for seasonality, you want to express demand in terms of how much the value varies from the total average. For the movie theater, over the course of one or more weeks, an average number of customers visit per day — X(average). Calculate this average by summing the number of customers over the course of a week and dividing that sum by 7 (the number of days open in the week). You may want to do this for more than one week to get an adequate sample. Then forecast X(average) using the moving average or exponential smoothing technique described in previous sections.

To calculate the movie theater's seasonality index for each day of the week, take the average number of customers for any one day and divide that number by the X(average). For example, if the theater serves an average of 1,600 customers a day and the average for a Monday is 400, then the seasonality index for Monday is 0.25 (400 ÷ 1,600). On a Saturday, the theater serves 2,400 customers and has an index value of 1.5 (2,400 ÷ 1,600).

After you calculate the seasonal index, you can forecast demand for each day by multiplying the index by the average forecasted demand, X(average). Monitor X(average) to identify any trends you may need to consider for future forecasts and business planning.

Figure 6-4 shows the forecast for a time series that exhibits seasonality.

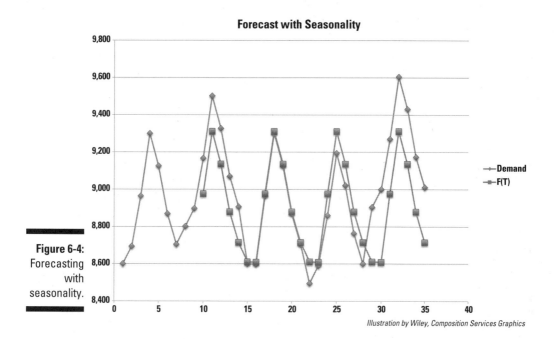

Figure 6-4: Forecasting with seasonality.

Illustration by Wiley, Composition Services Graphics

Lacking data: No problem

The forecasting methods described in the previous sections require past demand data. In many cases, this data isn't available. For example, when you introduce a new product or enter a new market, no record of past demand exists for forecasts.

In this situation, you can use qualitative techniques and build causal models to build a forecast.

Relying on qualitative techniques

Without past data, you must rely on judgment and opinion to derive a forecast. The key is to get as close to the customer (or potential customer) as you can. Here are some methods you can utilize:

✔ **Collaborative forecasting:** Collaborative forecasting involves gathering information about the marketplace from personnel at all levels of the organization and supply chain. This method works well for long-range planning and new product development.

✔ **Customer surveys:** Surveying current and potential customers can generate helpful information, but you must be careful when conducting the survey. Proper survey design and implementation could fill its own *For Dummies* book; it's beyond the scope of this book. Just be aware that survey information can be misleading.

✔ **Demand patterns of similar products:** When introducing new products to the market, looking at demand patterns of similar products in the past can provide a good starting point. Particularly for electronics, most new products seem to follow a similar demand curve as previously launched products in a given category. See Chapter 18 for details on how to manage new product growth.

✔ **Direct customer contact:** Your salespeople and customer service representatives are your lifeline into what customers are thinking. Direct input from customers provides the best information on potential demand when trying to forecast.

Identifying related variables

Another way to forecast demand for a product is to find correlations in demand between your product and other products. For example, demand for electric vehicles may exhibit a relationship with the price of gasoline.

Here, you can use a simple *regression model* which represents the statistical relationship between the two variables — in this case, electric vehicle demand and the price of gasoline. Figure 6-5 shows a sample relationship between the price of gasoline and the demand for electric cars.

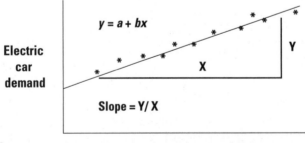

Figure 6-5:
Causal
relationship.

Illustration by Wiley, Composition Services Graphics

By plotting the variables, you can derive an equation that shows their relationship. The value of the second (or dependent) variable *(y)* is given by the following equation:

$$Y = a + bx$$

x is the value of the first (or independent variable), *b* is the slope of the line (the change in the *y* value divided by the change in the *x* value), and *a* is the value of *y* when *x* is 0.

For example, assume *a* is 40,000 cars and *b* is 10,000 cars per $1.00 increase in gasoline prices. If the price of gas *(x)* is $4.50, then the forecast for car sales is 40,000 + (10,000)(4.50) = 85,000 cars.

Acknowledging the Error of Your Ways

Forecasts tend to be inaccurate, and you need to find out how (in)accurate your forecasting model is. *Forecasting error* is the difference between the forecast and actual values. In this section, we point out the most common reasons that forecasts are inaccurate and give you metrics for determining how off target you are.

Hunting down the source of your error

Forecasts are inaccurate for many reasons. Here are some of the most common sources of errors:

- **Incorrectly identifying the relationship between variables:** In the "Identifying related variables" section earlier in the chapter, we give you a formula to identify the correlation between one variable and another. In reality, there may be more than one variable determining an outcome. For example, sales of electric automobiles can be related to not only the price of gasoline but also the price of the car itself and the availability of public charging stations in your town. Multivariate analysis is outside the scope of this book, but you should be aware that correctly identifying variables has an impact on your forecast.

- **Not recognizing trends in demand:** When you fail to recognize trends (either upward or downward) and don't account for them in your forecasting model, your forecast will significantly lag your actual demand. Trends can change quickly and be subtle and therefore be difficult to observe. Using the wrong trend line is a common mistake.

✔ **Not updating forecasting assumptions and techniques:** You should monitor your forecasting method on a regular basis to detect any changes in demand patterns. Fundamental shifts in demand may require you to change your forecasting technique. By monitoring your forecasting error, you can quickly detect changes in your demand.

✔ **Projecting past trends into the future:** When you use the time-series methods (moving average and exponential smoothing), you're making the assumption that past patterns will continue in the future. This can be dangerous, especially in rapidly changing markets, where products experience tremendous growth in demand or become obsolete quickly. For information on product life cycles, check out Chapter 18.

✔ **Reacting to random or special cause variations:** *Random* variation is the natural shifts that occur from many minor sources. It's the "noise" in your system that can't be explained. *Special cause* variation is fluctuation that can be contributed to an event that doesn't normally occur, such as a hurricane warning that forces evacuations and causes a rise in hotel stays in certain areas. Don't react to these variations, because they're unpredictable and nonrecurring. For more on the statistical nature of random variations, see Chapter 12.

✔ **Relying on biased information sources:** Sales performance is often measured based on actual sales as compared to the forecast. If actual sales exceed the forecast, salespeople are often rewarded, so low forecasts offer them a greater chance of exceeding it. Production staff, on the other hand, tend to prefer high demand forecasts so they have more resources available to meet the forecasted demand. Be sure to consider the source of information for your forecasts. Avoid or minimize bias to create accurate forecasts.

✔ **Using an insufficient number of data points:** Using time-series data often requires a significant amount of data, especially if trends or seasonality conditions exist. What may look like a pattern in your data may actually be random variation in demand. Accurately identifying seasonal shifts in demand requires a significant amount of past data. You want to make sure you have enough points to observe the pattern over several seasons. Exactly how much past data you need depends on the nature of your business and product. Choosing the number you need requires statistical analysis beyond the scope of this book.

Measuring how inaccurate you are

A company makes many important decisions based on what it anticipates future demand to be. These decisions include how much capacity to purchase and maintain, how many people to hire, and how much inventory to hold. Making these decisions on an inaccurate forecast can be very costly to the bottom line. If the forecast overestimates demand, the firm can spend money on unnecessary capacity and can end up with an excess of inventory that it can't sell. On the other hand, if the forecast underestimates demand, the company may find a growing backlog of orders or, worse yet, it may lose sales because of the unavailability of products. Because of the high stakes involved, it's important to monitor the accuracy of the forecast.

You have a few different options for measuring how inaccurate your forecast is. This section describes some of these methods and points out when you should think about changing your forecasting model. The first two methods measure the average error of the forecast in terms of the demand being forecast. The second pair measures the error in percentage terms, which is probably more important to the typical user of forecasts. Finally, we describe a way for you to determine if any systematic bias exists in your forecast.

Mean absolute deviation (MAD) and mean squared error (MSE)

One of the most common ways to assess the mean absolute error is to find the *mean absolute deviation* (MAD) with this formula:

$$MAD = \frac{\sum |Actual - Forecast|}{n}$$

In this equation, you average the absolute value of the error over *n* periods.

Mean squared error (MSE) is the average squared error and is calculated as

$$MSE = \frac{\sum (Actual - Forecast)^2}{n-1}$$

Here, the error is squared.

The difference between these two measurements is that MAD weights all errors evenly, and MSE weights the errors by their squared values. Because of this squaring, MSE is more sensitive (gives more weight) to outliers, and the units are the square of the variable's units, which is often confusing to interpret.

The primary use of these measures is to allow you to compare different forecasting methods. For example, you could forecast using exponential smoothing and compare the errors for different values of α, choosing the one that results in the lowest value of MAD or MSE.

Mean absolute percent error (MAPE)

One significant issue with MAD and MSE is that they produce a result in absolute terms, meaning that a product with greater demand gives a larger measure than a product with less demand. *Mean absolute percent error* (MAPE) takes care of this by providing the error in percentage terms. You calculate MAPE using this equation:

$$MAPE = \frac{\sum \left| \frac{Actual - Forecast}{Actual} \right|}{n} \cdot 100$$

MAPE is useful when comparing forecasting methods across products with different magnitudes of demand. For this reason, MAPE is a preferred measure of accuracy among experienced forecasters.

Tracking signal (TS)

Because of inevitable changes in demand patterns, it's necessary to have a way to tell when your current forecasting method is no longer working. One option is to use control charts that monitor your error over time; another option is to use a *tracking signal* (TS). (Check out Chapters 12 and 13 for details on how to make and use a control chart.)

Here's the equation for the tracking signal:

$$TS = \frac{\sum (Actual - Forecast)}{MAD}$$

The TS shows bias that may exist in your forecast. *Bias* is the tendency for the forecast to always be greater or less than the actual value of the demand. If the TS exceeds a predetermined value, you want to consider changing your forecasting model.

Typically, if your TS goes outside +/– 4, which closely corresponds to the three standard deviation limits used in control charts (see Chapter 12), you may want to change your forecasting methodology because the method is biased (it is consistently measuring too low if the TS is positive and too high if the TS is negative). In addition, if you experience five or more positive or negative error calculations (actual versus forecast) in a row, you may want to consider a change in the methodology.

Chapter 7

Planning Capacity

· ·

· ·

*I*n a perfect world, output would be designed to exactly meet steady demand at a low cost. However, demand variability is an unfortunate business reality, and operations managers have a number of ways to manage fluctuations. One of the most important is adjusting the *output rate,* or capacity.

Capacity is a company's maximum possible sustained level of output of goods or services. Part I of this book goes into detail about how to calculate and utilize process capacity. In this chapter, we take a closer look at capacity, focusing on how to leverage capacity by long-term planning (including appointment and reservation policies) to achieve company goals, such as maximizing profit. We also describe a process for determining how much capacity you really need. After all, more capacity costs more money, and a company doesn't want to build any more than it really needs. We also address how you can use inventory to reduce the need for capacity over the long term. Finally, we look at how capacity influences the issue of customer lines and wait times, which is a common issue in many service and some manufacturing industries.

This chapter is primarily meant to help you perform long-term capacity planning. After you determine capacity to match long-term demand trends, you need other techniques to help manage short-term fluctuations in demand. In Chapter 8, we cover inventory management, and in Chapter 9, we look at short-term aggregate demand planning. In many firms, different individuals perform each of these functions, yet each of these methods has a part to play in meeting variable demand.

Considering Capacity

No simple standard equation exists to tell you how much capacity you need — right now or in the future — or when exactly you should add capacity. Determining the correct capacity level for your business at any given time to satisfy customer demand takes a great deal of assessment and careful consideration because demand fluctuates, and adding capacity (which often involves building facilities, securing suppliers, and/or training employees) takes time and money.

When developing a capacity plan, start by answering these questions:

✔ **How variable is your customer demand?** When demand is smooth, operations are pretty simple. Unfortunately, however, demand tends to have a great deal of variability. The more variable your demand is over time, the more capacity and/or inventory you need in order to cover demand during the spikes. (In Chapter 9, find out how to smooth out the spikes with aggregate planning.)

✔ **How much inventory can you hold?** Answering this question requires you to understand the costs of holding inventory (see Chapter 8) and how time spent in inventory affects product quality (covered in Chapters 12 and 13). If your product is tiramisu, for example, the cake's quality may deteriorate as it sits in the freezer.

✔ **How expensive is acquiring and maintaining capacity?** Getting a handle on your how much your capacity costs to acquire and maintain is important because you need to know how much it costs to maintain extra capacity to deal with surges in demand. (We cover the costs of capacity in Chapter 5.)

✔ **How long is your customer willing to wait for your product or service?** You must know your customer's expectations when it comes to *delivery lead time,* or how long a customer must wait between placing the order and receiving the product. For service industries, this equals time spent waiting in line for service. Wait time is an important component of customer satisfaction.

✔ **How long does it take to expand or build new capacity?** If you have to hire people or buy equipment, expanding capacity may take a long time and require careful planning, as covered in this chapter. On the other hand, you may be able to cover small increases with overtime (see Chapter 9) or temporary increases with short-run inventory buildups, as described in the later "Balancing Capacity and Inventory" section. These topics are also covered in Chapter 9.

Matching supply and demand

Managing demand variability creates a perplexing problem for managers seeking to improve the return on investment (ROI) of their operation. Building and maintaining capacity (along with producing and holding inventory) is expensive; capacity and inventory represent a huge portion if not most of the costs associated with doing business. On the other hand, if you don't have the capacity or inventory you need to manage demand variability, you risk late shipments or not having product available when customers want it. So you can either spend money on extra capacity and/or inventory to meet demand surges or risk losing customer revenue.

Predicting demand, particularly over the long term, is difficult. Using the forecasting methods described in Chapter 6, you can obtain a *point forecast,* an actual expected demand that includes any expected growth, as well as a measure of how inaccurate this forecast may be. The greater the expected variability of demand, the more excess capacity and/or inventory you need to have available.

Choosing an appropriate capacity is difficult when you don't know for sure what demand will be. If demand occasionally spikes above process capacity, as shown in areas B and D in Figure 7-1, customers will either leave the line or cancel their order prematurely (reducing profit immediately) or not return to your company the next time they want your product. This reduces customer demand, revenue, and profit.

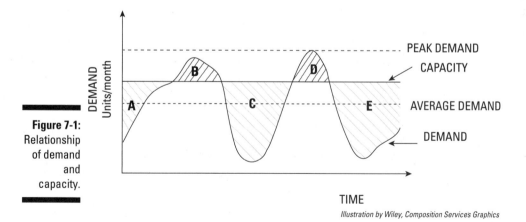

Figure 7-1: Relationship of demand and capacity.

Illustration by Wiley, Composition Services Graphics

If you're concerned about disappointing customers, you can increase capacity to the level of peak demand and always be able to service every customer.

But this may lead to further underutilization of your resources because they're already underutilized in the times shown by areas A, C, and E in Figure 7-1.

If you carry inventory, you can build up an inventory during area A in Figure 7-1, as the demand during that period is less than capacity. You can then sell off that inventory during period B, when demand is greater than capacity. Similarly, you can build up inventory during period C to cover a shortfall in capacity in period D, and so on. This approach allows you to satisfy most, if not all, demand while maintaining a high utilization of resources, hence improving ROI. We provide more information on balancing capacity and inventory levels later in this chapter in the section "Balancing Capacity and Inventory."

Timing adjustments just right

In most industries, capacity is typically added in chunks, known as *step increases,* because adding a single unit of capacity is impractical. If demand exceeds a company's current capacity, then the company must increase capacity by either acquiring more equipment or hiring additional workers.

The equipment or worker has the capacity to do a fixed amount of work, which steps up the company's capacity. For example, in an electronics firm, the smallest component placement machines (which put the integrated circuits, resistors, and transistors on the circuit board) produce several thousand parts per year. You can't buy a machine that only produces several hundred. In services, you simply cannot hire a nurse for less than half time, which means that you'll need to increase capacity in steps of about 120 patients per month.

Always make sure that when you add capacity, you add it to the correct parts of the process (often the bottleneck, as described in Chapter 3) to avoid allocating resources to improvement efforts that don't meet your goals.

The step process can make planning capacity decisions even more difficult, especially when you require new facilities because predicting demand gets harder as you consider time periods farther in the future. Keep in mind that a forecast for demand this month is likely to be much more accurate than a forecast for demand a year from now. The longer it takes to build additional capacity, the less certain you can be of actual demand at that time.

You may need several months or longer to build a new manufacturing facility or retail outlet, and training new employees also takes time. Building capacity at the right time ensures that goods and services are available when customers demand them. If your timing is off, you may miss sales or find yourself sitting on excess capacity.

Figure 7-2 shows capacity being added in a step function pattern to match increasing demand. Each new piece of equipment or worker adds to the capacity in defined amounts. A restaurant, for example, hires an additional server who can serve ten customers per hour.

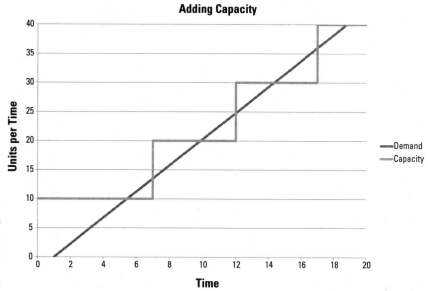

Figure 7-2:
Adding
capacity.

Demand can also decline. In this case, step issues are a problem for the same reasons they are for managing increasing demand; similar issues arise. If lower demand results in firing people, then problems with workplace morale, employee discontent, and so forth can also occur. Chapter 18 covers the product life cycle.

Balancing Capacity and Inventory

How do you manage your capacity to make sure you always have enough inventory to serve customers while keeping inventory levels as low as possible? Or, looking at it from the other direction, how much capacity should you have and exactly how much inventory should you build up during the periods when you have more capacity than demand?

When you set out to determine how much capacity and inventory you need, the first thing to do is analyze how inventory can build up over the long run, given a set capacity. Consider the process shown in Figure 7-3.

Figure 7-3:
Balancing
supply and
demand with
inventory.

Balancing Supply and Demand with Inventory

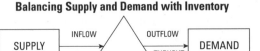

Think of the supply into and the demand from an inventory as a pair of operations. In this case, let the capacity of the supply operation, representing what you can produce during any time period, be equal to S, and for maximum efficiency, we will produce at maximum capacity for the entire time period. Let the capacity of the demand operation, or customer demand during the time period, be equal to D. The supply represents the inflow, and the demand is the outflow of the stock of inventory.

Ideally you want S to equal D, but because of variations in D, you encounter periods when D is either less than or greater than S. When S is greater than D, items accumulate in inventory; when D is greater than S, items are pulled from inventory. The following equation shows the amount of inventory at any time, represented by b, given an initial inventory at time a:

$$I_b = \int_a^b \big[in(t) - out(t) \big] dt$$

In the equation, $in(t)$ is the inflow from S, and $out(t)$ is the outflow from D.

If the sight of a calculus equation makes you sweat, relax; you don't need it to figure this out. Consider a simple example to illustrate how the concept applies: My favorite bakery in the North End of Boston makes tiramisu desserts that are world famous. The cakes are popular with the locals, and tourists are known to wait in the streets on a busy summer evening to purchase one. The demand for tiramisu during the first 6 months of the year is 1,800 cakes per month. Demand increases to 2,500 cakes per month the second half of the year, during the high tourist season and the holidays. The bakery has a maximum capacity to produce 2,000 cakes per month.

Figure 7-4 shows the demand and capacity over the course of a year.

The bakery has several operating alternatives for producing tiramisu:

- ✔ Produce cakes only as they're ordered and maintain no inventory, a strategy known as *make-to-order*. This is often referred to as *chase demand strategy* because the firm matches production to the expected demand for the period.

> ✔ Produce cakes all year at capacity and maintain an inventory to cover increased demand during the second half of the year, an approach known as *make-to-stock*. This is also often referred to as a *level production strategy* because the firm maintains a constant output.
>
> ✔ Increase capacity above current levels, which reduces inventory needs.

In general, carrying inventory is less expensive than carrying idle capacity, and inventory is more flexible if demand doesn't materialize because you don't need to build it up or you can save it for sale later. In comparison, idle capacity wastes money on excess equipment, floor space, maintenance, and possibly idle labor. But you also pay a price for inventory; inventory incurs the holding costs of tied-up capital for storage space, shrinkage, obsolescence, and quality. Flip to Chapter 8 for more on the true costs of inventory.

Capacity & Demand for Tiramisu Cakes

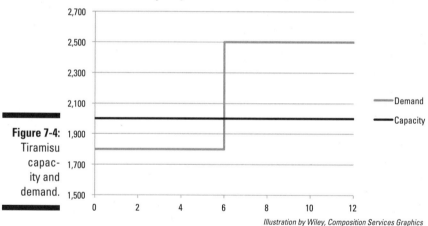

Figure 7-4: Tiramisu capacity and demand.

Illustration by Wiley, Composition Services Graphics

Producing to match demand

If the bakery described in Figure 7-4 chooses to produce cakes only at the rate of demand and maintain no inventory (chase demand strategy), then during the first 6 months of the year, it produces only 1,800 cakes per month. Its supply (or thruput) is less than its capacity, and its *utilization* (how busy resources are) is

$$Utilization = \frac{1,800}{2,000} = 90\%$$

During the second half of the year, the bakery works at a capacity of 2,000 cakes per month but loses sales of 500 cakes per month because it can't fulfill customer demand. Over the 6 months, the bakery loses sales of 3,000 cakes. Assuming that it makes a profit on each cake, this results in a considerable loss in profit.

In this case, if the bakery wants to avoid losing sales while maintaining a zero inventory policy, it needs a capacity equal to the maximum demand of 2,500 cakes per month. The bakery can avoid some of these lost sales without adding capacity if it uses the downtime in the first half of the year to produce cakes for inventory, as shown in the next section.

Producing at capacity

If the bakery doesn't want to send away 500 customers per month, it can produce at capacity and accumulate inventory over the first 6 months (level production strategy).

An inventory buildup diagram, or IBD, is a simple visual tool that shows the current level of inventory over time. Figure 7-5 shows the buildup of inventory over the year if the bakery described in Figure 7-4 produces at capacity, assuming that it begins the year with zero cakes in inventory.

Inventory (cakes)

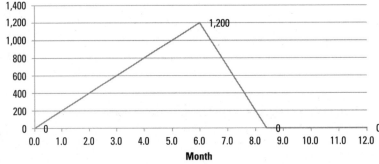

Figure 7-5: Inventory of tiramisu cakes.

Illustration by Wiley, Composition Services Graphics

If the supply and demand is constant between time a and time b, as is the case with the bakery in this example, then the inventory at time b is equal to

$$I_b = I_a + (T_b - T_a) \cdot (S - D)$$

During the first 6 months, the bakery produces 200 more cakes per month than demand (2,000 – 1,800), and these 200 cakes go into the inventory freezer. After 6 months, the inventory peaks at 1,200 cakes (200 × 6).

At month 7, demand for cakes increases to 2,500 per month. Because the bakery can only produce 2,000 per month, it needs to sell 500 cakes per month from the inventory to meet demand. Over the second half of the year, it needs 3,000 cakes in inventory to meet all the demand in the second half of the year.

This won't work because the bakery only has 1,200 cakes in inventory. At some point, the bakery will deplete the inventory in the freezer and be unable to meet demand. You can calculate the time at which the bakery no longer has inventory by rearranging the earlier equation:

$$T_b = T_a + \frac{I_b - I_a}{S - D}$$

If you then set I_b equal to zero and solve for T_b, you know that the bakery will run out of cakes at time equals 8.4 months. From month 8.4 on, the bakery won't be able to meet all its demand. During the last 3.6 months (12 – 8.4), the bakery won't be able to meet the demand of 500 cakes per month, resulting in total lost sales of 1,800 cakes. This number is a bit better than the loss the bakery incurs when not carrying inventory, but it still represents a significant loss in sales.

Increasing capacity

To minimize lost sales, the bakery could increase its capacity. To prevent any lost sales without carrying inventory, the bakery needs its capacity to equal the peak demand. In this case, it needs a capacity of 2,500 cakes per month to meet demand during the second half of the year. However, this leads to a low utilization of resources during the first half of the year — only 72% (1,800 ÷ 2,500).

The bakery could choose a capacity between the original 2,000 per month and the maximum of 2,500 per month, as long as it's willing to hold inventory during some point in the year. The bakery may decide to acquire capacity equal to its average demand of 2,150 cakes per month, operate at capacity all year, and allow inventory to accumulate.

Following this analysis, the bakery produces an extra 350 cakes each month during the first half of the year. This results in a maximum inventory level of 2,100 cakes. During the last 6 months, the bakery produces at capacity and pulls 350 cakes out of inventory each month, leaving zero inventory at the end of the year. Figure 7-6 shows the IBD for this scenario. At this capacity level, the bakery can meet all demand, but doing so requires that the bakery allow a maximum inventory level of 2,100 cakes.

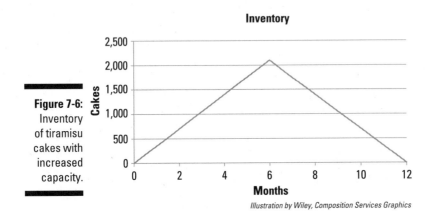

Figure 7-6: Inventory of tiramisu cakes with increased capacity.

Addressing Wait Time for Services

Doesn't it seem like you're always waiting for something, especially when it comes to service? You wait in line to purchase a movie ticket, to check out at the grocery store, and to get cash at the automated teller machine (ATM). While this problem is endemic to most face-to-face services, it also is present in some industries, such as make-to-order PC manufacturers.

Waiting is a critical component of a customer's perception of service quality. On the one hand, customers intensely dislike waiting. If they feel like they're waiting too long for service, they may leave the line (or cancel their order) prematurely and may or may not return. Both actions reduce customer demand, and eventually revenue and profit take a hit as a result. But that's not all; longer customer waiting times also increase the costs for doing business because waiting times equal more customers in a company's building, and this requires space and stress on employees who must deal with grumpy customers.

Managers can reduce waiting times by increasing capacity, which is also expensive and reduces profit. Finding a waiting time that customers find acceptable while keeping utilization reasonably high is thus critical to efficient operations. But the calculation is not intuitive, because average waiting times can be quite long, even when capacity is significantly greater than demand.

In this section we examine the mechanics of waiting: what causes it, how you calculate expected wait times, how you reduce wait, and how you can manage negative customer perceptions when they must wait.

Getting the why of waiting

When the demand for a service exceeds the capacity of that service, waiting is inevitable. Surprisingly, however, even when process utilization is less than 100 percent, waiting can still be part of the customer experience.

Here are the primary causes of waiting:

- ✔ **Insufficient capacity:** There's a direct link between wait times and resource utilization.

- ✔ **Variability and "lumpiness" in customer arrival rates:** Arrival rates vary from time period to time period and also within a given time period.

- ✔ **Variability in the time it takes to serve a customer:** Not all customers require the same amount of time with a server. Although companies often state an average service time, some customers take longer; some take less.

Lacking capacity

In any process, if average demand is greater than the average capacity, the line grows indefinitely as resources aren't able to keep up. Even if average demand is less than the capacity, expected *flow time* (the time a customer takes to get through your process, including wait time) grows with increasing resource utilization.

Figure 7-7 illustrates the relationship between utilization and wait times. The flow time remains fairly constant until about 80 percent utilization. When utilization reaches 85 percent, the flow time begins to increase exponentially (the shape of this curve comes from the Sakasegawa approximation covered later in the "Estimating waiting time with queuing theory" section).

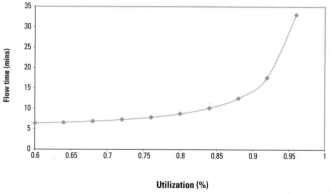

Relationship between Utilization and Flow Time

Figure 7-7: Relationship between utilization rate and flow time.

Illustration by Wiley, Composition Services Graphics

Accommodating differences in arrival time and service duration

Demand fluctuations are a major cause of waiting. Figure 7-1 shows, if demand equals customers arriving per hour, capacity is greater than the average customer arrival rate (average demand). Because firms can't perform services such as haircuts, medical appointments, and car repairs in advance during periods A, C, and E, they're unable to create "inventories" of services to await future customer arrivals when capacity exceeds demand. So customers arriving during periods B and D experience a wait. A client arriving during periods A, C, and E may also experience a wait due to the statistical nature of arrival rates.

Customers don't arrive in a predictable and steady pace. It varies. For example, a restaurant experiences a peak lunch demand between 11 a.m. and 2 p.m. If the average arrival rate during these three hours is 60 groups per hour, that doesn't mean that a group arrives every minute; instead, several groups may arrive within minutes of each other and several minutes may elapse with no arrivals.

Similarly, some customers take longer to process than others. A grocery store cashier takes longer to process a customer with a full cart than a customer with only a few items. A restaurant server usually needs more time to process a group of eight than a table of two.

This variation occurs because customers arrive independently of one another. Knowing one customer's arrival time tells you nothing about another's. This results in a something called a *Poisson arrival process*.

In Poisson processes, people do not coordinate their arrival times or needs for service with each other (that is, they aren't coordinated to arrive by appointments or reservations). Under these conditions, the time between individual arrivals is exponentially distributed.

Numerous studies of face-to-face services have shown that the time required to process each customer is also often exponentially distributed. If you don't know the distributions of either the times between arrivals or the durations of their service, the best default assumptions are that they both have exponential distributions.

Here are the important things to know about exponential distributions:

- ✔ They don't follow a normal or bell curve distribution. Most random phenomena are normally distributed, which unconsciously or not conditions people's intuition about random behavior. Because arrivals are exponentially rather than normally distributed, arrivals seem "clumpier" than what most people expect (despite the fact that they are indeed perfectly random). Because service times are exponentially (rather than normally) distributed, the number of horrible wait times is also much greater than most people would intuitively expect.

✔ The mean (expected value) of the distribution equals the standard deviation. This helps you out in the next section when you're figuring out waiting times.

Estimating waiting time with queuing theory

Wouldn't it be helpful if you had a way to know how many people you need to schedule for a shift to operate at full capacity and utilization or how long a customer needs to wait on a given evening to get a table in your restaurant? It turns out that you can use some relatively simple equations to calculate average expected line length and wait times. Queuing theory provides these equations.

Queue, by the way, is originally the British word for a waiting line. American operations management professionals use it as well.

Before you can understand how queuing theory works, you need to familiarize yourself with the following terms and their definitions:

✔ **Queue:** A line (or buffer or inventory) feeding a number of servers

✔ **Server:** An operation fed by a queue

✔ **Arrival rate (λ, *lambda*):** The mean number of arrivals per unit time, usually per hour or per day

✔ **Service rate (μ, *mu*):** The mean number of customers that can be served at 100 percent utilization by each individual server per unit time; at the individual workstation level, the service rate equals capacity

✔ **Thruput:** The number of customers actually served

✔ **Channel (*M*):** The number of parallel operations connected to an individual queue

✔ **Utilization (*u*):** A measure of how "busy" the system is — utilization is generally defined as the ratio of thruput to capacity

✔ **Phase:** A queue and its connected servers

✔ **Line length (L_q):** The average number of people in a line awaiting service

✔ **Wait time (W_q):** The average time a customer waits before being served.

Figure 7-8 shows a two-phase queuing system. Each phase has two servers or channels being served by the one queue.

Example of a two-phase queuing system

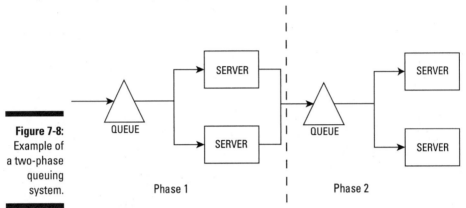

Figure 7-8:
Example of
a two-phase
queuing
system.

Illustration by Wiley, Composition Services Graphics

Connecting the dots little by little

A simple relationship exists between the average line length, the average customer arrival rate, and the expected waiting time. This relationship is known as *Little's law* and is represented by this equation:

$$W_q = \frac{L_q}{Thruput}$$

To illustrate the simplicity of this equation, consider the example in Figure 7-9. You arrive at a vending machine to find 8 people waiting in line ahead of you, and you estimate that each person takes 1 minute to complete his transaction, giving the vending machine a capacity to process 60 customers per hour. Because of the line, you can assume that the vending machine is 100 percent utilized (at least during the time you're in line). In this case, thruput is equal to capacity.

Applying Little's Law

Figure 7-9:
Applying
Little's law.

Illustration by Wiley, Composition Services Graphics

Using Little's law you can estimate your wait time:

$$W_q = \frac{8}{60} = 0.133 \text{ hours} = 8 \text{ minutes}$$

You've probably used this relationship without realizing it many times as you stood in line and wondered how long the wait was going to be.

You can apply Little's law in any system in which the mean waiting time, mean line length (or inventory size), and mean thruput (outflow) remain constant. Always measure the thruput as the number leaving the system, not entering it.

When using Little's law or other queuing equations, process utilization must be less than 100 percent. Otherwise, the line would grow forever because the process can't keep up with the arriving customers. With a utilization less than 100 percent, the average inflow equals the average outflow over time. Here is the variation of Little's law most often used in queuing problems in this case:

$$W_q = \frac{L_q}{\lambda}$$

Going beyond Little's law

If you don't know the line length or the waiting time, but you have the system's thruput value, then you can calculate average line length and waiting time if you make a few assumptions.

Hirotaka Sakasegawa, an operations management professor at Waseda University in Japan, empirically derived a formula to analyze waiting lines. Here is a simplified version of his formula:

$$L_q \approx \frac{u^{\sqrt{2(M+1)}}}{1-u}$$

This equation gives a good approximation of line length if the following conditions occur:

- Utilization is less than 100 percent.

    The equation shows that if u equals 1, then the line length is undefined. If u is greater than 1, then the line length is negative, which is impossible.

- A customer intending to enter the line does so no matter how long the line is.

- Customers don't exit the line until they're served.

✔ An infinite number of customers can enter the line.

✔ The distributions of the time between arrivals and the duration of the service times are both exponential.

To illustrate this equation, imagine that 72 customers arrive randomly each hour at a fast-food restaurant. Five cash registers are open, and each register has its own line. Assuming the customers distribute themselves equally across the 5 service lines, 14.4 customers per hour arrive in each of the 5 lines. The cashier requires an average of 4 minutes to process each customer.

The first thing you need to do is calculate the utilization of a cashier. Because a cashier has the capacity to process 15 customers per hour (60/4) and only has to serve 14.4 customers per hour, each cashier's utilization, u, is 96%. In this case, you have one line feeding each resource, giving you an M of 1.

Using these numbers in the earlier equation, find the average (mean) line length:

$$L_q \approx \frac{.96^{\sqrt{2(1+1)}}}{1-.96} \approx 23 \text{ people}$$

Now find the average wait time using Little's law:

$$W_q = \frac{L_q}{\lambda} = \frac{23}{14.4} \approx 1.6 \text{ hours}$$

In most cases, this wait time is much too long. To reduce the wait time to an acceptable level, how many cashiers do you need?

Figure 7-7 shows that wait times begin to explode when the system exceeds a utilization of around 85%. You can determine what arrival rate of customers gives each cashier a utilization of 85%:

$$\lambda = Utilization \cdot Capacity = .85 \cdot 15 = 12.75 \text{ customers per hour}$$

Calculate the number of cashiers you need to assure an arrival rate into each line of no more than 12.75 customers per hour by dividing the total number of customers arriving by this number: 5.65 (72/12.75) cashiers. Because you can't have a fraction of a person at any one time, the system requires 6 cashiers.

With 6 cashiers, each resource has a utilization of 80% (each cashier can process 15 customers per hour but only 12 [72/6] arrive in each line), and the new line length is

$$L_q \approx \frac{.8^{\sqrt{2(1+1)}}}{1-.8} \approx 3.2 \text{ people}$$

and the average wait time is

$$W_q = \frac{L_q}{\lambda} = \frac{3.2}{12} = 16 \text{ minutes}$$

By increasing the number of servers by just one, you can significantly reduce the line length and corresponding wait time.

However, adding more servers after you reach a utilization below 85% has diminishing returns. With the addition of a seventh cashier, cashier utilization drops to 68.6%, the average line length is approximately 1.5 customers, and the average wait time becomes 8.8 minutes.

Going single file

Reducing wait time without adding servers is possible by forming one line for all the servers instead of having a separate line for each resource. For example, at airline check-ins, you line up in a single, serpentine line with an attendant at the end directing you to an open agent.

One line and 5 servers (M = 5) produces this average line length:

$$L_q \approx \frac{.96^{\sqrt{2(5+1)}}}{1-.96} = 21.7 \text{ people}$$

Find the average wait time:

$$W_q = \frac{L_q}{\lambda} = \frac{21.7}{72} \approx .301 \text{ hours} = 18.1 \text{ minutes}$$

You may be wondering how we determined the utilization and arrival rates. Utilization remains unchanged, regardless of whether there are multiple lines or just one, because each resource still processes an average of 14.4 customers per hour.

The arrival rate is the number of customers arriving in a queue per unit of time. Because you have only one line, 72 customers per hour enter the line.

Whenever possible, you want to have multiple resources serving one line rather than each resource serving an individual line. By combining the lines into one, you can obtain results similar to those you got when you had 6 cashiers, each with an individual line. This approach also prevents the problem and frustration of "choosing the wrong line" at grocery checkout counters, fast-food restaurants, banks, and anywhere else there are multiple server stations to choose from.

Squishing variability to reduce waiting

There's another way to reduce waiting time. Waiting comes from the variability in the times between arrivals and the durations of the service times for customers. If you can reduce the variability in the arrival rates (through appointments or reservations) or service time duration (through standardizing the process), you can reduce waiting time still further.

Squishing variability in either situation means you'll no longer have exponential distributions. But you can modify the Sakesagawa approximation to account for this as follows:

$$L_q \approx \frac{u^{\sqrt{2(M+1)}}}{1-u}\left(\frac{CV_{TBA}^2 + CV_{ST}^2}{2}\right)$$

The coefficient of variation of the time between arrivals (CV_{TBA}) is the ratio of the standard deviation of the time between arrivals to its mean. In other words, the CV_{TBA} = Standard deviation (TBA)/Mean(TBA). The CV of service time duration (CV_{ST}) is, similarly, the ratio of the standard deviation of service times to their mean: CV_{ST} = Standard deviation (ST)/Mean(ST). Generally speaking, the larger a CV is for a random variable, the more spread out or random is its distribution.

You can also use this longer Sakesagawa approximation if you have some historical data for the two CVs. Note that exponential distributions always have a CV of 1.0, which is why the shorter form for L_q used in the prior two sections is really just a special case of this longer formula.

To see how squishing variability works, let's build on the case of the fast food restaurant in the earlier "Going single file" section, which has one line feeding 5 servers. First we introduce a reservation system, which we find out drops the CV_{TBA} from 1.0 to 0.4. We also work to standardize the process, so that the CV_{ST} goes from 1.0 to 0.5. The resulting line length becomes

$$L_q \approx \frac{.96^{\sqrt{2(5+1)}}}{1-.96}\left(\frac{0.4^2 + 0.5^2}{2}\right) = 4.45 \text{ people}$$

This is a reduction of over three-quarters in the line length. This results in a similar reduction in the wait time thanks to Little's law:

$$W_q = \frac{L_q}{\lambda} \approx \frac{4.45}{72} = 0.0618 \text{ hours} = 3.71 \text{ minutes}$$

Looking at these results, you can see that using reservations (or appointments for services, as doctors and dentists do) and standardizing processes
to squish variability are powerful tools to reduce wait times.

Waiting in more complicated processes

Many times you have to deal with entire processes having many stages, all of
which have waiting lines rather than just the one line. How do you calculate
the waiting times in these situations? It's easier than it looks.

So long as all the arrival rates are Poisson and the service times of all the
operations are exponentially distributed in a complex process, two facts let
you leverage the Sakesagawa approximation for line lengths described in
"Going beyond Little's law":

✔ The output rate of an operation is equal to the arrival rate if utilization is
less than 100 percent, and the output is also a Poisson process.

✔ The total arrival rate into a queue is the sum of the arrival rates feeding
into it.

Figure 7-10 illustrates the process at a popular cafeteria on a university
campus. A student enters one of three lines, depending on what he wants for
lunch. After he receives his food, he proceeds to one checkout line, which is
served by two cashiers.

If the student is hungry for pizza and wants to know how long he'll have to
wait for it, he can use these equations to calculate the average line length
and wait time for each of the server stations:

$$L_{pizza} = \frac{u^{\sqrt{2(M+1)}}}{1-u} = \frac{\frac{54}{60}^{\sqrt{2(1+1)}}}{1-\frac{54}{60}} = 8.1 \text{ customers}$$

$$W_{pizza} = \frac{L_{pizza}}{\lambda} = \frac{8.1}{54} = .15 \text{ hours} = 9 \text{ minutes}$$

To calculate the number of customers waiting for a resource and the average time they'll spend waiting, you need to know how many customers are
exiting the three server stations and entering the checkout line.

The exit rate from each of the server stations is equal to the arrival rate
because all utilizations are less than 100 percent. The arrival rate into the
checkout line is the sum of the 3 exit rates. So, in this case, 115 customers per
hour enter the line.

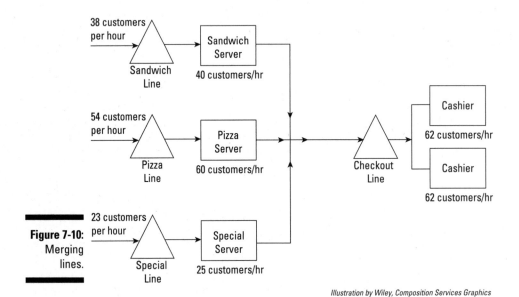

Merging Lines

38 customers per hour — Sandwich Line — Sandwich Server — 40 customers/hr

54 customers per hour — Pizza Line — Pizza Server — 60 customers/hr

23 customers per hour — Special Line — Special Server — 25 customers/hr

Checkout Line — Cashier — 62 customers/hr — Cashier — 62 customers/hr

Figure 7-10: Merging lines.

Illustration by Wiley, Composition Services Graphics

Because the checkout line has two cashiers, you can find the average line length and wait time for each resource:

$$L_{checkout} = \frac{u^{\sqrt{2(M+1)}}}{1-u} = \frac{\frac{115}{124}^{\sqrt{2(2+1)}}}{1-\frac{115}{124}} \approx 11.5 \text{ customers}$$

$$W_{checkout} = \frac{L_{checkout}}{\lambda} = \frac{11.5}{115} = 0.1 \text{ hours} = 6 \text{ minutes}$$

The total time that a pizza customer spends in the process is equal to the time he waits plus the time he's being processed. This time is often referred to as the *flow time* (see Chapter 2). For the average pizza customer, the pizza server takes 1 minute (1/60 of an hour) to prepare the order, and the cashier takes 0.97 minutes (1/62 of an hour) to collect payment. So the total flow time is 16.97 (9 + 1 + 6 + .97) minutes for the customer to get his lunch.

Altering customer perceptions

From a customer's perspective, two theories are in play: how long the customer waits in line and how long the customer *thinks* he's waiting in line.

If you must make a customer wait, you can make the time more comfortable and seem shorter than it really is by managing the customer's perception of the waiting time. Here are some things to know about managing customer perceptions so the wait doesn't negatively affect satisfaction:

✔ **Customers don't mind waiting as much if they're comfortable.** This is perhaps the most important way to influence customer satisfaction. Make sure that you have plenty of space, comfy chairs, and a pleasant atmosphere in your waiting room. Offering amenities such as refreshments, current reading material, and wireless Internet can go a long way toward softening the sting of waiting.

✔ **Preprocess wait time feels longer than in-process wait time.** You want to get your customers into the process as quickly as possible. This may involve something as simple as greeting them the moment they walk in the door. After they enter, they're less likely to leave before being served.

✔ **Unoccupied time feels longer than occupied time.** You may want to break up the processing time into smaller steps with a wait between each step rather than having a longer wait time upfront. The doctor's office is great at doing this. When you arrive at an appointment, a receptionist greets you and then you wait to be called, usually by a nurse who shows you to a room and takes your vital statistics. You then wait again in the exam room for the doctor. On average, you wait the same amount of time as if you had waited all at once at the beginning, but because the wait is interrupted, people often perceive it as being less.

✔ **Uncertain waits are perceived to be worse than certain waits.** By telling customers know how long the wait will be, you remove the anxiety associated with waiting. The customers can then relax, knowing when they'll be served.

✔ **Unexplained waits are worse than explained waits.** If your customers are going to have to wait longer than expected, let them know. For example, if the doctor is handling an emergency patient, inform the others who are waiting. Customers are more tolerant of these delays. However, if the wait is longer because the doctor took an extended lunch, you probably should avoid sharing this information.

✓ **Unfair waits are worse than fair waits.** Nothing is worse than feeling that other customers are cutting in line or getting preferential treatment. Having a well-defined process flow can minimize this effect.

These same principles can apply to back orders or customers waiting for build-to-order. For example, providing a website link so the customer can check the order status and a tracking number so the customer can check the shipping progress of the item can make the wait for an ordered item seem to go by faster.

Chapter 8

Managing Inventory

. . . .

. . . .

Inventory refers to all the forms of material eventually intended for sale that a business maintains, including raw materials, work in process, and finished products. In the past, maintaining large stocks of inventory was common practice in manufacturing because primary metrics for evaluating performance centered on *utilization,* or how busy the company's resources stayed, and order fulfillment (or back-order reduction), which emphasized the ability to fill customer orders immediately. These metrics led managers to produce more products than were needed, and these parts ended up in inventory. (See Chapter 3 for info on what happens when a process overproduces.)

Now, many business leaders no longer view inventory as an asset but as a liability that ties up a firm's working capital. Therefore, over the past several years, companies have made a tremendous effort using techniques such as *just in time* (JIT) to reduce the levels of inventory that they maintain (see Chapter 11 for more on lean manufacturing). But having too little inventory can be just as costly as having too much. Some inventory is necessary to maintain operations and ensure that products are available when customers demand them.

This chapter presents the basics of cost-effective inventory management. We point out why inventory is needed, explain the true costs associated with inventory, and describe three common inventory policies. But don't worry — it's inventory, not rocket science! Before all is said and done, we give you some specific methods for reducing inventory without sacrificing customer satisfaction. The chapter concludes with a discussion of inventory management across the supply chain.

Dealing with the Business of Inventory

Inventory has become the four-letter word of operations management. Balancing inventory to satisfy *customer demand* — that is, actual demand in the market for products and services — without exposing the company to unnecessary cost and risk is crucial. But this aspect of operations can be one of the toughest.

When the number of customers walking through your door ready to purchase your product or when the number of people adding your product to their online shopping cart is significantly different from what you expect, your business is exposed to *demand risk*. If customer demand exceeds expectations, then you don't have enough product or resources to fill all customer orders. If demand is lower than expectations, then you're left sitting with excess inventory.

Successfully balancing inventory with actual customer demand minimizes the risks of losing sales to the competition and of overinvesting in unneeded inventory.

The problem is that customer demand is variable and forecasts of demand are always inaccurate; in many cases, they're way off (see Chapter 6). You can never really predict what actual customer demand will be. To manage this uncertainty, companies use inventory and capacity to hedge their bets.

By *capacity,* we mean the amount of product you can produce during a specific time period — widgets per hour, for example. You need capacity to make inventory.

Chapter 7 covers how to manage capacity; for now, all you need to know is that, in order to meet unexpected surges in demand, companies need to have one of the following:

- ✔ Sufficient inventory available
- ✔ Sufficient additional capacity (often called *surge capacity*) to make additional products in a time period acceptable to customers

If fewer than expected customers want your goods, you'll be left with excess inventory in the first case or excess capacity in the second case. Keep in mind that extra capacity requires extra investment in facilities and capital equipment.

Holding inventory in your process so that product is available when customers demand it can help you reduce capacity levels. In other words, products can be assembled and held during periods of low demand in anticipation of high-demand periods. The key question is how much or how little inventory is really needed at any given time.

In this section, we point out why you need to have adequate inventory. We also lay out the real costs associated with this often-scary part of business.

Recognizing inventory's purposes

There's just no way around it for most businesses: If you're going to sell products, you need to have stuff available for customers to purchase.

The goods that are available for immediate sale make up just one type of inventory; it's known as *finished goods inventory* (FGI). The other two categories are *raw material inventory* (RMI), which are typically items purchased from a supplier and used to create the end product, and *work in process inventory* (WIP), or product that's still going through the production process.

Here are some of the important functions of inventory in successful operations:

- ✔ **Meeting customer demand:** Maintaining finished goods inventory allows a company to immediately fill customer demand for product. Failing to maintain an adequate supply of FGI can lead to disappointed potential customers and lost revenue.

- ✔ **Protecting against supply shortages and delivery delays:** A supply chain is only as strong as its weakest link, and accessibility to raw materials is sometimes disrupted. That's why some companies stockpile certain raw materials to protect themselves from disruptions in the supply chain and avoid idling their plants and other facilities.

- ✔ **Separating operations in a process:** Inventory of subassemblies or partially processed raw material is often held in various stages throughout a process. Work in process inventory (or WIP) protects an organization when interruptions or breakdowns occur within the process. Maintaining WIP allows other operations to continue even when a failure exists in another part of the process.

- ✔ **Smoothing production requirements and reducing peak period capacity needs:** Businesses that produce nonperishable products and experience seasonal customer demand often try to build up inventory during slow periods in anticipation of the high-demand period. This allows the company to maintain thruput levels during peak periods and still meet higher customer demand.

- ✔ **Taking advantage of quantity discounts:** Many suppliers offer discounts based on certain quantity breaks because large orders tend to reduce total processing and shipping costs while also allowing suppliers to take advantage of economies of scale in their own production processes.

Inventory is necessary to your business. It supplies your operations processes and meets customer demand.

Measuring the true cost of inventory

Maintaining inventory is expensive; it diverts resources from other areas of your business. But not having enough inventory can lead to lost sales and inadequate customer service. Therein lies the rub. Getting too far off the delicate balance of appropriate inventory for your business puts you in dangerous territory.

When deciding how much inventory to carry, an operations manager must balance the costs of having too much with the risk of coming up short. The different costs of inventory touch every area of business:

✔ **Ordering costs:** The costs of ordering and receiving inventory vary for each business, but these costs include the labor associated with placing an order and the cost of receiving the order. Ordering costs are usually expressed as a fixed dollar amount per order, regardless of order size.

✔ **Holding or carrying costs:** The cost of physically having inventory on-site includes expenses to maintain the infrastructure needed to warehouse the goods and insurance to protect it.

Additionally, the value of inventory can decline because of deterioration and obsolescence, which adds to the cost of storing inventory. This is particularly true of perishable goods such as food and medicine, but even nonperishable products can go out of style or become obsolete. And inventory can be damaged or "disappear" off the shelf when it's being stored, which in operations lingo is called *shrinkage*.

✔ **Lost sales:** If a product isn't available, then you can't sell it. Unless a customer is willing to wait for delivery while you produce and/or prepare the product of interest, you lose the sale and the resulting revenue and profit by not having an adequate supply to meet demand.

✔ **Goodwill costs:** Alienating customers if your product is out of stock rolls back a considerable investment that your company has likely made in establishing goodwill in the market. Your loss in this situation includes other items that the customer doesn't purchase when the product is unavailable as well as products he doesn't purchase from you in the future because of perceptions about your company related to the initial shortage.

Though ordering and holding costs are usually easy to calculate, estimating the actual cost of lost sales and goodwill is more difficult. Many companies don't have a way to track potential customers who wanted to buy a product that was unavailable and to determine whether the inventory snafu led to the loss of other sales. Nevertheless, accurately measuring these costs is important because they can significantly affect a company's inventory policies and, ultimately, the bottom line.

The best way to measure goodwill costs varies by industry and by the nature of your product, but good market research and acute familiarity with your customer base are critical.

Managing Inventory

Inventory management is one of the most difficult tasks in operations because it's hard to predict actual customer demand. You can approach inventory management in many different ways. The right one for any given situation depends on the specific business environment.

Establishing a cost-efficient inventory management system — a process that determines how much inventory you need and when — requires knowledge of three specific variables:

- **Customer demand forecast:** Because *point forecasts* (a single estimate for expected demand) are always inaccurate, your forecasts should always include information on expected average demand and a measure of the potential variability in demand (see Chapter 6).

- **Inventory costs:** Reliable estimates of inventory costs should contain expenses related to ordering and holding inventory and costs of lost sales and goodwill if insufficient inventory is available to meet demand.

- **Lead time:** Accurate estimates of expected *delivery lead time* for raw material and other manufacturing components (time between a placed order and delivery) and the variability of this time is critical to planning inventory levels. You also need to add in how long it will take you to process those materials into a finished product. Find out how to design your supply chain to meet delivery targets in Chapter 10.

Many different inventory management systems are available, but they all share one goal: Get the right products to the right place at the right time. To figure out which system is the right one for you to achieve this goal in light of your business environment and infrastructure, you need to answer four basic inventory questions:

- **Can I reorder?** In most cases, you can place orders to replenish stock that sells. But this isn't always the case. In the fashion industry, for example, restocking isn't usually an option. The best approach for managing inventory is fundamentally different for businesses that can and can't restock inventory.

- **When can I review inventory levels?** If you can reorder, choosing when to review inventory levels is crucial. Most often, inventory review can occur either continuously or periodically. If monitored continuously (hopefully this is automated), inventory can be ordered whenever a certain set point is reached. In many cases it's impractical to keep a constant eye on inventory, so you can set a designated time period to review inventory levels and place orders; this is called *periodic review*.

✔ **How much do I need to order?** Regardless of the review system you use, you need to consider expected demand, costs, and delivery times when deciding how much inventory to order at any one time.

✔ **When is the best time to place an order?** If you can reorder product, then you need to figure out when to place the reorder. This decision tends to go hand in hand with how you choose to monitor inventory levels.

Modern inventory software makes monitoring inventory much easier than it was in the old days of counting boxes. Computer programs have all but eliminated the need to take a physical count of inventory in most cases. Counting usually takes place only at tax time to value the inventory or to verify the accuracy of the software count. This means you can now maintain a near-constant tally of inventory and even link with supplier systems, thereby automating the ordering process.

The periodic review system, despite requiring slightly higher inventory levels, offers many advantages over continuous review systems. It simplifies operations because you can set a specific time for a resource to place all necessary orders. It allows you to consolidate shipments if you purchase multiple products from the same supplier, and it simplifies life for the supplier because the supplier knows when to expect an order from you.

Just because you place orders periodically doesn't mean you don't continuously track inventory through a point-of-sales system or bar coding. It only means that you've set a designated time to place an order rather than placing an order when the level reaches a set point.

Effective inventory management hinges on choosing the best process for reviewing inventory levels, which depends on your particular business. Basically, inventory review can be continuous, periodic, or isolated as a single period. Most of today's inventory review programs are based on one or more of these basic systems.

Continuous review

In *continuous inventory review,* you monitor inventory on an ongoing basis. You set a predetermined inventory level as the reorder point (ROP) and typically place a consistent order.

Figure 8-1 shows a continuous inventory review system, and on average, inventory falls by the average demand rate. If demand becomes higher or lower than normal, inventory levels change at a different rate.

Regardless of timing, when inventory falls to a specified point (represented by ROP) in the figure, an order is placed for a certain amount of goods (represented by Q in the figure).

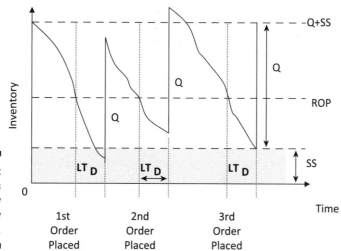

Continuous Review System

Figure 8-1:
Continuous
inventory
review
system.

Illustration by Wiley, Composition Services Graphics

Depending on the nature of the products, a certain length of time (also known as *lead time*) passes between the time of order placement and delivery. Remember that demand can vary from the average during this time, and you may run out of inventory if demand is unusually high. To avoid inventory depletion, many companies maintain some inventory to cover above-average demand that may occur during the lead time; this inventory is known as *safety stock* (SS).

After the new order arrives, inventory is boosted beyond the reorder point, and continuous monitoring resumes.

Calculate the ROP using this formula:

$$ROP = (\text{Average Demand} \cdot \text{Average Delivery Lead Time}) + \text{Safety Stock}$$

Use this formula to determine how much SS you need to cover the risk of above-average demand during reorder lead time:

$$SS = Z\sqrt{\text{Average Lead Time} \cdot \text{Std Dev of Demand}^2 + \text{Avg Demand}^2 \cdot \text{Std Dev of Lead Time}^2}$$

In this formula, z is the number of standard deviations above the mean in normally distributed demand. Its value depends on the *service level* (SL) — the probability that demand won't exceed supply during the lead time — that the company wants to maintain. The SL increases as the risk of a *stock out* (running out of inventory) decreases.

Using Excel or some other table-based software, you can find z using this equation if you know the desired service level:

SL=normsdist(z)

z =normsinv(SL)

Make sure to express SL as a decimal when entering this value into Excel. In other words, use 0.95, not 95 percent, because this is standard Excel notation.

Figure 8-2 provides the z value for some common service levels.

Values for Common Service Levels

Service Level	Z
50%	0
75%	0.67
84%	1.00
90%	1.28
95%	1.64
98%	2.00
99%	2.33
99.9%	3.00

Figure 8-2: Common service level z values.

Illustration by Wiley, Composition Services Graphics

Choosing a desired SL is a big decision, mainly because as the SL increases, so does the required safety stock. A normal distribution curve shows that achieving a 100 percent SL isn't possible, and getting close to 100 percent is increasingly expensive because it requires more and more inventory.

The *economic order quantity* (EOQ) — how much inventory you order when the ROP is hit — represents an order that minimizes total inventory costs.

In the following equation, D is the annual expected demand, S is the ordering cost, and H represents annual holding costs per unit. An order of EOQ is placed every time inventory falls to the ROP.

$$EOQ = \sqrt{\frac{2 \cdot D \cdot S}{H}}$$

When calculating the EOQ, make sure that you state the values for demand and holding costs in annual quantities. If they're not in the same time units, your EOQ will be incorrect.

Periodic review

Continuously keeping your eye on inventory numbers can be inconvenient. After all, you have other things to do. Using *periodic review,* you can schedule time to assess the need to place an order for any additional inventory.

The periodic review approach is especially useful if you purchase more than one product from a single supplier. Placing a single order for more than one product may reduce shipping costs, allow you to take advantage of quantity discounts from the supplier, and make receiving your inventory easier.

In a periodic system, you order inventory at certain time periods (T) to bring the total back to a designated target inventory (TI). Between the time you place and receive an order, higher-than-expected demand can cause a stock out. This situation is even more dire than in a continuous review approach because you must also account for the demand variability that occurs before the next review time.

The equation for the TI is similar to the ROP except TI must also account for the monitoring time interval. Here's the formula to calculate TI:

$$TI = \text{Average Demand} \cdot \left(\text{Average Lead Time} + T \right) + SS$$

Use this equation for calculating SS as part of a periodic inventory review system:

$$SS = z \cdot \sqrt{\left(\text{Avg Lead Time} + T \right) \cdot \text{Std Dev of Demand}^2 + \text{Avg Demand}^2 \cdot \text{Std Dev of Lead Time}^2}$$

Figure 8-3 illustrates a periodic review system.

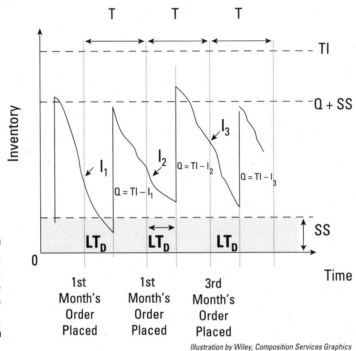

Periodic Review System

Figure 8-3:
Periodic
inventory
review
system.

Illustration by Wiley, Composition Services Graphics

Often, you don't have a choice about the monitoring time interval. For example, you may have to place orders every Friday. However, if you have the freedom to set a monitoring time interval, use the following equation to select a monitoring time interval that minimizes costs:

$$T = \frac{EOQ}{Average\ Demand}$$

Regardless of how you determine T, every T time periods, you place an order for Q according to the following equation (where I is the current level of inventory):

$$Q = TI - I$$

When using these equations, make sure that you state the values for demand and lead time in the same time units. For example, if you're using average demand per week, then you must also state lead time in weeks.

Single period review

Sometimes, you need to make a one-time decision on how much to order, such as with seasonal items like snowblowers and swimsuits. At the end of the season, you typically liquidate any unsold items at significant price discounts to make room for new products for the next season.

In the *single period inventory review* model, the optimal quantity of inventory to order balances both the costs of understocking (Cu) and overstocking (Co) product. Cu is the sum of the *lost profit per unit* (usually price minus variable cost/unit) and the associated *goodwill cost*, which is the net present value of not having a unit of inventory on hand when a customer wants to purchase it. Co is the difference between the variable cost/unit of a product and its salvage value — often equivalent to the end-of-season clearance price.

Goodwill costs can be difficult to measure, but try to get an accurate estimate (perhaps with help from a marketing expert), because this consideration greatly influences the amount of inventory a business needs to order in a single period review system.

You can calculate the desired service level for the product using this equation:

$$SL = \text{Probability of Not Stocking Out} = \frac{C_u}{C_u + C_o}$$

As defined, the *service level* is the probability that you won't stock out given a certain order quantity. If the demand is normally distributed, you can find z as described in the earlier "Continuous review" section.

After you find z, use this equation to determine the optimal quantity to order:

$$Q = Expected\ Demand + z \cdot Std\ Dev\ of\ Demand$$

Looking back to understand a name

The *single period review* policy is often referred to as the *newsboy* or *newsvendor* problem because newspapers are generally printed once a day in a certain quantity. A seller typically needs to tell the printer how many issues she wants to buy, and she can only order once.

At the end of the day or when a new issue is released, the old newspapers are obsolete and must be discarded or sold at a steep discount to anyone looking to line a bird cage or enjoy a campfire that evening.

Comparing the options

A company may want to use more than one review process depending on the nature of the products they need to purchase. Figure 8-4 presents a side-by-side comparison of the three inventory review policies.

Comparison of Inventory Policies

Inventory Policy	Continuous	Periodic	Single Period
When to review	Ongoing	At selected review time (T)	One time
When to order	At established reorder point (ROP)	At review time (T)	Before the start of the season based on supplier lead time
How much to order	Fixed economic order quantity (EOQ)	Variable: order up to target inventory (TI) minus quantity on hand	Optimal stocking level determined by service level

Figure 8-4: Comparison of inventory policies.

Illustration by Wiley, Composition Services Graphics

Getting Baseline Data on Performance

How effective is your inventory management process? In this section we provide common metrics used to measure how well a company is controlling inventory levels and meeting customer demand.

Assessing the inventory management system

To find out how well an organization is managing its inventory, you must be able to measure it. Here are some common inventory metrics:

✔ **Average inventory level:** As the name implies, this is the average inventory levels maintained in the system. Your goal is to reduce this without negatively impacting the other metrics.

✔ **Line item fill rate:** This is the total number of line items filled divided by the total number of line items. This metric applies to products or orders that contain multiple products. Again, you want this as high as possible without sacrificing average inventory levels.

- **Order fill rate:** This is the number of orders filled on time divided by the total number of orders during a time period. You want this to be as close to 100 percent as possible. Order fill rate and average inventory levels can be conflicting. Trying to maintain a high fill rate typically means maintaining more inventory.

- **Service level:** This represents the likelihood of having available stock in a replenishment cycle. You use the service level to calculate the safety stock in the inventory models. You usually set this value based on your customer expectations.

- **Turnover ratio:** This ratio tells you whether average inventory levels are in line with sales. Calculate turnover by dividing annual sales by average inventory level. You typically want this number to be large. For example, a ratio of 5 means that your sales are 5 times greater than your average inventory levels. In this case, many operations managers say they're carrying 5 *turns* of inventory.

  Many industries publish the average turnover ratio for companies in the industry. This allows firms to compare their performance to their competitors. If your ratio is lower than your competition's, then the other companies are doing a better job of keeping their inventory levels low.

  The inverse of the ratio gives you the average time period of supply on hand. If a company has a turnover ratio of 6, for example, it has, on average, 2 months of inventory in stock.

If an order contains more than one item, the order fill rate will be lower than individual product fill rates.

Evaluating the quality of customer service

As a manager, knowing how many customers you're serving, particularly in context of how many you're sending away, is extremely helpful. The ratio of sales (how many products you sold) to demand (how many customers wanted to buy) provides a much better picture of how you're satisfying customers than the service level does.

The term *service level* is thrown around by operation managers, but it doesn't exactly represent what it seems to. The service level tells you only how likely it is that you'll have inventory on hand for all the customers who want it. For instance, a company that sets it service level at 95 percent has a 5 percent probability of running out of inventory. But this doesn't mean that you'll disappoint 5 percent of your customers by not having inventory.

The service level also tells you nothing about when the stock out will occur, and this matters. Experiencing a stock out just before a new shipment arrives or during the last days of the season isn't as damaging as stocking out just after you place an order or midway through the season. The service level number doesn't account for the fact that if you do stock out at some point, you've potentially still served many, if not most, of your customers. Therefore, the number always underestimates how many customers you're actually serving, sometimes significantly.

A better measure of customer service is *fill rate,* or how many customers you serve on average (expected sales) as a percentage of the average number of customers who want your goods (expected demand). Here's an equation to calculate your fill rate:

$$Fill\ Rate = \frac{Expected\ Sales}{Expected\ Demand}$$

Depending on what inventory review system you use (single period, periodic, or continuous), the process of calculating the fill rate varies a bit.

Single period review

If your demand is normally distributed, expected sales are a function of the z you use to calculate your order quantity. (See the section "Single period review" earlier in this chapter.) Solve for L(z) to discover the number of sales lost due to inventory stock outs in relation to the standard deviation of demand:

$$L(z) = \frac{Expected\ Number\ of\ Lost\ Sales}{Std\ Dev\ of\ Demand}$$

To find L(z), program the following function into Excel or a similar spreadsheet program:

$$L(z) = NORMDIST(z, 0,\ 1, 0) - z \cdot \left(1 - NORMDIST(z, 0, 1, 1)\right)$$

See Figure 8-5 for values for L(z) for some common service levels.

After you solve for L(z), you can find the fill rate using this formula:

$$Fill\ Rate = 1 - \frac{L(z) \cdot Std\ Deviation\ of\ Demand}{Expected\ Demand}$$

For example, if the service level for a swimwear company is 60 percent and the expected demand is 200 bathing suits, with a standard deviation of demand of 40 bathing suits, you can find the fill rate with this process:

1. **A service rate of 60 percent corresponds to an L(z) of 0.285.**

2. **Calculate fill rate using this equation:**

$$Fill\ Rate = 1 - \frac{0.285 \cdot 40\ \text{suits}}{200\ \text{suits}} = 0.942$$

3. **In this case, 94.2 percent of customers can be satisfied from inventory, and only 5.8 percent (100 – 94.2) of customers arrive to find no inventory on hand to fill their demand.**

Note that the fill rate of 94.2 percent is significantly greater than the 60 percent service level.

Common L(z) Values

Service Level	z	L(z)
50%	0.000	0.399
55%	0.126	0.339
60%	0.253	0.285
65%	0.385	0.236
70%	0.524	0.190
75%	0.674	0.149
80%	0.842	0.112
85%	1.036	0.078
90%	1.282	0.047
95%	1.645	0.021

Figure 8-5:
L(z) values
for common
service
levels.

Illustration by Wiley, Composition Services Graphics

Continuous review

Under a continuous review policy, the odds of a customer arriving during a stock out are considerably less than in the other policies because the only time a stock out can occur is between the time a reorder of inventory is placed and when it arrives.

In this case, you calculate the L(z) the same as you do in the single period review, but you calculate the fill rate to account for the lead time:

1. **First, find the standard deviation of demand during the lead time:**

   $Std\ Dev\ of\ Lead\ Time\ Demand =$

   $$\sqrt{Average\ Lead\ Time \cdot Std\ Dev\ of\ Demand^2 + Avg\ Demand^2 \cdot Std\ Dev\ of\ Lead\ Time^2}$$

2. **Now calculate the fill rate using this formula, where LT is the lead time, D is the average demand, and EOQ is the economic order quantity:**

$$Fill\ Rate = \frac{LT}{EOQ/D}\left(1 - \frac{L(z)\cdot Std\ Deviation\ of\ Lead\ Time\ Demand}{LT\cdot D}\right)$$

Periodic review

Calculating the fill rate when using a periodic review policy is similar to the process for figuring fill rate for a single review policy, but finding the exact fill rate in this case is extremely difficult. You can get a reasonably accurate approximation by using a modified version of the single period equation:

1. **Find the standard deviation of the demand over the lead time:**

$$Std\ Dev\ of\ Lead\ Time\ Demand =$$
$$\sqrt{\left(Avg\ Lead\ Time + T\right)\cdot Std\ Dev\ of\ Demand^2 + Avg\ Demand^2 \cdot Std\ Dev\ of\ Lead\ Time^2}$$

2. **Use the value of the standard deviation of the demand in the following formula, which is essentially the single period fill rate formula:**

$$Fill\ Rate = 1 - \frac{L(z)\cdot Std\ Deviation\ of\ Lead\ Time\ Demand}{D(T + LT)}$$

Generally speaking, continuous review policies have significantly higher fill rates than periodic review policies.

Reducing Inventory without Sacrificing Customer Service

A company's financial health depends on its ability to reduce inventory, but its viability as a business relies on doing so without sacrificing credibility as a supplier and its customer service. Accomplishing inventory reduction in customer-friendly ways requires well-designed processes (covered in Part 1), accurate demand forecasting (see Chapter 6), implementation of lean strategies (flip to Chapter 11), and production of quality products (turn to Chapter 13). Just as waiting is undesirable to customers in service operations, as shown in Chapter 7, waiting for a product to become available can be devastating to your business. Customers may cancel their order and buy elsewhere, and your business may lose those customers for good.

In this section, we point out how to use commonality and postponement strategies to reduce inventory levels without sacrificing customer service.

Multitasking inventory: The commonality approach

A manufacturer producing several products made from multiple components can reduce its overall inventory levels by using each component in more than one product. For instance, a major automobile manufacturer uses up to 85 percent of the same components in its luxury model and its economy name plate. By reducing overall demand variability for the component, the company reduces inventory requirements.

To put this in practical terms, let's say that the demand variability for the luxury vehicle is 20 cars per week and the demand variability for the economy model is 10 cars per week. If each model utilizes its own ignition switch and the company strives to maintain a service level of 98 percent, then z equals 2.05 from the normal distribution curve.

If you assume that lead time is 1 day, the safety stock (SS) needed for each model would be as follows:

$$SS\ Luxury = z \cdot Std\ Dev\ of\ Demand \cdot \sqrt{Lead\ Time} = 2.05 \cdot 20 \cdot \sqrt{1}\ switches =$$
41 switches

$$SS\ Economy = z \cdot Std\ Dev\ of\ Demand \cdot \sqrt{Lead\ Time} = 2.05 \cdot 10\ switches \cdot \sqrt{1} =$$
20.5 switches

Total SS for switches is 61.5 (41 + 20.5), or 62 switches.

It's common practice to always round up in inventory calculations.

If the company can use a common switch for both cars, then the combined standard deviation for the switch would be

$$Std\ Dev\ of\ Common = \sqrt{Std\ Dev\ of\ Luxury^2 + Std\ Dev\ of\ Economy^2}$$

$$Std\ Dev\ of\ Common = \sqrt{20^2 + 10^2} = 22.36\ switches$$

You can't simply add standard deviations. You must add variances. That's why we square the standard deviation in the equation to get the variance. Sum the variances and square the root to get back to the standard deviation.

The safety stock for the common switch would be

$$SS\ Common = z \cdot Std\ Dev\ of\ Demand \cdot \sqrt{Lead\ Time} =$$
$$2.05 \cdot 22.36 \cdot \sqrt{1}\ switches = 46\ switches$$

By using the same components across multiple models, known as *commonality,* the manufacturer can reduce inventory. In the car example, the number of switches needed is reduced by 16, or about 26 percent, and the company can still maintain the original service level with this lower level of inventory.

Choose common components carefully to avoid hurting other aspects of customer satisfaction. Customers expect performance and comfort in a luxury vehicle to be better than an economy model. If a buyer doesn't perceive the luxury model to be better than the economy model, he won't be willing to pay the premium price and may instead buy a competitor's luxury offering.

Holding on: The postponement strategy

By delaying product differentiation or customization for specific customer requests, a company can provide products according to buyer specifications while reducing overall inventory levels. *Postponement* involves strategically placing work-in-process inventory in the pipeline before customization points.

In addition to reducing inventory levels, postponement holds inventory in the state of lowest possible cost and reduces customer lead time for custom products. Postponement must be a consideration inherent in product design, and the benefits of postponement require a commonality strategy.

For example, consider a company that manufactures three different models of Super Dog action figures. Through the use of commonality, the models are the same except for their exterior armor and color. The non-optimized manufacturing process is illustrated in Figure 8-6.

Assume these conditions for this sample scenario:

- ✔ Daily demand for each action figure stays at 100 with a standard deviation of 10.
- ✔ The firm desires a 95 percent service level (Z = 1.64).
- ✔ Total lead time from start to FGI is 0.4 days.

In this case, the safety stock of the FGI for each action figure needs to be

$$FGI\ SS\ = z \cdot Std\ Dev\ of\ Demand \cdot \sqrt{Lead\ Time} = 1.64 \cdot 10 \cdot \sqrt{0.4} = 10.37 = 11$$

Total FGI for the three models is 11 x 3 = 33 total items.

Manufacturing without Postponement

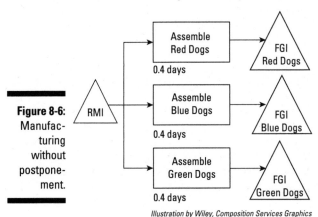

Figure 8-6: Manufacturing without postponement.

Illustration by Wiley, Composition Services Graphics

If, however, the company implements a postponement strategy and delays customization by holding common dog figures in a WIP prior to attaching armor, as illustrated in Figure 8-7, the lead time to assemble the common models reduces to 0.3 days and the lead time from the WIP to FGI for each item becomes 0.1 days. The amount of safety stock in each of the three FGIs becomes

$$FGI \; SS \; = z \cdot Std \; Dev \; of \; Demand \cdot \sqrt{Lead \; Time} = 1.64 \cdot 10 \cdot \sqrt{0.1} = 5.19 = 6$$

The total FGI for the three models is now 6 x 3 = 18 dogs.

Manufacturing with Postponement

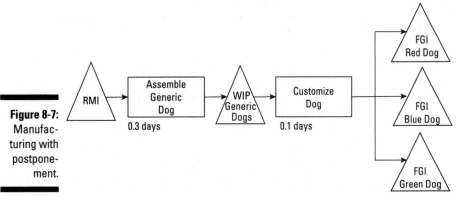

Figure 8-7: Manufacturing with postponement.

Illustration by Wiley, Composition Services Graphics

Employing a postponement strategy can reduce the amount of inventory in finished goods and protect a company against variability in demand for an individual product. The finished goods inventory drops from 33 dogs to 18 dogs with the implementation of a postponement strategy. If the customization lead time is small enough, the firm may consider not customizing the product until a customer order is received, thereby eliminating the need for an FGI altogether. Find ideas on how to reduce lead time in Part I of this book.

Before implementing a postponement strategy, be sure that you understand your customer requirements concerning acceptable lead times. If you decide to postpone customization until the order is actually received, be sure you can customize the product and get it into the customer's hands within a time frame that's acceptable to the customer. Also be aware that the addition of an additional WIP may increase the flow time through your process.

Managing Inventory across the Supply Chain

So far this chapter has focused on managing inventory within an individual firm. However, cost-effective inventory management also involves looking at total inventory across your entire supply line. After all, you do eventually pay for the excess inventory your supply holds or pay if your supplier stocks out and can't supply you the parts you need in a timely manner. In this section we show you how important the entire supply chain of inventory is. (For details on the ins and outs of managing other aspects of the supply chain, see Chapter 10.)

Keeping track of the pipeline inventory

When assessing inventory, a firm not only has to take into account the inventory it has on-hand but also needs to be aware of the inventory being held by its suppliers. Figure 8-8 shows the typical supply chain for a product. Let's assume that you're the maker of an end product (OEM), and you purchase a subassembly for your product from supplier T1. T1 purchases components for the subassembly from T2, and T2 purchases raw materials for the component from T3. Your inventory costs are determined by how well you manage your on-site inventory and also by how well your suppliers manage their inventory levels. Inventory in the supply chain is often referred to as *pipeline inventory* because it will eventually emerge out the end.

Figure 8-8:
Supply
chain
inventory.

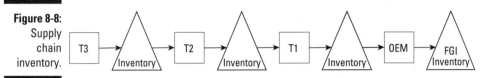

Illustration by Wiley, Composition Services Graphics

Unfortunately, managing this pipeline inventory isn't an easy task and involves coordination across an often diverse supply chain. (See Chapter 10 for more on supply chain management.) Two important questions that a firm needs to address are where in the pipeline to hold inventory and how much should be at each stocking point. Answers to these questions vary based on production and shipping lead times.

Some techniques can be used to manage supply chain inventory if the inventory costs across the chain are accounted for. Figure 8-9 illustrates a firm that buys a component from a supplier. The buying firm has a setup cost of $100 to order and a holding cost of $10 per component per year. The supplier produces the component only when an order from the buyer is placed and ships the component as soon as it's manufactured, and thus, the supplier has no holding cost for the final component. The supplier, however, incurs a $300 per-order setup cost.

Figure 8-9:
Optimizing
supply chain
inventory.

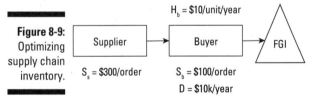

Illustration by Wiley, Composition Services Graphics

If the buying firm only looks to optimize its costs and uses an EOQ model with annual demand of 10,000 per year, then it would place an order for (to simplify the example we assume a constant demand):

$$\text{EOQ} = \sqrt{\frac{2(10,000)(100)}{10}} = 448$$

You can calculate total supply chain inventory costs by multiplying the sum of the average inventory (EOQ/2) times the annual holding cost per unit, plus the number of orders place per year (D/EOQ) times the setup cost per order. Given an EOQ of 448, total supply chain cost would be

$$\text{Total Supply Chain Cost} = \frac{EOQ}{2}H + \frac{D}{EOQ}\left(S_{Buyer} + S_{Supplier}\right)$$

$$= \frac{448}{2}(10) + \frac{10,000}{448}(100 + 300)$$

$$= 2,240 + 8,929 = \$11,169$$

Because in real-world situations you have demand variability, you must add your safety stock into the average inventory.

However, if you optimize taking into account the supplier's costs when determining your EOQ, your new recommended order quantity is

$$EOQ = \sqrt{\frac{2(10,000)(300 + 100)}{10}} = 895$$

Total supply chain costs then become

$$\text{Total Supply Chain Cost} = \frac{EOQ}{2}H + \frac{D}{EOQ}\left(S_{Buyer} + S_{Supplier}\right)$$

$$= \frac{895}{2}(10) + \frac{10,000}{895}(100 + 300)$$

$$= 4,465 + 4,469 = \$8,944$$

In this example, you can reduce your total supply chain inventory costs by $2,225 ($11,169 − $8,944), or approximately 20 percent. As you can see, being aware of all inventory costs across your supply chain can lead to significant savings.

Setting service levels with multiple suppliers

As if setting service levels isn't hard enough with one supplier, doing so is even more difficult if you have multiple suppliers providing materials that all must go into your product. Figure 8-10 shows a manufacturer that has multiple suppliers. (For more on the tiered structure of a supply chain, see Chapter 10.) If the OEM sets a service level of 98 percent for each of its suppliers, then the end service level will be much lower at 90 percent. In general, the end product service level is calculated as

$$\text{End Product Service Level} = \text{Individual Service Level}^{\text{Number of Suppliers}}$$

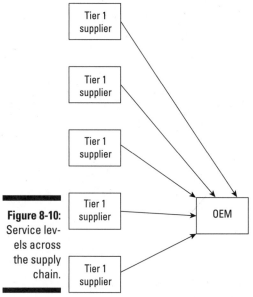

This lower-end product service level occurs because each supplier has a
2 percent chance of stocking out, and you can't produce your product unless
you have product from every supplier. As you can imagine, the more suppliers you have, the higher your individual service levels must be to maintain an
acceptable end product service level.

Chapter 9

Planning for Successful Operations

●●

In This Chapter

▶ Putting together an operations plan

▶ Creating an aggregate plan and master schedule

▶ Conducting material requirements planning

▶ Performing operations planning in service-based companies

▶ Implementing an enterprise resource planning system

●●

*B*en Franklin said, "If you fail to plan, you are planning to fail." This is particularly true of operations management because of the interdependencies of all the various components, including resources, materials, and processes. Trying to manage complex business operations with a seat-of-your-pants approach, hoping that the process will somehow evolve into something efficient without planning, is a losing proposition. To win at the game of operations, you need to plan.

In this chapter, we show you how to plan operations with a hierarchical approach. We describe tools you can use to plan operations at both the corporate and facility levels and point out how to apply your plans to process scheduling. Near the end of this chapter, we also cover software systems that are particular popular in the operations management set.

Planning from the Top Down

The planning and control of operations usually occurs in a hierarchical manner. Figure 9-1 illustrates the typical organization for operations planning. Strategies and goals are determined at the corporate level; detailed plans for meeting the firm's objectives are developed at the facility level; and operations are executed at the plant-floor (or, for services, front-line) level. In this section, we examine these three levels of planning and look at the decisions made in each.

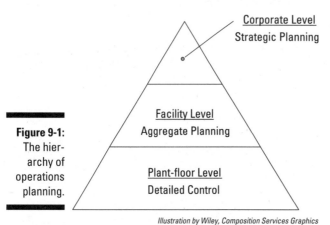

Hierarchy of Planning

Figure 9-1:
The hier-
archy of
operations
planning.

Determining corporate strategy

At the top of the pyramid is the corporate strategy, which ideally establishes the organization's direction and the basis upon which the business will compete. Michael Porter, a leading expert on corporate strategy and competitiveness, proposed basic strategies for competitive advantage. They include a focus on being the low-cost provider (Walmart), a focus on being the leader in innovation (Apple) or product quality (Toyota), or a focus on the differentiated needs of the customer (American Express). Each of these strategies requires a different approach to operations management. For more details on how strategy choice and product life cycles influence your operations, see Chapters 5 and 18.

The key to executing the corporate strategy is the *business plan,* which answers the core questions of running the business, such as what products or services the firm wants to provide and where and how it will produce, market, and distribute them. The business plan also describes market dynamics and competition.

The business plan has a long-term effect on the health of the company and its shareholders. It covers many aspects of running the business, including these:

- ✔ **Goals:** What financial and performance goals will the company set?
- ✔ **Markets:** What markets and which customers will the firm pursue?
- ✔ **Product portfolio:** What products will the business offer, and how quickly will the company introduce and update the products?

The business plan also covers the key strategic operations management decisions within the scope of this chapter on operations, including these considerations and others:

- ✔ **Facility location:** Will the company have multiple facilities, and if so, where will they be located?

- ✔ **Long-term capacity:** What is the forecast for expected demand, and how much capacity will the firm need to meet the demand (see Chapters 6 and 7)?

- ✔ **Outsourcing strategy:** What will the company produce or provide itself and what will it outsource (see Chapter 17)?

- ✔ **Production allocation:** What facilities will make which products, and will a product be produced at multiple facilities or will a facility make multiple products? Chapter 4 covers flexibility in processes.

- ✔ **Production policy:** How will the firm face the market? Will the company make its product to order or make it to stock (see Chapter 5)?

These high-level decisions have long-term implications and must be considered over a long time horizon. Given the long-term nature of corporate strategy decisions, company leaders must look into the future and create a shared vision of what the company will be before making those decisions.

Preparing for success

After a firm determines its corporate strategy and establishes its long-term capacity needs and production policies, focus shifts to intermediate planning, which is often referred to as *aggregate planning*. Aggregate planning usually presents a detailed plan for sales and operations that covers a period of 2 to 12 months. A company's aggregate plan typically addresses the following three specific operational considerations:

- ✔ **Employment levels:** How much manpower is needed to meet the set production rates?

- ✔ **Inventory levels:** How much inventory (both raw material and finished goods) does the company need (see Chapter 8)?

- ✔ **Production or output rates:** How much will the company produce in the designated time period? For a detailed discussion on long-term capacity planning and the effects of different production strategies, see Chapter 7.

Develop an aggregate plan by following these steps:

1. **Determine demand for each time period covered in the plan.**

   You can use the forecasting methods described in Chapter 6 to predict demand.

2. **Determine the available capacities for each time period.**

   Be sure to calculate capacities for all resources, including labor and machine capacities.

3. **Identify corporate policies and external constraints such as regulation and market forces that may influence the plan.**

   These policies include limitations on workers over time, inventory targets, and outsourcing policies.

4. **Determine product cost, based on direct labor and material costs as well as indirect or overhead (fixed) manufacturing expenses.**

5. **Develop contingency plans to account for surges and downturns in the market.**

   For example, each plan may utilize different levels of overtime, outsourcing, and inventory to meet the demand requirements, thus resulting in a different product cost and availability.

6. **Select the plan that best meets the corporate objectives.**

   Compare your various plans and determine how well each one meets your business objectives. Some plans may present tradeoffs in different performance metrics such as utilization versus inventory levels.

7. **Test the plan for *robustness* (its ability to perform well under varying conditions).**

   This may involve changing the demand requirements or the unit costs for things such as overtime to simulate different scenarios. If the outcome of the plan varies greatly from your ideal scenario, revisit one of the alternative plans available in Step 5.

Aggregate planning is an ongoing process. A plan usually provides details at the monthly level over the course of a year, and you should update it as conditions change. For example, you need to account for changes in expected demand as well as unexpected events such as material shortages and production disruptions.

Avoid the temptation to change your aggregate plan too often. The purpose of the plan is to provide an intermediate path into the future. Reacting too quickly to perceived changes in demand or variability in production output can create unnecessary disruptions in your overall plan, such as layoffs, unnecessary hiring, or changes in supply purchasing contracts. Until you recognize an undisputable, reoccurring change in demand or production output, allow your short-term planning to accommodate the blips in demand that are only temporary because of such things as weather events or short-term shifts in customer preference.

Executing the plan

Armed with the aggregate plan, plant personnel or those who schedule and control actual production develop the short-term detailed plans for implementation. This level of planning generally includes the weekly and daily schedules for specific tasks:

- ✔ **Inventory levels:** How much raw material, work-in-process, and finished goods should be in the operation (see Chapter 8)?

- ✔ **Machine loading:** What items will be processed by what resources and when?

- ✔ **Production lot sizes:** How large should batch sizes be, and how should changeovers be scheduled (see Chapter 4)?

- ✔ **Work schedules:** What are the staffing needs, including overtime?

A critical aspect of successful operations is managing bottleneck operations (covered in Chapter 3). Because the bottleneck is the resource that limits the processes output, start your detailed planning with a focus on the bottleneck. This increases the likelihood that the facility will use its resources in the best way possible.

The detailed plan needs to be responsive to sudden changes in conditions such as a rush order for a product, a disruption in material supply, or an unexpected equipment failure. The operations manager can schedule over-time or reassign workers to different tasks to adjust for many of these issues.

Exploring the Components of an Aggregate Plan

An aggregate plan provides the road map for business operations; it translates corporate strategy into a plan that can be implemented on the plant floor or on the front-line of service. For companies that sell physical products, this map details the production process. For service-based companies, the aggregate map identifies staffing levels and other resources needed to accommodate customer demand. In this section, find out how the aggregate plan evolves from the corporate strategy and how it becomes a detailed plan for production.

Putting together a plan

The operations planning process starts at the corporate level with a strategic plan for the company. The overarching corporate strategy guides the aggregate operations plan; this relationship is shown in Figure 9-2.

The purpose of the aggregate plan is to match the firm's capacity with anticipated customer demand to ensure that the company is utilizing its available capacity to best meet anticipated demand. An aggregate plan requires two sets of information:

✔ **Strategic capacity plan:** A *capacity plan* emerges from the corporate strategic plan and provides aggregate planners with details on current and future capacity levels.

✔ **Forecast of anticipated demand**: The demand forecast provides an overview on how much product the facility needs to manufacture in the coming months to satisfy anticipated customer demand. (Find details on forecasting in Chapter 6.)

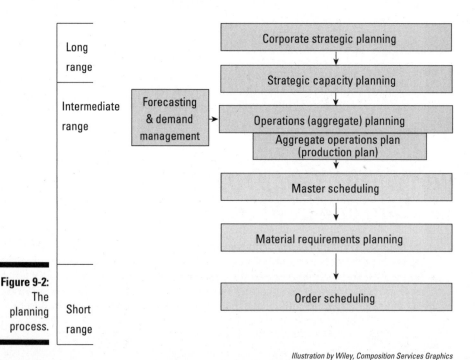

Figure 9-2: The planning process.

Illustration by Wiley, Composition Services Graphics

In their general form, aggregate plans deal with the total demand. They typically don't focus on individual models or items. For example, when allocating space in a grocery store, the aggregate plan would indicate a certain amount of space to be used for breakfast cereals, but the plan wouldn't address how much shelf space each type or brand of cereal gets. In some cases, the plan may allocate a specific amount of space to a particular manufacturer, such as Kellogg's, but this is usually as specific as it gets.

The end product of aggregate planning is the production plan, which guides the development of a master schedule (MS), which informs detailed schedules for operations. These relationships are illustrated in Figure 9-2.

Creating the master schedule

Based on the production plan, facility personnel (such as a retail store manager) create a detailed schedule to give specific direction on what to do when to employees who are actually doing the work or providing the service. The master schedule shows the quantity and timing for a specific product to be delivered to customers over a specific period of time, but it doesn't show how many products actually need to be produced because the demanded products can be provided using inventory in some cases.

The master schedule and inventory levels provide information for the master production schedule, which communicates how many units need to be produced at a given time. Chapter 8 covers how to calculate desired inventory levels, and Chapter 7 provides details on balancing production with inventory.

For example, a computer manufacturer's production plan may show that the company forecasts sales of 1,200 portable computers in September, 1,500 in October, and 1,700 in November. But it doesn't give any information about what quantity of each model is needed. The master schedule shows how many of each model is needed and when it needs to be produced.

Figure 9-3 shows the aggregate plan and the master schedule for a company that manufactures three different models of a product.

Getting to the specifics of the master schedule can be difficult. Breaking a production plan into the number of specific models to produce isn't always easy. Because disaggregate forecasts are less accurate than aggregate forecasts, it's often difficult to predict what actual models the customer will desire. You must take care when developing the forecast (flip to Chapter 6 for info on forecasting techniques). Because short-term forecasts are typically more accurate than long-term forecasts, the longer you can delay making the line item (model) forecast, the better off everyone will be. When creating a master schedule, follow a structured method (such as the one described earlier in this chapter in the "Preparing for success" section).

Disaggregating the Plan

Aggregate Plan	Month	September	October	November
	Planned Output	1,200	1,500	1,700
Master Schedule	Month	September	October	November
	Planned Output			
	Model 360	500	700	800
	Model 183	450	500	575
	Model 71	250	300	325

Figure 9-3: Disaggregating the plan.

Illustration by Wiley, Composition Services Graphics

Considering Materials

A company's master schedule focuses on creating the product or delivering the service that a company is in business to sell. This commodity often requires materials and processes, and the collection of parts and activity can become complicated very quickly. In this section we present the basics of material requirements planning (or MRP).

Gathering information for the system

Material requirements planning (MRP) is a computerized information system designed to help manage the ordering and scheduling of the components, parts, and raw material that make up a company's end product. Demand for these components is often referred to as *dependent demand* because the quantity demanded depends on the consumer demand for the end product.

An MRP system requires these major inputs:

✔ **Master production schedule:** This input is described in the section "Creating the master schedule" earlier in this chapter.

✔ **Product structure:** This diagram shows all inputs needed to produce the product. It may also show assembly order. Figure 9-4 shows an abbreviated product structure for an automobile. The automobile consists of two axle assemblies: one body and one engine assembly. Each axle assembly consists of two wheels and one axle subassembly.

✔ **Bill of materials (BOM):** This input is a listing of all the items needed to produce an end product. It's much like the list of ingredients in a recipe.

✔ **Inventory record:** Tallies of all the raw material, parts, subassemblies (partial assemblies), and assemblies for each time period are included in this input. Here are the primary data points contained in this file:

- **Gross requirements:** The total demand for the item during the time period

- **Scheduled receipts:** The orders that have been placed but not yet received, often referred to as *open orders*

- **Expected on-hand inventory:** An estimate of the inventory that's on hand

- **Net requirements:** Actual amount needed

- **Planned receipts:** Quantity expected to be received

- **Planned releases:** Quantity expected to be ordered

For MRP, you must also know the expected *lead time,* the time between the ordering of parts and their delivery.

Product Structure for an Automobile

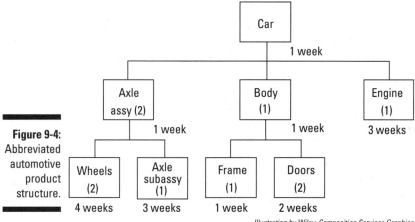

Figure 9-4: Abbreviated automotive product structure.

Illustration by Wiley, Composition Services Graphics

Getting system results

The MRP system takes the master production schedule, product structure, BOM, inventory record, and lead time information and creates a material requirement plan for each item. The process starts with the number of end products desired in any given period. The software uses the product structure and the BOM to determine how many of each assembly and subassembly are needed — and when — to make the end product. Using current inventory levels, the system provides the manufacturing staff with a work release, which points out how many items they need to actually produce. This process repeats down to the raw material level.

To visualize this process, consider the BOM in Figure 9-4. If you need 100 automobiles in week 7 and 120 in week 8, then the MRP system breaks out the master schedule into separate plans for the automobile, the axle assemblies, the subassemblies, and the wheels. Figure 9-5 shows a traditional output from an MRP system.

MRP Output

	Week Number	1	2	3	4	5	6	7	8
	Quantity							100	120
Automobile	Gross requirements							100	120
LT 1 week	Scheduled receipts								
	Expected on hand								
	Planned receipts							100	120
	Planned releases						100	120	
Axle									
Assembly	Gross requirements						200	240	
(2 required)	Scheduled receipts								
LT 1 week	Expected on hand								
	Planned receipts						200	240	
	Planned releases					200	240		
Axle									
Subassembly	Gross requirements						200	240	
(1 required)	Scheduled receipts								
LT 3 weeks	Expected on hand								
	Planned receipts						200	240	
	Planned releases		200	240					
Wheels	Gross requirements					400	480		
(2 required)	Scheduled receipts								
LT 4 weeks	Expected on hand								
	Planned receipts					400	480		
	Planned releases	400	480						

Figure 9-5: MRP output.

Illustration by Wiley, Composition Services Graphics

Figure 9-5 shows that the company needs 100 automobiles in week 7. Because the company has a one-week lead time, it needs to release the required materials into the plant during week 6, which means that 200 axle assemblies must be ready at this time. (Each automobile needs two axle assemblies.) Given the one-week lead time to produce an axle assembly, the company must release the material needed to produce the assemblies at week 5. Notice that producing a subassembly takes 3 weeks, so the company must release materials for 200 axle subassemblies at week 2. For the same reasons, it needs to release materials for 400 wheels at week 1 (two wheels per axle assembly; four-week lead time). These calculations are repeated for the 120 automobiles needed at week 8, although, because of the 20 percent increase in demand, all the quantities grow by 20 percent.

MRP reporting makes it quick and easy for an operations manager to see the required timing for future operations. For example, if you're managing the axle subassembly operations, you know that at week 2 you need to begin production for the 200 subassemblies required for a week-5 delivery to the axle assembly area.

Taking MRP data to the factory floor

MRP releases raw material onto the factory floor as needed but doesn't schedule the individual resources (machines and people) needed to produce the product. Scheduling jobs can be problematic when specific resources are required for multiple products or jobs. Which jobs do you schedule first?

Several methods to prioritize jobs are available. Here are some of the most common options:

- **First-come, first-served (FCFS):** Process jobs in the order that they arrive. Also known as *first-in, first-out* (FIFO).

- **Shortest operating time (SOT):** Start with the job that has the shortest processing time.

- **Earliest due date first (EDD):** Begin with the job that has the earliest required date.

- **Critical ratio method (CR):** Calculate the time remaining until the due date and divide it by the total processing time remaining. Start with the job with the smallest ratio.

The metrics you use to evaluate the advantages of each scheduling method include the flow time and the job lateness. *Flow time* (covered in Chapter 2) is the length of time a job spends in the facility. It includes not only processing time but also the time the job waits to be processed. Measure lateness against the promised due date to the customer; that is, calculate job lateness as the difference between the actual completion date and the due date.

Unfortunately, no one method is better than the others in all circumstances. Evaluate all the methods for each series of jobs to find the best approach for a given situation.

Here are some general trends:

- ✔ FCFS is the worst performer in most situations because long jobs often delay other jobs behind them in the process. However, FCFS is often used in service operations because it's the simplest method to implement and perceived to be the fairest to customers.

- ✔ SOT always results in the lowest flow time for a group of jobs. This typically results in lower work-in-progress inventory because jobs move through the process quickly. The major drawback is that long-processing-time jobs often spend much more time waiting than with FCFS or EDD.

- ✔ EDD usually minimizes the number of jobs missing their delivery date, but it also can increase the flow time of jobs through the system because they aren't processed until the last possible moment.

Planning for Services

Aggregate planning is rooted in the manufacturing sector, but many of its concepts apply to service industries, too. In this section, we point out how operations planning typically happens in service-based companies. We highlight the factors that make planning for service unique and describe how to develop a plan for serve operations.

Seeing the difference in services

All sorts of businesses sell services, and some service products — such as those provided by restaurants and retail stores — contain many of the same operational elements as manufacturing-based organizations. For starters, these particular service industries require a business to maintain inventory. In fact, much of the activity in the banking industry (think processing deposits and withdraws) can be automated in a way that's quite similar to what you may see on a production line. However, other kinds of service-based businesses, including healthcare, are significantly different from a manufacturing operation because patients cannot be inventoried and their care cannot be automated.

Most service industries share a handful of characteristics that don't apply to most manufacturing operations:

- ✔ **High level of customization:** No two customers are alike in most service environments, and each requires at least some level of customization, if not complete customization.

- ✔ **No inventory:** Customers cannot be inventoried for services, and the service process cannot be initiated until a customer expresses demand for the service. For example, a bank cannot approve a mortgage loan until an applicant finds a house he wants to purchase and submits the loan application. Similarly, a doctor cannot perform most medical procedures until a customer is present.

- ✔ **Variable arrival rates:** In manufacturing, the operations manager has a fairly high level of control over the arrival rates of material. This isn't the case for services, where the arrival of customers is often difficult to control. Even with the use of appointments and reservations, customer arrival rates are difficult to predict and control. If a manufacturing company produces using a make-to-order system (only producing when an order is received), its arrival rate variability will be more like that of a service operation.

- ✔ **Variable service times:** In services, the *cycle time* (time to complete the task) can vary significantly, much more than in a typical manufacturing operation. Service time variability makes capacity planning more difficult in service industries (see Chapter 7).

 Because inventory isn't present in most service-based operations, capacity becomes the prime leverage point when managing "product" availability, and the variability in arrival rates and service times makes capacity management difficult, resulting in potentially significant waiting time for customers, which often impacts customer satisfaction.

Establishing the service plan

Service planning is usually completed in a hierarchical manner. At the corporate level, company leaders decide what types of services to provide and set goals and metrics. These parameters are communicated to the facility level where detailed plans are made. As in manufacturing, these plans are then carried out on the service floor, or front line.

In services the primary focus is on capacity, and service capacity is usually of the human variety, so the goal of planning is to determine how many people are needed for certain periods of time and when individual employees should work. See Chapter 7 for processes to determine capacity. In aggregate planning terms, customer demand is specified for each time period and employees are assigned to meet this demand. For example, when staffing a restaurant, additional kitchen and wait staff are scheduled during lunch and dinner hours to meet the increased demand.

Though an MRP system isn't too useful in services, many services utilize a scheduling optimization software program that can help managers best utilize resources and provide better customer service.

Consider a popular retail chain. At the corporate level, the strategic plans for the company are established. Corporate leaders determine what customer market to target and what products to sell. Each facility takes these strategic plans and determines how to implement them at its local branch. In the clothing industry, for example, a store in southern Texas has limited need for winter parkas, so the store's managers may decide to carry a larger stock of lightweight jackets instead.

Though general management employment levels are established at the strategic level, it is typically up to the facility management to determine how many employees are needed on the store floor to service customers. These employees are usually assigned to departments based on projected demand. For example, the days before Mother's Day, more employees may be assigned to the women's apparel and jewelry departments to service the anticipated increase in demand in these areas.

Applying Information to the Entire Organization

MRP led to the development of *enterprise resource planning* (ERP). As the name implies, ERP integrates an entire company into one information system that operates on real-time data it receives from throughout the organization. The shared database ensures that every location and department can access the most reliable and up-to-date information (see Figure 9-6).

An ERP system incorporates many of the topics covered in this book, including process design and management, aggregate planning, capacity and inventory management, scheduling, quality control, and project management.

An ERP system has many advantages, but beware of the silver bullet perception. ERP systems require significant investments, including purchasing the system and then implementing and maintaining it. Many companies underestimate the amount of time and money involved with implementing and maintaining an ERP system.

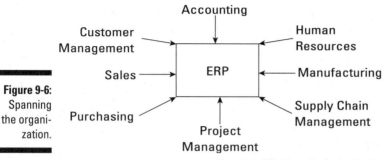

Figure 9-6:
Spanning
the organi-
zation.

Accounting

Customer
Management

Human
Resources

Sales ⟶ ERP ⟵ Manufacturing

Purchasing

Supply Chain
Management

Project
Management

Illustration by Wiley, Composition Services Graphics

We recommend the following steps for implementing a successful ERP system:

1. **Assess your needs.**

   Do you really need such a sophisticated system? The system itself won't fix all the problems of an organization. Often, some process re-engineering and communication across the organization can do the trick, and you can handle data management in a much simpler and inexpensive way. Many world-class manufacturing and service operations use relatively simple, unsophisticated systems to manage their ERP needs.

2. **Fix your processes.**

   Implementing an ERP system won't fix broken, inefficient processes. Before investing in an ERP system, evaluate and, if needed, redesign your processes using the methods described in Part I of this book.

3. **Acquire and verify consistent data.**

   When you begin populating an ERP system with data, remember that the outputs are only as good as the data going in. If different departments are operating on different sets of data — say, sales data in one department is different from sales data in another — then the software system isn't going to produce accurate data for the company.

4. **Customize your software.**

   ERP vendors offer highly standardized software, typically with optimized modules for particular industries. One of the major concerns companies have about implementing an ERP system is that it locks the company into standardized processes. This inhibits process innovation within a company because deviating from the ERP's process ends up requiring many software work-arounds. When setting up an ERP, make sure the system can accommodate process improvements from Step 2 and not force you into the standard processes that have been built into its software.

When customizing software to accommodate an improved process, be sure your competitors don't get ahold of the same programs and eliminate any competitive advantage you've gained.

5. **Train your employees.**

   Employees must understand the purpose of the system and how to input data and interpret the reports that the system generates.

6. **Continuously improve your processes.**

   Continuous improvement is the heartbeat of all successful companies, and changing processes almost certainly involves modifications to ERP software. Many companies find themselves locked into their current processes to avoid the time and money needed to update their software. Avoid stagnation by developing a good relationship with your software provider.

Chapter 10

Managing the Supply Chain

· ·

· ·

*Y*ou may have heard the saying "You're only as strong as your weakest link." Nothing is truer for a company's *supply chain* — the businesses that provide the materials that you need to do business. Sometimes, the failure of just one supplier can drastically affect your ability to deliver quality goods and services to your customers in a timely manner.

The importance of efficient supply chain management has significantly increased as companies outsource more and more functions that go into their products and services. In the past, companies were traditionally *vertically integrated,* meaning that they produced a great majority of the components in their products. Today, however, firms now take on a horizontal structure, with many suppliers providing the products and services that once were done in-house. The costs associated with the purchase of goods and services now makes up a large portion of a firm's cost of goods sold. By efficiently managing this supply chain, a firm can realize big savings and make a significant impact on its bottom line. For more on vertical integration and how business evolved into its current structure, see Chapter 11.

Among the most well-known businesses that are thriving in part because of smart supply chain decisions are Toyota, which made suppliers an integral part of its operations as part of its quest to get lean; Walmart, which relies on suppliers to keep shelves stocked with products at the lowest possible prices; and Dell Computer, which rose to market dominance by managing its supply chain to provide components quickly to fuel a custom manufacturing model. The importance of a reliable supply chain to businesses has even prompted many universities to establish supply chain management majors.

In this chapter we describe the basic structure of supply chains and point out how you can establish a supply chain that meets the particular needs of your product. We also explain supply chain dynamics and reveal the major issues that arise from these dynamics. But don't worry; we tell you how to prevent and manage these issues, too, and even highlight a few methods that real companies are using to bring suppliers into the fold of their business to strengthen the supply chain.

Seeing the Structure of Supply Chains

Most supply chains have a basic structure that resembles the pyramid shape of a typical organizational chart. Here, one person is in charge. Several people report to the head honcho, and each of these people has direct reports as well, and the chain of command continues down to line workers. In a supply chain, the main business — also known as the *original equipment manufacturer* (OEM), a general term that describes the organization that makes the end product for customers — is supported by supply tiers that become increasingly specialized as you move down the structure. That is, Tier 1 suppliers provide the most refined, market-ready components for the end product — whether the business sells widgets or services. Tier 2 suppliers provide direct support to Tier 1 companies and so forth down the layers. Figure 10-1 represents a real supply chain.

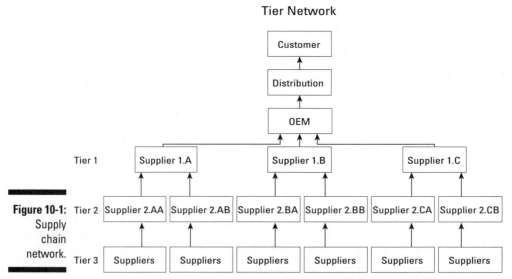

Figure 10-1: Supply chain network.

Illustration by Wiley, Composition Services Graphics

Tier 1 suppliers receive support from their suppliers, companies that enable them to provide materials or services to their customers. From the OEM's perspective, the suppliers to the Tier 1 suppliers are Tier 2 suppliers; yet these companies are Tier 1 suppliers to the OEM's Tier 1 suppliers. Sounds like the old "Who's on First" scenario, right? Well, this support system continues with Tier 3 suppliers supporting Tier 2 suppliers and so on. And the chain eventually leads to the raw material providers.

In this section, we describe the tiered structure of a supply chain and point out how support services link into a company's supply chain.

Getting through the tiers

It's important for the OEM to determine how many tiers it wants to manage. As you progress down the chain, management of suppliers (and the suppliers of the suppliers' suppliers) can get pretty complicated. A business may have only a few Tier 1 suppliers but many more Tier 2 and Tier 3 suppliers. As you can see, the number of suppliers grows quickly.

 Most OEMs rely on their Tier 1 suppliers to manage the lower layers of the supply chain. However, very large and successful companies such as Toyota have been known to work with Tier 2 suppliers, lending their quality expertise to help improve the quality of products delivered to Tier 1 suppliers.

Linking in support services

A company's supply chain may extend beyond the suppliers that contribute components for a specific product or service. The distribution network is also a critical component of many supply chains and ensures that products get to the customer. For example, Amazon relies on United Parcel Service (UPS) to deliver customer orders quickly and reliably. This distribution function is outside the core competency of most companies, so it's often an important support service. (Find more on outsourcing in Chapter 17.)

Keep in mind that the tiered structure of a supply chain also applies to service-based commodities. For example, in order for a financial lender to provide a customer with a mortgage, the company performs a series of operations that involve other businesses. In this case, the mortgage lender is the OEM. To approve a loan, the company utilizes several other business (Tier 1 suppliers), which may include a credit reporting agency to determine whether a customer is creditworthy, a title company to confirm there are no other claims to the property, a property appraiser to assess the value of the property, and a surveyor to determine property lines and infringements.

Each of these Tier 1 suppliers for the OEM may require its own set of suppliers; these are the OEM's Tier 2 suppliers.

An OEM or end customer is often unaware of every supplier involved with the commodity being purchased. Figure 10-2 illustrates this mortgage supply chain.

Figure 10-2:
The mortgage service supply chain.

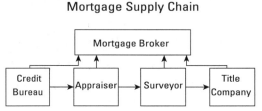

Mortgage Supply Chain

Illustration by Wiley, Composition Services Graphics

Service supply chains have different requirements from their manufacturing cousins because service supply chains have no way to inventory their services. In other words, a mortgage provider and its suppliers can't perform its functions until a property has been identified for purchase.

In Chapter 7, we point out that companies in a service supply chain must manage demand variability by maintaining excess capacity, which often means having employees work overtime.

Service-based companies can smooth the demand for their suppliers' services by pulling as much as they can forward in the process. For example, mortgage companies often recommend that clients get preapproved for a mortgage before they find the property they want to purchase. This takes the time crunch off of the resources in the process.

Aligning the Supply Chain with Business Strategy

One size doesn't fit all when it comes to building a supply chain. Each company needs to consider its goals and business strategy when designing a supply chain. Companies also need to account for the cultural aspects of their suppliers because communication is key to any successful relationship. Language barriers and the meaning of different phrases can vary across cultures, leading to misunderstandings in directions. Management of both a company and its suppliers must work toward the same goals and objectives, and both must understand what is expected.

In this section, we describe the relationship between a product or service and a company's business strategy and point out how this relationship influences the supply chain.

Defining product demand

Before developing a supply chain, a company needs to understand the nature of the demand for its products (find more on demand in Chapter 6). The supply chain needs for a product with stable demand (a well-established or mature product) are different from those for a product with less predictable demand (an innovative product).

Functional products typically have a demand stream that's well-known and predictable. For your local grocery store, these products include staple food products such as breakfast cereals and milk. Functional products typically have a long product life cycle, meaning that the products don't change dramatically over time. Functional products also often have low profit margins because they're considered a commodity, and many substitutions (generic products) are available.

Innovative products, on the other hand, are new and often revolutionary products that have a demand stream that's not well-known and unpredictable. Innovative products are characterized by variable demand, shorter product life cycles, and higher profit margins. Examples of innovative products include most consumer electronics, computer games, and fashion apparel.

Choosing the right supply chain strategy

Depending on the type of product that a business sells, supply chain development may take on one of two basic looks. Here are the primary supply chain categories:

- **Efficient supply chain:** Usually a make-to-stock (MTS) producer that draws from a large finished goods inventory. Functional products usually benefit from an efficient supply chain because demand for these products is stable, allowing the company to maintain inventory with minimal risk of overstocking or being left with inventory that doesn't sell.

- **Responsive supply chain:** Usually produces make-to-order (MTO) products. With their high demand variability, innovative products benefit from responsive supply chains that can deliver products quickly without maintaining a finished goods inventory. Flip to Chapter 8 for a discussion of the risks associated with inventory.

We describe MTS and MTO production strategies in Chapters 5 and 11.

Figure 10-3 illustrates how a product's demand influences supply chain choice.

Choosing a Supply Chain Strategy

	Functional Product	Innovative Product
Efficient Supply Chain	Match	Mismatch
Responsive Supply Chain	Possible Match	Match

Illustration by Wiley, Composition Services Graphics

Figure 10-3: Choosing a supply chain strategy.

You can implement a responsive supply chain for functional products under certain circumstances. Because responsive supply chain companies don't maintain inventory, they must be able to quickly produce the products needed. These companies must embrace the lean principles described in Chapter 11.

A major supply chain mismatch is an innovative product trying to operate in an efficient supply chain, although many companies find themselves in this situation. This pairing is especially common in markets where companies find that the life cycle of their products are rapidly decreasing, such as mobile phones. (How many versions of the iPhone exist?)

Efficient supply chains tend not to serve innovative products well because they benefit from long production runs that result in the buildup of inventory. If a product's demand is highly variable and unknown, this inventory presents a sizable risk (see Chapter 8 for details on inventory risk).

When a firm sells both functional and innovative products, designing a successful supply chain gets tougher. In this case, the firm may have different supply chains for different product offerings.

Just be aware that not all the vendors in a firm's supply chain need to operate exclusively as an efficient or responsive supplier. For example, a consumer electronics firm may require that its Tier 1 suppliers be responsive to accommodate the variability in demand. However, because a particular supplier can provide a certain component to more than one firm, the supplier may operate according to the efficient approach because its demand variability can be reduced across multiple customers.

Exploring the Bullwhip Effect

The layered structure of a supply chain (shown in Figure 10-1) generates variability in the supply chain that increases with each new layer, a dynamic known as the *bullwhip effect.* Figure 10-4 illustrates the bullwhip effect.

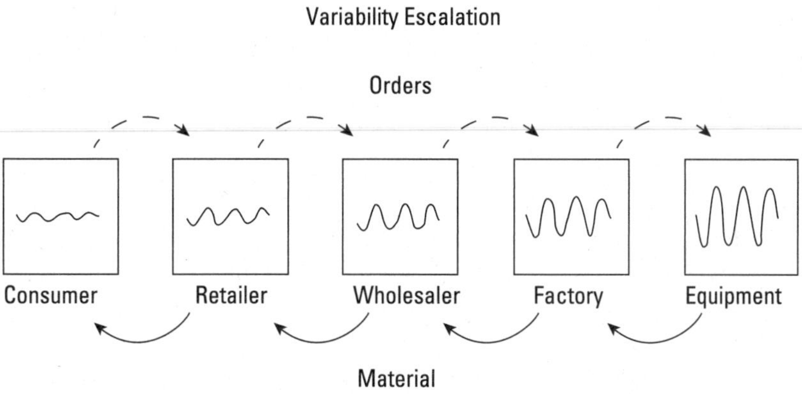

Variability Escalation

Orders

Figure 10-4:
Supply
chain
variability
escalation.

Consumer   Retailer   Wholesaler   Factory   Equipment

Material

Illustration by Wiley, Composition Services Graphics

In Figure 10-4, the consumer demands product from the retailer, the retailer places an order with the wholesaler, and the wholesaler in turn orders from the factory. Farther down the supply chain line, the factory, experiencing an increase in demand, places an order with an equipment supplier for machines to increase its production capacity. The escalation in the demand variability is the result of several policies that locally seem to be sensible but, when examined from a systematic point of view, result in the bullwhip chaos.

The bullwhip effect exists in all supply chains — it's the root of the boom and bust cycles that occur in many industries — and it can be devastating if not properly managed. Fortunately, you have ways to manage the bullwhip and minimize its impact. Find out more about these maneuvers later in this section.

Figure 10-5 shows actual data for the machine tool supply chain. The GDP in this graph looks relatively stable compared to the variability experienced in the demand for automobiles and the supply chain for automobiles. Figure 10-5 shows that the variability in orders for machine tools is even greater than for automobiles. This makes practical sense because automotive manufacturers purchase machine tools to assemble automobiles. When demand for automobiles increases, the firm may desire to increase capacity and go out and place orders for more machines to assemble the autos. Just like the end of a bullwhip can exceed the speed of the sound barrier, resulting in a sharp "crack" while the handle of the whip is moving more slowly, relatively small changes in GDP resulting in noticeable changes to auto demand can be magnified into far more dramatic changes for machine tool demand. Hence the term *bullwhip*.

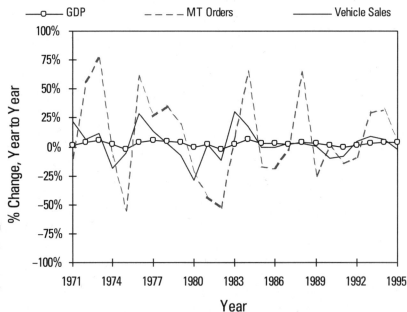

Figure 10-5: The machine tool supply chain.

Illustration by Wiley, Composition Services Graphics

Variability in demand makes managing business operations difficult. Planning capacity, managing inventory, and making staffing decisions are tough when you're riding the demand roller coaster of the bullwhip, especially as you move along the supply chain away from the customer. (Find more on how to manage capacity and inventory in Chapters 7 and 8.)

In the next section, we point out what causes the bullwhip effect and how you can keep your supply chain bullwhip-free.

Finding the bullwhip triggers

The bullwhip effect is triggered by several different causes. We describe four of the most prevalent causes here.

Delivery delays and pipeline inventory

Delivery delay, also called *lead time,* is the span of time between when an order is placed and when it's received. If you don't maintain sufficient inventory, you need to account for the time it takes your suppliers to produce and/or deliver goods.

For example, consider a beer supply chain in a city hosting the Super Bowl for the first time. During the week before the game, end customers purchase the beer from a local retailer. By Tuesday, when supplies of beer on the shelf get low, the retailer places an order with the wholesaler. When the wholesaler receives the order from the retailer, it prepares the beer for shipment and ships it. Processing the order and delivering it to the customer take time. This time is considered the delivery delay.

While the order is being shipped, the retailer continues to sell beer; as stock disappears, the retailer orders even more beer from the wholesaler on Thursday. The wholesaler in turn experiences a decrease in inventory and places additional orders with the brewers. The factory, located in Germany in this case, has a long lead time to ship the beer, which may inspire the wholesaler to order even more beer as inventory decreases in order to avoid empty shelves in other cities.

The greater the delivery delay, the more prone your supply chain is to the bullwhip effect because orders increase across the supply chain as everyone waits for delivery. If all participants in the supply chain don't account for the *pipeline orders* (outstanding orders) and continue to order normally as inventory is depleted, when the ordered shipments start arriving, the participants will end up overshooting their desired inventory levels and decrease future orders. This leads to large variation in demand experienced throughout the supply chain.

Be sure to modify the basic inventory equations in Chapter 8 to include orders that have been placed but not received by customers. For example, in a periodic inventory review system, the amount of inventory that a firm should order is revealed by this formula:

$$\text{Amount to Order} = \text{Demand} \cdot \text{Lead Time} + \text{Safety Stock} -$$
$$\text{Amount on Hand} - \text{Amount on Order}$$

Order batching

Depending on how frequently you order from your supplier, your supply chain will likely experience varying levels of bullwhip effect. Placing frequent orders for small quantities is better (creates less bullwhip) than placing larger orders less frequently. Figure 10-6 shows demand for a product at a retailer. The demand is continuous (not constant) over the month, and the retailer places orders with its supplier once per month. This creates very inconsistent demand for the supplier over time.

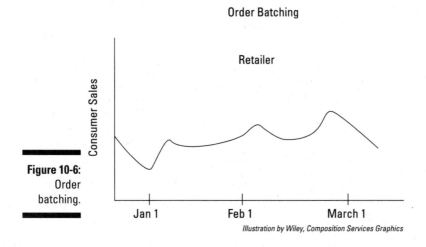

Order Batching

Retailer

Figure 10-6:
Order
batching.

Jan 1   Feb 1   March 1

Illustration by Wiley, Composition Services Graphics

The demand stream to the supplier can be smoothed if, instead of once a month, the retailer places an order to the supplier every week.

Sales and price discounts

Many supply chain experts believe that promotional price discounts and sales are the worst marketing ploys ever created when it comes to managing a supply chain. When things you use and buy on a regular basis go on sale, a bullwhip effect often occurs because sales create a boom-and-bust cycle. Lots of product moves during the promotional period, which is followed by lower levels of sales. This cycle ripples through the supply chain.

Promotional sales also lead to retail outlets running out of inventory, which means that customers hoping to purchase the product on sale can't get it. If offered, customers can wait in line at the customer service counter to receive a rain check for the product, but in most cases, customers leave disappointed, with a lower opinion of the operation.

Another unintended consequence of promotional sales, especially if a company offers them frequently, is that customers come to expect a sale, and they won't purchase items unless they're on sale. Companies also believe that they must offer the sales to attract customers.

Shortage gaming

Shortage gaming occurs when customers place multiple orders for a product with one or more suppliers or when they place an order for more than what they want. Customers often do this if they know inventory will be in short supply.

Consider the release of a hot new product such as a video game. You know you must have it the day it's released to the public and realize that it may be in short supply. So you place a preorder with several retailers, knowing that you'll purchase only one and will cancel orders from the others (or you may buy every item and resell them on some Internet site for a profit).

This *double* or *phantom* ordering creates a false demand picture for the product provider. Demand can often be exaggerated, leading the producer to increase output. This very real problem occurs often in businesses where shortages are expected, and the effect ripples throughout the supply chain. Many companies, especially those in the retail industry, have tried to combat this by making the customer place a small deposit on ordered items.

Dodging the bullwhip

Most companies are aware of the bullwhip effect and the damage it can inflict on their business. Yet many managers still fall into the traps that trigger bullwhips, which are described in the previous section. Here, we introduce basic techniques for avoiding the bullwhip effect. These techniques may seem simplistic, but many companies don't follow them.

Sharing information

Demand exists at every level of a supply chain, but the only demand that really matters is the end customer's demand for the final product. As shown in the tier structure presented in Figure 10-1, every tier should be aware of the end customer demand (sometimes called *pull-through*) and not just of the orders placed by its upper tier. Businesses at each tier should also be aware of the pipeline (outstanding) inventory.

Technology systems, such as point-of-sales product scanning and vendor-managed inventory, make sharing these information points fairly painless. We describe these systems in the later section "Improving Supply Chain Management."

Aligning your supply chain

Reducing the number of suppliers and the number of tiers in your supply chain can facilitate better communication and decrease the oscillation that creates the bullwhip effect. The restaurant industry has reduced the number of Tier 1 suppliers, which facilitates communications because restaurants have only one supplier they need to communicate with. Another advantage is that the Tier 1 suppliers may supply many restaurant chains, allowing them to reduce the overall variability they experience in demand. Pharmacies have long benefited from the same structure, with specialized wholesalers (Tier 1 suppliers) that stock medicines and medical devices from all the manufacturers.

Implementing an everyday-low-price policy

Promotional sales are a major contributor to the bullwhip effect. To avoid it, successful retailers such as Walmart have adopted the everyday-low-price strategy. If you look at your local Walmart's weekly advertisement, you may notice that many, if not most, of the products in the ad are listed at their normal prices.

This marketing approach is quite useful. Customers may actually think they're getting a price discount when they're not, and Walmart can strategically advertise products they have in excess inventory with the hope that consumers will see the low price and come into the store to purchase the product.

However, the Walmart approach may not work for some products and industries. Recently, one major retailer, suffering from lackluster sales, embarked on an everyday-low-price strategy. Instead of participating in the weekly sales and discount coupons that its competitors use, this retailer started to offer its products at a low fixed price and had monthly special pricing on certain items. Unfortunately, this strategy didn't have the desired effect. But why? Most consumers refuse to buy many products unless they're on sale, and this has an effect on how retailers promote and advertise their products. This appears to be the trend in the fashion retailing and cosmetics industries.

Establishing long-term contracts with suppliers

Many successful companies have made their supply chain an integral part of their core business processes. Toyota's treatment of its supply chain is a major contributor to its success. The best way to embrace your suppliers is to establish long-term relationships with them. This long-term relationship makes the supply chain vested in your success and helps align the goals of both companies.

In Chapter 11 we point out that lean companies view their suppliers as an extension of their company. One way to embrace the supplier is with long-term contracts based on shared goals and shared performance standards. Long-term purchase contracts give the supplier confidence to invest in long-term improvements, knowing that the revenue stream will be available. To be successful, though, this relationship depends on mutual trust between the buyer and the supplier.

Long-term contracts also make suppliers vested in the contracting company's success. Most suppliers realize that improvements in their products and processes potentially improve the customer company's position in the market, increasing sales and leading to increased demand for the supplier's products.

Improving operational efficiency

The supply chain is only as good as its weakest link. Therefore, improving the processes of your supply chain companies improves your operations. (See Part I of this book for info on how to improve processes.)

Improving your processes and your supply processes reduces your delivery lead times and helps reduce the pipeline inventory. The reorder point and desired inventory levels are a direct function of your delivery lead time. As you reduce this lead time, you can reduce the total amount of inventory in your process. Reducing this pipeline inventory lessens the bullwhip effect described earlier.

Improving Supply Chain Management

Most companies know that designing and maintaining a strong and reliable supply chain is vital to profitability and long-term survival. In this section we describe how to improve supply chain management through better communication, accountability, and inventory management. (Find out why a strong supply chain matters to a lean organization in Chapter 11 and how to manage supply chain inventory in Chapter 8.)

Communicating better

Through modern information technology, companies are now able to share two critical data points with their suppliers: actual customer demand and the amount of inventory on hand.

Fortunately, modern scanners used at retail outlets enable suppliers to access consumer demand instantaneously. Your local grocery store probably utilizes this scanning system — to tally your order and to facilitate stock-replenishment orders. That is, companies can use this *point of sale* (POS) information to trigger the ordering of inventory (covered in Chapter 8).

In addition, if suppliers can access a company's POS data, they can anticipate when you'll likely place an order before you actually place it! The bar coding of inventory facilitates this constant monitoring throughout the supply chain. Concepts such as collaborative planning, forecasting, and replenishment (CPFR) strive to increase supply chain integration by increasing the visibility of demand at every point on the supply chain.

Outsourcing inventory management

More and more companies are putting the responsibility of inventory management on their suppliers. This practice, known as *vendor-managed inventory* (VMI), is quite common in major retailers.

Here's how it works: A major retailer gives a certain amount of shelf space in its store to a supplier, which keeps its products stocked there. Armed with the retailer's POS data, the supplier can restock its products without direct involvement by the retailer. This saves the retailer time and money because it avoids the job of managing the inventory.

VMI requires trust in a supplier. For VMI to work, a company must give the supplier access to sales information so it can restock the shelves as necessary. In many cases, especially retail, the supplier also supplies competitor retailers. Given actual sales and inventory levels, the supplier could inadvertently (or possibly on purpose) provide sales data to the competition. So trust and integrity are necessary conditions for a sound relationship that benefits both parties.

In addition, a company must be certain that the supplier knows how to efficiently manage inventory. (Hey, perhaps you should provide a copy of this book to your suppliers!) And the supplier must have the technical capability to perform VMI. Its computer systems and programs need to be compatible with the partner company to enable the necessary information exchange to execute VMI.

For more suggestions on how a firm can manage supply chain inventory, see Chapter 8.

Simplifying the chain by consolidating shipments

Managing a supply chain can get complicated quickly. From the OEM standpoint, the more Tier 1 suppliers that are involved, the more time someone must spend coordinating them. Many companies try to minimize the number of suppliers they use.

For example, consider a restaurant's dependence on food distributors. The burger joint down the street needs many separate items to prepare and serve a meal consisting of a cheeseburger, fries, and drink. If the restaurant uses a different supplier for each component, imagine the traffic jam of delivery trucks that'd amass around the facility! Figure 10-7 shows all the deliveries a restaurant would require from different suppliers, each providing different items to the restaurant.

Restaurant Supply Chain

Figure 10-7: The restaurant supply chain.

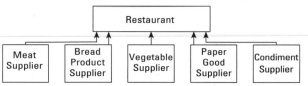

Illustration by Wiley, Composition Services Graphics

In the restaurant business, supply chains no longer rely on multiple suppliers with specialty support. All-in-one restaurant supply companies have emerged to simplify the material management process for restaurants. This new Tier 1 supplier purchases core supplies from specialty suppliers (now Tier 2 suppliers) and delivers them in one shipment to the restaurant, as shown in Figure 10-8. Reducing the complexity of the supply chain eases the burden on restaurant management to keep ingredients and supplies in stock, and, because fewer trucks are making deliveries, this simplification decreases traffic congestion at the facility and the number of deliveries the restaurant must receive.

Another method for simplifying a supply chain, *cross-docking,* reduces a company's inventory levels and the need for warehouse space. Cross-docking is a logistics network approach used to minimize warehousing costs and reduce inventory. This is a popular process for big retailers and grocery store chains.

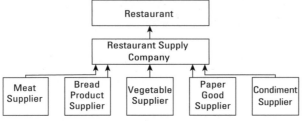

Simplified Restaurant Supply Chain

Figure 10-8:
Simplified
restaurant
supply
chain.

Illustration by Wiley, Composition Services Graphics

Figure 10-9 shows how cross-docking works. The OEM maintains a shipping dock where supplier trucks arrive and park. The trucks are unloaded, and instead of placing the inventory in a storage warehouse, the goods are placed directly on the firm's truck (or another supplier's truck), which delivers the inventory directly to the facility. The end delivery truck may contain goods from multiple suppliers.

Cross-docking reduces pipeline inventory and also the need for warehouse space. It functions similarly to the simplified restaurant supply chain shown in Figure 10-8, but cross-docking leaves direct control over suppliers in the hands of the OEM instead of an all-in-one middleman supplier.

Cross-Docking

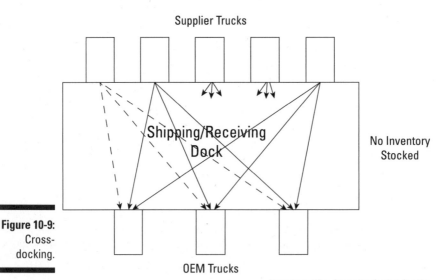

Figure 10-9:
Cross-
docking.

Illustration by Wiley, Composition Services Graphics

Part III
Improving Operations

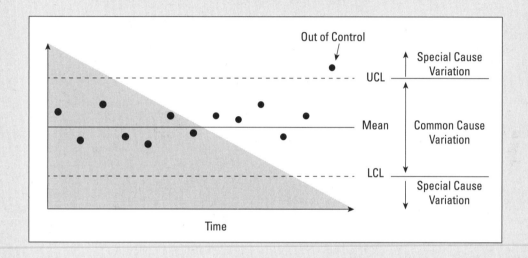

In this part . . .

✔ Find out how to become lean and mean as a business, so that you eliminate waste and produce only what your customers want. If you need help getting lean, take a look at some tools that will help your business trim the fat.

✔ Take a deeper look at quality, including what it means, how it's measured, and what it costs. Understand the necessary operations that lead to a quality product or service.

✔ Determine whether your company has a quality-oriented culture throughout — not just in the manufacturing department. If it doesn't, get familiar with the tools that are necessary for building a quality-focused organization.

Chapter 11

Becoming Lean

In This Chapter

▶ Tracing the history of craft and mass production

▶ Examining the principles and tools of lean businesses

▶ Explaining push systems, pull systems, and the customer interface

Most doctors advocate lean human bodies and point out the health benefits of high-functioning physical activity, including extended life and improved quality of life compared to the heavier alternative. This is true in body and also in business.

The lean philosophy centers on doing more with less by eliminating waste and producing only the products that customers demand. The lean approach to business has changed manufacturing throughout the world, and it applies to all aspects of business.

In this chapter, we describe the concept of lean from a business perspective. We explore the principles of lean and offer a brief history of how businesses came to embrace the lean approach. We also present useful tools for becoming lean.

Evolving to Lean

The techniques described in this chapter that have become known as *lean manufacturing* dramatically changed manufacturing industries. The concepts and techniques that the Japanese implemented to save their failing industries after World War II revolutionized manufacturing everywhere and had a profound effect on the world economy. In this section, we explore the evolution to lean. Why did businesses need it and how did the lean revolution begin?

Mastering the craft

The human race has always made things. Even back in the Stone Age, cave dwellers made spears and other tools they needed to survive. The Egyptians managed large-scale projects when building the Pyramids and created ornamental artifacts they placed in the tombs. The Romans constructed viaducts, paved roads for their chariots, and also produced elaborate furnishings and decorations to adorn their homes.

In the beginning, humans made only what they needed to survive and usually made everything on their own. As societies developed, some people started to specialize in a particular field, such as blacksmithing. *Craft production* is the term often associated with the first manufacturing movement.

Craft production yielded one-of-a-kind products that were completely customized. Craftspeople made products for specific customers when they received an order. Craft workers were highly skilled, and the processes they used were very flexible; even when made by the same craftsperson, each piece varied slightly from the next. They used general-purpose tools, the facilities were usually small, and a business served its local market.

Craft production dominated until the mid-19th century, when several innovations emerged and paved the way to mass production. These innovations include interchangeable parts (one part can be swapped out for another), coal power, and the construction of the railroads.

Before interchangeable parts, mass production wasn't possible. Eli Whitney, the American inventor of the cotton gin, was the first one to prove that it was possible to produce parts with enough precision to assure that parts could be interchanged from one product to the next. This made the division of labor not only possible but desirable, as companies could train workers on one specific task rather than requiring them to have the skills to complete all the process steps.

Prior to the mid-1800s, the establishment of large-scale industries was impossible because a reliable energy source was lacking. The availability of coal and steam power after 1840 opened the door to the creation of factories that were large enough to mass-produce products. Coal and the steam it produced offered an inexpensive and reliable means to fuel production.

Even with a reliable energy source and the interchangeable parts necessary for standardizing products, mass production wasn't feasible until people found a way to get raw materials to the production site and then move finished products out to a large market. The massive railroad building that started in earnest in the 1830s provided the transportation solution, and the construction of the railways and rail cars provided a large demand for railroad-related mass-produced products. The railroads needed mass production and mass production needed the railroads. It was a marriage made in heaven.

Producing in mass

The availability of interchangeable parts, an inexpensive energy source, and reliable transportation provided the foundation for mass manufacturing, but it wasn't until Henry Ford integrated the moving assembly line that true mass production began.

Ford realized that, to be most profitable, speed was of upmost importance. He needed to produce more product from the resources he had available. His moving assembly line removed the waste associated with workers needing to go to the product to perform their task; the product came to workers! And by controlling the speed of the line, Ford controlled how fast an employee worked, removing timing variability from the process. This emphasis on reducing processing time and eliminating waste is still at the heart of all modern operations improvement initiatives.

The Ford production system embodied the following characteristics:

- ✔ **Standardized product:** The Ford plant in Highland Park, Michigan, made one automobile, the Model T, using identical parts with no customization. Ford held firm to his policy of producing identical products and is well-known for his famous quote: "The customer can have any color as long as it's black." (Black spray paint was the only color that dried fast enough to keep the line moving at Ford's ideal pace.)

- ✔ **Dedicated equipment and tooling:** Ford set out to automate as much of the process as possible. This was financially possible because the standardized product allowed high volumes of parts to be produced by machinery dedicated to the task. The long production life of the Model T allowed the equipment to be used over many years, thus spreading the investment cost. Between 1909 and 1927, more than 15 million Model Ts were sold, and all were produced on the same equipment. (Most of the customization on the automobile, if there was any, was added after assembly as add-ons.)

- ✔ **Standardized gauges:** The use of interchangeable parts launched a rudimentary quality movement. In craft production, the craftsperson would adjust the parts on each assembly so that the parts would work together. Because this capability wasn't possible on the moving assembly line, parts had to be more standardized and required much tighter measurement tolerance. Parts were inspected using *go/no-go gauges,* which were standardized and revealed whether the part was good or bad. This method allowed for quick evaluation of production quality.

- ✔ **Simplified, easy-to-understand tasks:** The moving assembly line required that each station take approximately the same amount of time to complete its task. The line needed to be balanced (each operation requiring the same amount of time), and it could move only as fast as the longest operation took. The emphasis on speed meant that tasks needed to be easy to understand and perform.

- ✔ **Unskilled workers:** A worker on an assembly line performs the same limited tasks repetitively. This division of labor requires little training, and workers are interchangeable, just like parts. However, breaking down the process into a sequence of tasks and determining how long each task takes requires intimate knowledge of the process; this way of looking at the production process led to the creation of what would become known as *industrial engineering*.

- ✔ **Vertical integration:** The Ford River Rouge complex, which was completed in 1928, consisted of more than 90 buildings spanning 1.5 miles. The facility contained everything necessary to produce the Model A. It even had its own docks along the river where raw material was delivered, as well as its own railroad track for transportation within the complex, and an electrical plant produced energy for the plant on demand. This self-reliance is known as *vertical integration*, and it facilitated the rise of the Ford Motor Company and became the model for manufacturing industries in the decades that followed. This vertical integration was slowly replaced after World War II as companies became more reliant on other business to provide the items they needed.

- ✔ **Continuous improvement:** Despite mass production's bad reputation as being inefficient and wasteful compared to the production concepts of lean manufacturing, Henry Ford was a master of efficiency and was always looking to improve his operations. He reduced the time required to produce a Model T from 12.5 hours to only 1.5 hours, and the price of the vehicle dropped from the original price of $850 in 1910 to $290 by the 1920s.

The manufacturing model that Ford implemented was duplicated throughout the world, and it became the standard that powered the military machines of World War II and the consumer frenzy that followed.

After the war, America was left with excess manufacturing capacity that was no longer needed for the war effort. In addition, consumers who had survived the Great Depression and war rationing were ready to go on a buying spree. Using mass-production techniques, manufacturers started producing everything from underwear to appliances and every gadget imaginable.

This boom was also fueled by the shift of Americans to the suburbs. Neighborhoods sprung up throughout the country, many of which were centered around the growing number of manufacturing plants that were being built in what was once farm or vacant land. These newly built houses needed everything from refrigerators to TVs to washing machines. The move to suburban living also resulted in the need for families to have two cars; people could no longer walk to a shop to buy supplies and groceries.

Responding to the times

The term *lean* is credited to James Womack, who in 1990 wrote *The Machine That Changed the World* with co-authors Daniel Roos and Daniel Jones. (Many sources also cite MIT graduate student John Krafcik as actually coining the phrase while working as a researcher for the book.) This book documents the manufacturing success of Toyota. The original principles of lean manufacturing are often referred to as the *Toyota Production System*.

To see how lean evolved, you need to examine the conditions that existed in Japan after World War II. Japan was devastated after its defeat in the war. As the economic recovery progressed, a new way of production was necessary because the conditions that fostered the mass manufacturing industries in the United States were very different in Japan. These conditions included

✔ **Limited space:** Unlike America, Japan didn't have the availability of large land masses upon which to build sprawling manufacturing facilities. Japan has only approximately 146,000 square miles and is slightly smaller than Montana (147,000 square miles).

✔ **Limited capital investment:** Mass manufacturing required significant upfront investment in capital equipment and facilities. This investment wasn't easy to acquire in post–World War II Japan.

✔ **Limited supply of raw material:** Unlike America's, Japan's supply of raw materials was limited. Imports into Japan were also controlled after the war, making it difficult for them to acquire the materials needed for manufacturing.

✔ **Limited but highly skilled workforce:** The workforce in Japan, although a limited population, was considered highly skilled because of the increased emphasis on education and training.

✔ **Demanding consumers:** Though Americans were buying anything that manufacturers could get onto store shelves, Japanese consumers were more demanding about what they purchased.

These conditions required Kiichiro Toyoda to look for a new way to save his failing company, Toyota. Enter Taiichi Ohno and Shigeo Shingo.

Ohno, an engineer at Toyota, was inspired when he visited America in 1956. Sent to visit automotive plants, he was inspired most by his visit to the supermarket. He was impressed at how the shelves were stocked and the inventory was replenished. He took the idea of providing frequent replenishing of small lots of inventory back to Japan and applied it to the manufacturing floor. *Just-in-time manufacturing,* or JIT, was born.

Shingo, a production consultant, took another idea that Ohno observed on his trip and developed *rapid changeover* (changing production from one product to the next) techniques. While in the United States, Ohno attended the Indianapolis 500. During the race he was amazed at how fast the race cars were serviced during a pit stop. Ohno shared these ideas with Shingo, and they were able to apply these techniques on the factory floor. This allowed Toyota to quickly change production machine setup from one product to the next, a process that in traditional mass manufacturing plants would take hours, if not entire work shifts, to do.

Using these techniques and others, Ohno led what would become the lean revolution.

Post-World War II conditions in America were the perfect environment for the growth of mass production: vast areas of undeveloped land, abundant natural resources, a growing population, and insatiable consumer demand. American manufacturers flourished. However, on the other side of the Pacific, the seeds for a major manufacturing paradigm shift were being planted.

Trimming the Fat

Lean means different things to different people. In essence, lean means doing more with less. It's a philosophy for adding value to the customer while reducing waste from the process. From this philosophy, companies have developed and implemented a series of tools.

In this section, we examine the principles of lean and present the tools necessary for successful implementation.

Eliminating the waste

Eliminating waste, or *muda* as the Japanese call it, is the core of the lean approach to business. Waste exists in any process, and the goal of smart business is to identify it and get rid of it. For a detailed definition of the types of waste in a process, see Chapter 2.

The *process flow diagram* is a useful tool for identifying waste. The flow diagram is a visual representation of the process that you can use to identify those activities that don't add value to the end product. These are the activities on which you want to focus your efforts.

An organized work environment is essential for the identification, elimination, and prevention of waste. "A place for everything and everything in its place" is a philosophy of lean companies. Applying the *5S approach* helps provide and maintain an organized work environment. The 5S approach consists of these five elements (that all begin with S):

1. **Sort:** Identify what's necessary to do the job and get rid of the rest.
2. **Set:** Place the needed items in a convenient, easily accessible place.
3. **Shine:** Keep the work area clean and free of clutter.
4. **Standardize:** Organize all work areas in the same manner if possible.
5. **Sustain:** Establish procedures to keep the clutter clear and the workplace organized. Put everything back in its designated place when done with it.

Involving everyone

Everyone must be involved in a lean organization. Implementing and maintaining a lean environment requires a high level of training at all levels. In lean companies, decision-making is delegated to lower levels of the organizational chart. The workers are responsible for discovering issues and are empowered to take the appropriate action when problems are discovered.

Workers are expected to stop production when they identify mistakes. In traditional manufacturing facilities, the idea of stopping production is unheard of, even if a quality problem exists, because of the emphasis on utilization and getting the most out of the high fixed-cost resources. Stopping production to address a problem requires the full support of management at all levels.

Line workers in lean organizations are trained to have their eye on the big picture. They're exposed to and learn the entire manufacturing process. This way, each employee knows what it takes to get the product to his station and the potential consequences to the next station of not doing his job correctly. This education puts employees in a better position to identify process errors and to diagnose the cause of those errors. The emphasis on understanding and training is critical for the successful implementation of lean. Workers cannot be expected to perform to the added demands of a lean work environment if they don't have the skills required.

Leveling production

Heijunka is the Japanese term for production leveling. The goal of heijunka is to reduce batch size as much as possible while still meeting production volume targets. Heijunka facilitates just-in-time (JIT) production and significantly reduces all levels of inventory in a system. This contrasts with traditional production that tended to increase batch sizes to reduce downtime due to setups.

In Chapter 4, we describe the effect of batch sizing and setup times. In short, the longer it takes to change production from one model or product to the next, the larger the batch size needs to be. That's why reducing setup times is a prime concern of lean organizations.

Here are some benefits of reducing the batch size:

> ✔ **Easily identified problems:** Removing the clutter created by large batch sizes allows you to quickly identify problems such as machine breakdowns because subsequent operations will soon run out of inventory if the machine feeding them breaks down and there's no inventory for it to work on.

✔ **Improved quality and reduced waste:** Small lot sizes allow you to discover quality problems quickly and prevent an operation from producing a large number of defective parts.

✔ **Less space requirements:** With all the inventory eliminated, you need less production space. You can place operations closer together, which can enhance communication and process awareness.

✔ **Reduced inventory:** Small lot sizes reduce not only the amount of in-process inventory (WIP) but also the requirement for raw materials (RMI) and the amount of finished goods inventory (FGI).

✔ **Reduced process flow time:** Speed is a critical factor in a lean organization. Minimizing the batch size significantly reduces the wait time in the process. For a complete analysis on the effect of batch size on the process, see Chapter 4.

As Shigeo Shingo, a Japanese industrial engineer who was considered a leading expert on manufacturing practices during the lean revolution, discovered at Toyota, a major impediment to reducing batch sizes is the changeover time required to prepare the machinery for a different part. In Chapter 4, we point out that long setup times reduce active processing time and significantly reduce the capacity of the equipment because no parts are produced during the setup. Looking for a way to reduce the downtime, Shingo devised the *single-minute exchange of die* (SMED) method for changeovers. (*Single minute* doesn't mean one minute but that the setup can be accomplished in less than ten minutes.)

We use the terms *changeover time* and *setup time* interchangeably. Other authors differentiate between the two. In the strictest sense, the setup time is the time spent actually converting the equipment, while the changeover time includes the removal of all the old materials and products from the line and the time spent adjusting the equipment after it has been changed, before actual production begins. In this book, we consider the setup or changeover time to be all the time the equipment isn't operating.

SMED was first applied to change the dies on the stamping machines that shaped the metal of automobile body parts. These dies are very heavy, and the tolerances on the parts are less than a millimeter, making installation time-consuming because the machines need to be perfectly aligned. Although originally designed for die changes, the SMED method has applications for all types of machine setups. Here are the steps to SMED:

1. **Observe the current methodology.**

   Document all the steps currently taken to accomplish the changeover. This can be in the form of a process flow diagram.

2. Separate the internal and external activities.

External activities are those activities that can be completed before the machine is shut down for the setup, and internal activities are those activities that can only be done when the machine is stopped.

3. Eliminate all non-value-added steps.

Are any steps in the process unnecessary?

4. Turn internal activities into external ones.

By taking activities off-line, you can reduce the time the equipment isn't operating.

5. Simplify the internal activities.

For example, eliminate nuts, bolts, and screws, and replace them with clamps if a fastener is really needed. Use pins and jigs to simplify adjustments.

6. Simplify the external activities and make sure that they don't delay any internal activities.

7. Document the new process and measure improvement.

8. Repeat the process.

Continuously reduce the setup time. You'll likely need several cycles to get to a single digit setup time.

SMED reduced the time for die changes at Toyota to less than ten minutes per die, an improvement of over 40 times in most cases.

Embracing your supplier

One of the major characteristics of a lean company is the relationship it maintains with its suppliers. Lean organizations such as Toyota view their supply chain as an extension of the company, not as an adversary, as is common in traditionally managed companies.

For a healthy relationship with suppliers, follow these rules:

- **Minimize the number of suppliers.** The smaller number is easier to manage and allows you to develop closer relationships.

- **Establish long-term relationships.** Long-term contracts provide assurance to suppliers that they'll have revenue and allow them to focus on long-term improvements that will improve the product they produce for you.

✔ **Establish clear expectations on cost, quality, and responsiveness.** These expectations must be both clearly understood and obtainable.

✔ **Share the risks and rewards.** Provide incentives for improved supplier performance.

✔ **Develop effective lines of communication.** Share operational information such as process times and demand forecasts. Provide an environment where suppliers are encouraged to inform you of potential problems so that you can be prepared to act and implement solutions.

✔ **Invest in supplier continuous improvement and development.** When a supplier improves, either by increasing quality or reducing waste, this benefit is automatically passed on to you in an improved product. Lean manufacturers have been known to send their own employees into supplier facilities to help them increase quality and reduce costs.

Toyota embraced these supply chain principles. While researching his book *The Machine That Changed the World,* author Jim Womack found that the average number of suppliers for a Japanese plant was 170, compared to the average of 509 that supplied American plants. He also found that suppliers do benefit from multiyear contracts that allow them to focus on production rather than procurement.

For more information on how to create and manage a lean supply chain, see Chapter 10.

Focusing on quality

Quality is a pillar of any lean organization. Poor quality contributes significantly to the waste that lean companies strive to eliminate. In lean organizations, quality is the responsibility of everyone. Line workers are trained to detect poor quality, identify the causes of poor quality, and implement improvements. The quality process follows these steps:

1. **Detect the abnormality.**

   Part of workers' jobs is to identify poor quality as it occurs.

2. **Stop the process.**

   Line employees have the power and are expected to stop the line.

3. **Fix or correct the immediate condition.**

   Action is required to put in place a quick fix so that production can resume as quickly as possible.

4. **Investigate the root cause and solve the problem.**

You must implement a permanent solution to replace the quick fix of Step 3.

A radical concept found in truly lean organizations such as Toyota is the ability of workers to stop the production line when a quality issue is identified. The worker pulls an andon cord, which stops the line and sends a signal to an andon board that notifies management and other workers where the problem is.

This ability to stop the line can also be programmed into the equipment itself. *Jidoka,* sometimes referred to as *autonomation,* meaning automation with human intelligence, enables a machine to detect when a defect occurs and allows the equipment to stop the line automatically. For example, if a machine jams, the machine will not only shut itself down but also stop the entire line. The andon board then lights up, signaling for help at the machine. This eliminates the need to have an operator at each machine.

The first priority after you detect a defect is to implement a quick fix so that production can resume. This may involve the addition of another step in the process, such as manual machine adjustments or inspecting parts.

Because the quick fix usually adds some waste into the system, you don't want it to become permanent. What separates lean organizations from those trying to be lean is a relentless effort to identify the root cause of quality problems and implement permanent solutions. Many companies get lazy, allowing the quick fix to become permanent.

A common excuse for this behavior is that people are too busy with other things, and the fix is working. This *firefighting,* as it's often referred to, is what a lean organization is trying to eliminate.

The best way to correct a mistake, of course, is to prevent it from happening in the first place. This is why lean firms embrace *poke-yoke,* which means "preventing mistakes." Lean organizations focus on designing a simple process and training workers to function in the process. Always remember to simplify.

Implementing continuous improvement

Kaizen is the Japanese word for continuous improvement. It applies not only to quality but to everything one does in life. Any process can be improved, and your primary mission should be to improve it.

Kaizen, as it applies in a lean organization, follows a circular path that's nearly identical to the Deming wheel and Six Sigma's DMAIC methodology (see Chapters 12 and 13). You identify a problem or possible improvement area, gather information, conduct experiments, analyze the results, and, if improvement is verified, implement the solution. You measure the process again and the cycle continues.

The primary difference is that *kaizen* (often called a *kaizen event*) focuses on making quick improvements with a series of changes to the exiting process, while methodologies such as Six Sigma place a greater emphasis on large-scale projects that often require an arsenal of tools.

Producing Just in Time

Push and pull systems are two common types of production control strategies. In this section, we define these production strategies and point out the difference between them with regards to the customer interface. We also cover the conditions for implementing a pull system.

Be aware of terminology. Many sources use the term JIT to mean lean, incorporating all the concepts covered in this chapter. We consider JIT only as a component pillar of a lean organization. When we refer to JIT, we're referencing what occurs on the product production line. A lean organization may actually produce using a push system but release the material JIT into the process.

Knowing when to work

A process is made up of several operations. Each operation has a particular task to perform, and as one operation completes its task, the part is moved on to the next operation in the process until a finished product is made. As an operations manager, you must decide how to release raw material into the process and how this material, the work-in-progress (WIP), will flow through the production facility.

Push and pull are two possible production strategies for moving material through the manufacturing facility. (We get to what triggers material to be released into the process a bit later.) Find out more on the inventory effects in Chapter 8.

Defining push

In a *push system,* work-in-process is pushed to the next operation as soon as it's completed. The operation works as long as it has parts to process. A push system controls the *thruput* (what is actually produced) of the system and isn't concerned with level of the WIP. If the operation has inventory to work on, it will work.

Figure 11-1 shows how a push system works. As long as the upstream WIP has inventory, the operation will continue to produce, regardless of the inventory levels in the downstream WIP.

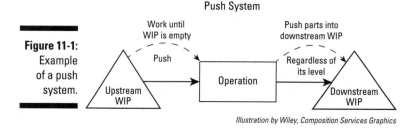

Figure 11-1: Example of a push system.

Illustration by Wiley, Composition Services Graphics

Defining pull

In a *pull system,* the operation pulls products only as they're needed. The operation works only when the next station signals that it needs parts. A pull system in essence controls WIP and observes the throughput.

Figure 11-2 shows how a pull system works. Operation 1 works only until the downstream WIP is full. As Operation 2 takes parts from the WIP, Operation 1 works to replace them.

A *kanban* system can be used to establish the desirable inventory levels in the downstream WIP. A kanban system is in effect a scheduling system. The kanban system determines how much inventory is in the process and products are only produced as indicated by the kanban. For details on kanban, refer to the section "Implementing pull" later in this chapter.

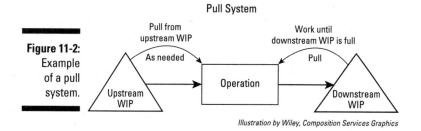

Figure 11-2: Example of a pull system.

Illustration by Wiley, Composition Services Graphics

Differentiating the customer interface

It's important to distinguish between a push and pull system and a make-to-order (MTO) or make-to-stock (MTS) system. MTO and MTS refer to the interface between the customer and the production system. In Chapter 5, we describe an MTO system and point out that it maintains no *finished goods inventory* (FGI). An MTO system produces only when a real customer order is received. Conversely, an MTS system generally produces to a forecast of demand and maintains an FGI for customer purchases.

Push and pull refer to how production in the facility is conducted. MTO and MTS can both use a pull or push system. Table 11-1 describes the steps to implement each of the four possible combinations:

 ✔ An MTO system utilizes push.

 ✔ An MTO system utilizes pull.

 ✔ An MTS system utilizes push.

 ✔ An MTS system utilizes pull.

Table 11-1	Implementing Customer Interface with Push and Pull	
System	**Make to Order**	**Make to Stock**
Push	1. Customer order received	1. Demand forecast developed
	2. Production schedule developed	2. Production schedule developed
	3. Raw material released into the facility based on production schedule	3. Raw material released into the facility based on production schedule
	4. Parts pushed from operation to operation	4. Parts pushed from operation to operation
Pull	1. Customer order received	1. Demand forecast developed
	2. Raw material released into the system only when first operation needs parts	2. Raw material released into the system only when first operation needs parts
	3. Parts pulled from operation to operation	3. Parts pulled from operation to operation

Implementing pull

The key to implementing a pull system is to determine when the operation should work. In most cases, a pull system utilizes what's called a *kanban,* which is a Japanese word meaning "signal." Kanban isn't an inventory control system but a scheduling system that determines when to produce and how much to produce. For details on other scheduling systems, flip to Chapter 9.

A kanban system uses a kanban card or other device (an empty bin, for example) to signal to the operation that it needs to produce. Figure 11-3 shows how a kanban system works.

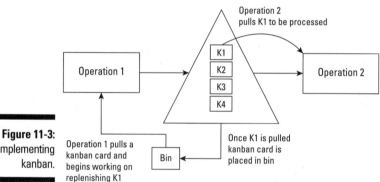

Kanban Illustration

Operation 2
pulls K1 to be processed

K1
K2
K3
K4

Operation 1

Operation 2

Operation 1 pulls a
kanban card and
begins working on
replenishing K1

Bin

Once K1 is pulled
kanban card is
placed in bin

Figure 11-3:
Implementing
kanban.

Illustration by Wiley, Composition Services Graphics

The downstream WIP contains four containers (K1, K2, K3, and K4) each containing the same part. When a container is removed by Operation 2, a card is placed in Operation 1's production box. As soon as the card arrives, Operation 1 begins working to fill an empty container to bring the downstream WIP up to the preset level.

Setting the levels of the WIPs in a kanban system isn't an easy task. It takes a lot of time and requires that you have intimate knowledge of the capacity of each operation in the system (see Chapter 2 for information on how to determine capacity levels) and the demand for the product.

In a kanban system, the levels of inventory, and thus the kanban, are set based on demand. To be successful, product demand needs to be relatively constant, and any variation (changes) in demand needs to be known. If demand isn't stable, then the number of kanban in the system need constant monitoring and updating to adjust to increasing and decreasing demand.

To determine the number of *kanban* needed, you first need to determine how big your WIP should be. The total number of parts in any WIP is given by the following equation:

WIP Level = Demand during the lead time + Safety stock

For a detailed discussion of this equation, turn to Chapter 8. In summary, you should set the amount of inventory to the demand expected during the time required to produce the parts (lead time) plus some inventory (safety stock) required to accommodate for demand and lead time variability.

Next, to determine the number of containers, divide the calculated WIP level by the number of parts each container will hold:

$$\text{\# of Kanban} = \frac{\text{WIP Level}}{\text{Size of Container}}$$

Knowing when to JIT

Pull systems aren't always better than push systems. A well-executed push system (see Chapter 9) can be just as efficient as the best-run pull system. A pull system does work better in environments with the following characteristics:

- ✔ **A dedication to preventive maintenance:** The low levels of inventory within the plant make each operation more susceptible to breakdowns anywhere in the system. If one operation experiences any unplanned downtime, then the operations before it quickly stop working because they don't have any parts to replenish and the operations following soon run out of inventory to work on. A pull system ties each operation closely together. A preventive maintenance program can help eliminate these disruptions.

- ✔ **A limited menu of product options:** A pull system operates most efficiently when the number of product configurations is limited. Increased differentiation of product requires a kanban system for each different part used in the product, which increases the inventory levels.

- ✔ **A reliable supply chain:** A lean supply chain is necessary for a firm to get the most out of its lean efforts. Because inventory is maintained at such low levels, any disruptions in the supply of parts can cripple production. Recently, after a devastating earthquake in Japan, the supply of parts for electronic and automotive products to assembly plants throughout the world was cut off, and all production came to a sudden halt. The stock of finished goods was quickly depleted, and customers experienced a shortage of goods.

✔ **A stable and smooth demand pattern:** Because of the time required to set up the *kanban* in a pull system, it's beneficial if demand is relatively predictable, with limited fluctuations.

Seeking the Silver Bullet

Despite what many operations management consultants may tell you, there's no easy way to build an efficient organization. As continuous improvement implies, there is always work to be done.

We describe different operation management approaches in this book. In this chapter, we cover lean. In Chapter 12, we describe Total Quality Management (TQM), and in Chapter 13 we cover Six Sigma. Still, no operations management book would be complete without mentioning the theory of constraints, which is basically the art of managing based on your bottleneck. We cover that in Chapter 3. All these strategies share the intents of eliminating waste, reducing inventory levels, cutting flow times, and improving quality. These strategies are also not exclusive. Most lean companies also embrace the techniques offered by Six Sigma.

Whichever approach you choose to implement, success depends on the ability of your organization to stay focused and adhere to the principles of your approach. Many companies fail when they attempt to implement a strategy because they don't follow the entire program and choose to implement only the easy parts. Some companies achieve success from the low-hanging fruit but give up when they actually have to get down to the hard work of redesigning the processes and changing the policies that they have utilized in the past to get results. As with dieting, getting started is easy; it's finishing the plan and sticking with it until you hit your goal that's usually difficult. And it's even harder to maintain the results as a lean maintenance plan is required.

Chapter 12

Managing Quality

. . . .

In This Chapter

▶ Understanding how the customer views quality

▶ Exploring the costs and payoffs of quality

▶ Managing quality efforts

▶ Building quality into the product design process

▶ Using various tools to measure quality

. . . .

*Q*uality is an aspect of a product that leaps to the forefront of a customer's attention when something doesn't perform as expected. Yet producing a quality product or providing a quality service must center on well-considered operations; it doesn't happen by accident. As an operations manager, you must ensure that quality drives every process and decision. This is sometimes a thankless effort because you'll likely only hear about quality issues from dissatisfied customers.

In this chapter, we take an in-depth look at quality — how to define it, how to measure it, and how to determine the costs associated with it.

Deciding What Matters

When assessing quality, the first question you need to ask is, "What is a quality product?" Only your customer can answer this question because quality is what the customer says it is. A quality product means different things to different people, and expectations differ from product to product. When asking potential customers to define a quality car, for example, you get an array of answers, ranging from "A quality car starts each and every time, gets good gas mileage, and has a high safety record" to "A quality car goes from 0 to 60 in 4.5 seconds and has a sleek design."

Making matters even more challenging is that customers, in addition to having different expectations of quality, perceive and define each of those dimensions differently. Turning those perceptions into metrics that an operations manager can act on is one of the trickiest parts of managing quality. The wrong metrics can lead to a lot of wasted effort on improving aspects of a product that the customer doesn't value. For example, if a car company uses the wrong metric (measures the wrong aspect) to assess its pickup truck's acceleration, then their attempts to improve this feature will be misdirected and wasted. By finding a metric that matches customer expectations, they could begin to make headway in improving the quality of this type of vehicle.

Moreover, a customer doesn't usually define the quality of a product or service by a single metric. Instead, quality is defined across a range of dimensions. According to David Garvin of the Harvard Business School, these are the attributes that customers most commonly consider when defining quality:

- ✔ **Performance:** The primary operating characteristics as perceived by the customer. Common performance metrics for an automobile are miles per gallon (MPG) and time to accelerate from 0 to 60 mph. Performance characteristics can often conflict because different customers value different factors.

- ✔ **Features:** The secondary operating characteristics or the "bells and whistles." These are the features that surprise the customer. Features often evolve and become primary operating characteristics — for example, anti-lock brakes, which were once considered features on a car, are now standard and considered part of performance quality.

- ✔ **Reliability:** The consistency of the product's performance. This dimension indicates how often the product malfunctions and doesn't deliver on performance expectations. For an automobile, reliability is typically determined by how often the car must go back to the dealer to fix a problem. But customer perception plays a role here as well. For example, if a car company makes its power locks as quiet as possible and customers don't like this, they may consider it a defect.

- ✔ **Durability:** How long the product provides acceptable service. In automotive terms, "Do I trade in the vehicle when the warranty expires or hold onto it because it will probably outlast me?"

- ✔ **Aesthetics:** How the product looks, feels, and sounds. Some types of products, including cars and computers, often sell better purely based on looks.

- ✔ **Safety:** The risk of harm or injury from using the product. Safety relates to the risk of using the product correctly as well as the risks associated with using it in ways for which it wasn't designed. How the auto performs in government crash tests is an important consideration to many customers.

✔ **Conformance:** How well a product or service meets its design standards during actual use by the customer. For cars, a good example of a conformance requirement is advertised MPG versus MPG actually experienced by the customer. Few (if any) drivers actually get the posted MPG because the specification was obtained under ideal driving conditions with a professional driver. In other types of manufacturing, conformance can be tested in the factory. The conformance metric can be crucially important because the firm often advertises the product based on these metrics, and if the product doesn't perform, the customer is disappointed.

✔ **Serviceability:** How well the product is serviced after the sale. This attribute relates to the speed, competence, and courtesy of customer service as well as to how the product was designed to accommodate service when a malfunction occurs.

✔ **Perceived quality:** How the public perceives the quality of the product or service, which affects a company's reputation in the marketplace. Brand loyalty is a potential outcome of perceived quality; many pickup owners strongly prefer either a Chevy or a Ford, and most are repeat buyers. An important point about perceived quality is that studies show a brand can lose it much more quickly than acquire it.

These attributes of quality provide a common language for assessing a product. You can measure and compare every product along these lines. And the key to developing quality products is knowing what customers expect and identifying actionable metrics for improvement based on these expectations. Reach out to the company's marketing department to gather reliable information on these data points.

Testing the power of perception

In a project comparing the acceleration of two pickup trucks made by two different manufacturers, one truck had a quicker 0-to-60-mph acceleration time. However, customer focus groups stated that the other pickup had better acceleration, which seemed to contradict the data. It turned out that most customers evaluate the concept of acceleration in terms of how quickly a vehicle can pass another vehicle. Therefore, the important metric was how long it took the truck to accelerate from 55 to 65 mph, which the second truck did more quickly.

To test perceptions concerning acceleration, researchers removed the driver's seat from the first pickup and replaced it with a seat from the second pickup without telling respondents. They thought they had improved the acceleration of the first pickup. They hadn't; they only changed the seat. Because acceleration often causes the sensation that you're being pushed back, customers felt like they were accelerating more quickly because they sank more deeply into the newly installed seat. In other words, the researchers hadn't improved acceleration but had modified only how far you sank into the seat during a given acceleration, which gave the driver the perception that the vehicle had greater acceleration.

It just goes to show the power of perception!

Recognizing the Value of Quality

You may have heard the saying "Quality is free." Implementing an effective quality system is anything but free, but the alternative usually proves to be much more expensive. This section explores the true costs and payoffs of quality.

Producing a quality product or service requires the whole organization to be onboard and involved. Quality begins in product design, requires attention in production, and must be at the forefront of customer service. A sincere focus on quality requires time, energy, and commitment; without it, a business risks lost sales and revenue, potential product liability claims if a product fails, and lowered productivity.

The primary burdens of poor quality are failure costs, detection costs, and prevention costs, which we cover in this section.

Assessing the cost of failure

Failure costs are those costs associated with producing a defective product. Two types of failures exist: those that are discovered internally and those that are detected externally.

Internal failures

Internal failures are defects discovered during the production process. When a company discovers an internal failure, it needs to discard or repair the defective part. The costs associated with internal failures are the wasted resources (labor and material) used to produce the product if it's discarded, or the additional costs to correct the defect if it's repaired. To see how reworking defective products affects process performance, visit Chapter 4. Internal failures also occur in service operations. A good example would be an accountant who discovers an error in a tax return before it's forwarded to the customer and eventually the IRS.

External failures

External failures are defects discovered after delivery to the customer — either identified by the manufacturer after the product ships or discovered by the customer during normal use.

Numerous types of costs are associated with external failures, and they go well beyond a company losing money because defects are visible to the customer. In other words, the manufacturer must not only repair and replace the product but also deal with the loss of reputation, customer goodwill, and eventually market share. The actual impact of external failures varies depending on the type of customer that discovers the defect. If the customer is the end consumer, then repairing or replacing the product can quickly provide an opportunity for the company to improve or retain good quality perceptions. When the customer is a business, however, replacing or repairing the product(s) is much less likely to undo the business disruption caused by the failure.

In the worst case, whether it's a runaway automobile, a spontaneously combusting computer battery, or a child's toy that becomes a choking hazard, external failures can cause serious injury to customers and incur litigation and liability costs — along with a severe blow to corporate reputation.

This also applies to services; it may be very difficult to regain the trust of a client if a faulty tax return is sent to the IRS and the customer is called in for an audit as a result.

Detecting defects

Expenses associated with detecting poor quality before, during, or after production are known as *detection* (or appraisal) *costs*. Inspection and testing are the primary ways a company can find product defects.

Ideally, you want to design quality into the process for creating a product. Sometimes, in addition, inspection and testing are necessary to ensure that the process is operating as designed. To establish an inspection process, you need to decide how many products to inspect and when and where in the process to conduct the inspection.

How many products to inspect is a trade-off between the cost of inspection (which can be high if the test destroys the tested unit) and the cost of external failures if customers purchase the defective products. Most firms test a small percentage of total product output. Some statistical implications are associated with the sample size; for details, see the "Measuring Quality" section later in this chapter.

You have three options when choosing when to inspect a product:

- **Incoming inspection of raw materials from suppliers:** Monitoring incoming materials prevents a company from wasting resources on material that's already defective. Proper management of the supply chain (see Chapter 10) should minimize these inspections.

- **Inspection during the production process:** Monitoring quality throughout the process is possible with a convenient and easy-to-use statistical technique we describe in the later section "Measuring Quality."

Where in the production process you conduct inspections is important to minimize waste. You generally want to inspect before the bottleneck operation (bottlenecks are covered in Chapter 3) to avoid putting any unnecessary burden on the resource that's already limiting capacity. Other good points of inspection include before an expensive operation (such as gold-plating) and before an irreversible operation (such as heat treating or cutting).

✔ **Inspection of the finished product:** Monitoring quality before products ship out to customers can prevent defects reaching customers. This is usually the most expensive inspection point because the product is complete and has thus already incurred all manufacturing costs; but it may prevent external failures, which can be devastating.

Getting the perks of high quality

Producing and delivering high quality products and services has beneficial external and internal effects.

Internal effects

The most important internal effect of high quality is the increased ability to further improve quality. How is this so? If you have a lot of quality problems, they tend to mask one another. It's much like a detective solving a murder case with many suspects. You can't focus much time on any single suspect. In addition, because all suspects are being scrutinized, they're probably unwilling to come forward with information that may help eliminate other suspects.

External effects

Externally, high quality results in a perception of reliability and value with customers over time. Customers are known to pay a premium for products — ranging from hotel rooms to vehicles — that they know they can rely on. Moreover, high quality tends to have a halo effect. In other words, if several of your products are known to be of high quality, customers will automatically assume that your other products are as well. This helps to increase a company's market share across the board.

Preventing defects in the first place

Make every effort to prevent defects from occurring in the first place. Doing so requires that quality is designed into the product *and* the process that makes it. Most firms have some type of quality program in place. These programs go by many different names, including Total Quality Management (TQM) and Six Sigma. We explore the fundamentals of TQM and related concepts in the next section, and Chapter 13 describes the revolution known as Six Sigma.

Addressing Quality

The best way to manage quality is not to make defects in the first place. To do this, companies are finding that they must shift their entire focus away from who's responsible for defects to how the process is creating defects.

Quality guru W. Edwards Deming once stated, "Workers are responsible for 15 percent of the problems; the system, for the other 85 percent. The system is the responsibility of management." When Deming said *system,* he meant *process* as it's typically called today. In other words, workers can only perform as well as the process allows them. Table 12-1 shows the difference in approach from the traditional to the process focus.

Table 12-1	Process Approach to Quality
Traditional Focus	*Process Focus*
Who?	How?
Doing my job	Getting things done
Knowing my job	Knowing the process
Motivate	Removing barriers
Measure the workers	Measure the process

The Toyota process improvement methodology (also known as *kaizen*) and its offspring, including Total Quality Management (TQM) and Six Sigma (see Chapter 13), are all movements toward improving quality with a process approach. They provide a new way to look at quality and focus on changing the culture of an organization to achieve continuous improvement. Without the cultural changes these concepts propose, companies can't realize maximum quality improvements.

Kaizen, TQM, and Six Sigma encompass three fundamental principles: a focus on customer satisfaction, participation by everyone across the organization, and an endless quest for continuous improvement and innovation. In this section, we look at each of these principles.

Considering the customer

As we mention earlier in the chapter, quality is what the customer says it is. Worse yet, customers' expectations are always changing (and usually ratcheting upward!). So to define quality, you must know what's important to your customers and keep updating that knowledge over time. Automobile customers, for example, vary greatly on the attributes they want a car to have. It's the rare vehicle that can deliver to all customers on all dimensions, especially when price is an important factor in the purchasing decision. Delivering a product the target customer wants requires a concerted effort among marketing, product design, and operations/production.

Getting all hands on deck

Participation by everyone across the organization is critical to the success of any quality improvement project. Line workers are often the first to recognize process problems that contribute to poor quality. They perform the operations day in and day out and are the best source for identifying and implementing improvements. Maximizing the potential of line workers requires that they're well trained and educated on the entire process, not just their individual jobs.

Upper-management support is also critical. Implementing quality improvement projects often requires significant time and resources. Management must be willing to suffer potential short-term productivity losses for the sake of long-term improvement. For example, in many innovative manufacturing facilities, line workers have the power to pull a cord and stop the assembly line if they observe poor quality. This could never occur if management is more concerned with the volume of daily production than the end quality of the products.

Others need to participate as well. Stopping the line frequently requires that employees, including maintenance and supervisors, can be dispatched quickly to the problem area and that they have the training and ability to resolve quality issues quickly so that production can resume. See Chapter 11 for details on the attributes of companies that have successfully implemented this policy.

Sticking to the improvement effort

Kaizen, TQM, and Six Sigma all focus on continuous improvement, which is the crux of any successful quality-focused program for two reasons:

✔ Quality is much like learning to play a musical instrument. If you give up practicing every day, then you won't improve anymore, and you'll actually get worse.

✔ Customer expectations tend to increase over time, so quality needs to improve to keep up.

But how do you actually accomplish continuous improvement? Figure 12-1 illustrates the cycle that underlies all continuous improvement efforts.

Plan-Do-Study-Act Cycle

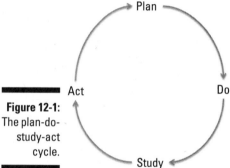

Figure 12-1:
The plan-do-study-act cycle.

Illustration by Wiley, Composition Services Graphics

This figure, known as the *plan-do-study-act cycle,* is also called the *Deming wheel* or the *PDSA cycle.* It represents the circular nature of continuous improvement. As you solve one problem, you continue on to the next problem. The process has four steps:

1. **Plan: You must plan for improvement, and the first step is to identify the problem that you need to solve or the process that you need to improve.**

   After you identify the problem/process, you need to document it, collect data, and develop a plan for improvement. (For more information on how to identify and select problems, see Chapter 13.)

2. **Do: You then implement and observe the plan.**

   As in Step 1, you should collect data for evaluation.

3. **Study: You need to evaluate the data you collect during Step 2 (the do phase) against the original data you collected from the process to assess how well the plan improved the problem/process.**

4. **Act: If the evaluation shows improved results, then you should keep the plan in place (and implement it more widely, if appropriate).**

Then it's time to identify a new problem and repeat the cycle. On the other hand, if the results aren't satisfactory, you need to revise the plan and repeat the cycle. Either way, you repeat the cycle!

This PDSA cycle is also the foundation behind the DMAIC method of the Six Sigma process improvement methodology, which we describe in Chapter 13.

Designing for Quality

Quality begins with a product's design, which determines how well the product will meet customers' needs and, to a large extent, drives the cost of production. Therefore, it's critical that marketing, product design, and manufacturing work together.

Quality function deployment (QFD) is a structured approach for integrating customers' requirements into a product; it's also the process used to create the product. The *house of quality* (HOQ) is a tool to accomplish this integration.

In this section, we introduce the concepts behind the HOQ and show you how to develop a cascade of such houses to take you from your customers' requirements to a process capable of producing a product that meets those requirements.

Starting with the end in mind

Just as two of the three little pigs learned, if you don't build a quality house — in the case of these famous pigs, a quality house is one that can survive a wolf's huffing and puffing! — then you may find yourself without shelter. The same principle of building in quality applies when designing any other product. The HOQ ensures that quality is designed into a product from the start. Figure 12-2 illustrates an HOQ.

When building your house, you want to start with the customer requirements, which are usually called the *voice of the customer* (VOC). This is what the customer needs and wants from your product. Generally, VOC is expressed in qualitative terms such as, "I want a house that will keep a wolf out." Later, you put quantitative measures on the requirement: The house must withstand a 100-mph wind gust.

House of Quality

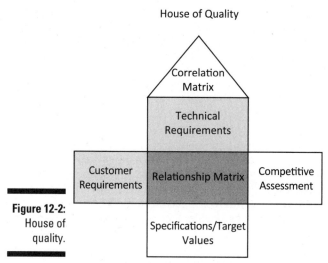

Illustration by Wiley, Composition Services Graphics

Figure 12-2: House of quality.

Developing a VOC that captures exactly what your customer expects requires market research and an intimate knowledge of your potential customers. Be aware that some of the customer requirements may conflict with each other. For example, requirements to keep the wolf at bay and to take advantage of the mountain views from the living room may conflict. Because of the potential conflicts, ranking requirements based on their importance to the customer is often necessary.

After capturing the VOC, you need to establish the product's technical requirements — how you're going to deliver the customers' wants. These are listed in the top "room" of the house and are general characteristics of the design. For the pigs' house, technical requirements may be wall thickness and number of windows.

The specifications or target values associated with the technical require-ments are detailed in the lowest level of the house, as shown in Figure 12-2. Here, you list quantitative specifications, such as 6 inches for wall thickness and at least 5 windows.

The main room of the house is the relationship matrix; it shows the correla-tion between each VOC and technical requirements. Typically, four possible conditions exist: strong, medium, small, and negligible. For example, a strong relationship exists between the take-advantage-of-the-mountain-views VOC and the number-of-windows technical requirement. The more windows, the more open the view.

The triangular attic at the top of the house contains the correlation matrix and shows the relationship among the product's technical requirements. Each requirement can have a negative, strong negative, positive, strong positive, or no relationship with the other requirements. For example, wall thickness has a strong negative relationship with the number of windows because windows are relatively thin, while an insulation requirement has a positive relationship with wall thickness.

The correlation matrix helps identify key requirement conflicts. Product designers must find ways to overcome the conflicts or decide what trade-offs they need to make in the design. In the case of the pigs' house, the designer may be able to add shutters to the windows that the pigs can open in the absence of the wolf to provide the view, and they can close them when the wolf threatens. Shutters, however, add to the cost of building the house, which may dissatisfy the customer, especially if cost is one of the important customer requirements.

The last room of the house is the competitive assessment. This room allows you to rank yourself against your prime competitors and highlights weakness in your product. Typically, you want to access your existing product (if one exists) and several other products in the marketplace. You usually gather the measures in this house from customer surveys. The first measure is the importance rating (often displayed in room 1). This metric has the customers rank each requirement on how important the requirement is to them. The second measure is a satisfaction rating that indicates how satisfied the customer is with the existing products along each requirement. Scales for the measures vary. A typical scale may be 1 to 5 or 1 to 3, with the higher number indicating greater importance or greater satisfaction.

Developing the HOQ requires cross-functional communication among marketing, design, and manufacturing. Marketing must be able to communicate the VOC to the designers, who must translate the requirements into a design with specific metrics that the manufacturing folks can meet.

Cascading to production

Most often, one house isn't sufficient to translate the VOC down to actual production. You can use QFD to build cascading houses where the technical requirements of one house are transformed into the customer requirements of the next. Figure 12-3 shows cascading houses that start with the customer requirements of the first house and end with the development of a house for production.

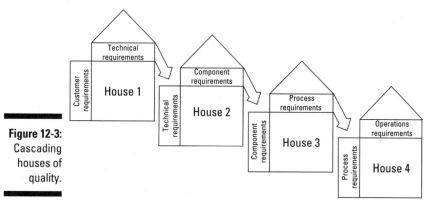

Figure 12-3:
Cascading
houses of
quality.

Illustration by Wiley, Composition Services Graphics

Building starts with developing the initial HOQ as described in the preceding section. You repeat the process by using the first set of technical requirements (product requirements) as the new VOC and then developing a house for the part (or component) requirements. This house assigns the product technical requirements to the component responsible for providing them.

This continues to the process planning house, where the hows from the parts house become the whats for the new one, and a new set of requirements is developed. The final house, using the process requirements as the VOC, provides the manufacturing requirements that are used to produce the product. The end result is a structured way to connect the actual wants of the customer through product and process design to the manufacturing floor.

Measuring Quality

Much of process improvement is about reducing defects. A defect results when some aspect of the product or service falls outside of the customer specifications. The causes of defects include a production process that is *out of control* — or unstable — and poor design objectives that did not incorporate customer requirements.

This section describes how to measure a process to determine whether it's out of control and to see how prone a process is to producing a defect. We examine the concept of variation and its effect on product quality. We also introduce a common tool for measuring process variation (you can find more tools in Chapter 13) and present methods for controlling the process.

Understanding variation

No two products are exactly alike; many sources of variation exist in the processes that create a given product. *Variation* is the change or difference in condition, amount, or level of some aspect of a product or process. From a process and quality perspective, two types of variation exist: common cause variation and special cause variation.

Common cause variation is the random variation that occurs naturally in a system. Countless and unavoidable factors create variation. For example, a machine used to drill a hole in a piece of material won't always produce a hole with the exact same diameter. Some natural variation is inevitable. This variation is generally tolerable within a certain range.

The output from any process can be characterized by an arithmetic mean and a standard deviation. The *mean* of the process is simply the sum of all observations divided by the total number of observations. The standard deviation is a measure of how the observations differ around the mean, which is the square root of the variance of the distribution.

Special cause variation, on the other hand, is variation that can't be explained by common cause variation. It can be assigned to a specific source, though, and then eliminated. For example, in the drill machine example, if a drill bit breaks, the machine will produce holes with diameters that can't be explained by common cause variation. After you identify the cause of this variation, you can fix it — in this case by replacing the drill bit. Variation should return to the common cause range after the special cause issue is addressed.

Process variation is a core aspect of most quality problems. Moving the mean of a process is much easier than reducing the variation of the process. For example, look at the targets of two hunters presented in Figure 12-4. Hunter 1 shoots consistently to the right of the bull's eye. Although he's off of the bull's eye, his shots have very little variation in location. On the other hand, the shots of Hunter 2, though centered around the bull's eye, are spread considerably (high variability in location).

Figure 12-4:
Target
practice.

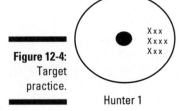

Hunter 1

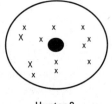

Hunter 2

Illustration by Wiley, Composition Services Graphics

Hunter 1 simply needs to move the mean of his shot to correct the variation; he can probably accomplish this by adjusting his scope. This would be an example of a special cause variation. Hunter 2, on the other hand, appears to have a twitchy trigger finger or some other problem that causes him to jerk the gun barrel when he shoots. He'll have a harder time identifying and correcting the cause of his missed shots.

You can expect a process to operate within the common cause variation. When the observed variation deviates from this, you know that the system is out of statistical control or not behaving as it should. Read on to discover an easy way to measure the variability of a process.

Measuring "goodness" of a process

Assuming that the process is operating within common cause variation means that no special causes are active. Thus, the process is stable. However, this doesn't mean that the process is "good." For example, a process may consistently make Oreo cookies with a certain amount of filling, but this amount of filling may not satisfy the customer.

The typical way to measure a process is to determine its *capability* — or the process's ability to satisfy the customer. You can determine process capability in a number of different ways, but the most common way is to use standard deviations (often called *sigmas* by operations management personnel) from the mean.

Consider, for example, how long it takes to fly from Austin, Texas, to New Orleans, Louisiana. If you measure the length of a couple of hundred flights, using statistical equations you find that the mean of this process (μ or mu) is 90 minutes and that the standard deviation (σ or sigma) is 5.75 minutes. If you assume that the distribution of times is normal, then you'd expect flight times to exhibit the pattern shown in Figure 12-5.

What you don't know is whether this process produces acceptable results in terms of customer specifications. To find out, you need to place some specifications on the process.

Generally, airlines believe that being 15 minutes late doesn't upset customers, but anything more results in dissatisfaction. So if the flight exceeds 105 minutes (90 + 15), then it's considered a defect. Similarly, arriving more than 15 minutes early is problematic because customers may need to wait for their ride home or other reasons, so arriving in less than 75 minutes (90 – 75) is also defective.

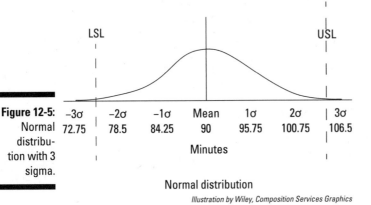

Figure 12-5:
Normal
distribu-
tion with 3
sigma.

-3σ	-2σ	-1σ	Mean	1σ	2σ	3σ
72.75	78.5	84.25	90	95.75	100.75	106.5

LSL

USL

Minutes

Normal distribution

Illustration by Wiley, Composition Services Graphics

These two parameters (75 and 105 minutes) are referred to as the *lower* and *upper specification limits* (LSL and USL) for the process or the range of "good" flight times as specified by the customer. Whenever a process results in a measurement outside the two specification limits, a defect exists. The LSL and USL for flight times are also shown in Figure 12-5.

Calculate the capability of the process to meet specifications by examining how many sigmas the specification limits are away from the mean. Because the process can vary by plus or minus 15 minutes and the observed standard deviation is 5.75 minutes, the specification limit is 2.6 sigmas away from the mean (15/5.75). Given the normal distribution, 2.6 sigma capability statistically means that 1 percent of the flights will be considered defective. Check out Chapter 13 to further explore the significance of the standard deviation on quality.

Calculating the process capability ratio (C_p)

Many kinds of businesses, including those in the automotive industry, use metrics that are different from the sigma level to measure process capability. The first one is the capability ratio (C_p). Calculate the process capability ratio using the following equation:

$$C_p = \frac{USL - LSL}{6\sigma}$$

If the ratio is less than 1, the process creates products that are outside the specifications assuming a normal distribution, which means it will produce some defects even though no special cause variation exists and the process is *in control*, meaning that the process is stable over time and has no active special causes. The smaller the C_p, the greater the number of defects.

Not many people use this measure because, unlike the sigma capability described in the previous section, it doesn't account for whether the mean of the parameter is off-center (the mean value the process is creating is not the mean value of what the customer expects). However, a modification of this calculation, called the $\left(C_{p_k}\right)$, accounts for the parameter being off center and is more popular.

Calculating the process capability index $\left(C_{p_k}\right)$

The process capability index accounts for the fact that a process doesn't necessarily operate at the center of its specification limits. This can be a problem because a process with a very small standard deviation can produce parts outside customer specifications because the mean of the process is off-target.

As an extreme case, if the mean lies right on top of the LSL, then half the parts would be outside the specification limit. So a metric that accounts for the potential of defects resulting from the mean lying near the USL or the LSL is necessary. Most firms address this problem by calculating the process capability index using the following equation:

$$C_{p_k} = Minimum \ of\left[\frac{\mu - LSL}{3\sigma}, \frac{USL - \mu}{3\sigma}\right]$$

The $\left(C_{p_k}\right)$ is simply the minimum value of the difference between the mean μ and the LSL divided by 3σ or the difference between the USL and the mean divided by 3σ.

The higher the process capability index, the less likely parts will be defective. Nominally, if the solution is greater than 1, then the number of defects is very low. However, some firms require the index to be greater than 1.33, or $C_{p_k} \geq 1.33$.

The process capability index is simply the process capability measured in sigmas, as described earlier, divided by 3. For example, a 4-sigma quality process has a C_{p_k} of 1.33 (4/3).

After determining how a process is expected to perform, how do you evaluate further output from the process to determine whether it's performing as it should? Find out in the next section!

Controlling processes

Statistical process control (SPC) is a set of statistical techniques that determine whether processes are behaving as expected. If a process is behaving as expected, it is *in control*. Being in control is the same as having no special cause variation present (described earlier in the section "Understanding variation"). In other words, a process that's in control is behaving the same today as it was yesterday; it's stable. On the other hand, if the process is not behaving as expected, then it's *out of control.*

A process's status as in control doesn't mean that it's necessarily producing good parts, merely that it's behaving as it has in the past without any special cause variation. A process can be in control and still produce a large number of defective parts. The reason it matters whether a process is in control is because this status determines that it's stable. If the process isn't stable, a number of problems can exist.

The most common SPC tool is a *control chart*, which is a plot of samples taken from the process over time. A control chart provides a simple visual to help operation managers monitor a process to see whether it's performing as expected.

You can use control charts for variables or attributes. Variables can be measured (diameter of a hole); attributes are counted (number of cookies in a box).

The idea is simple. After you establish the initial control limits, you can take a sample from the process at the specified time period — every day or every hour, shift, or week — and then plot results on the chart. You look for measurements that lie outside two calculated control limits. If no measurements lie outside these control limits, then theoretically the process is in control. If a measurement is outside the limit, then the process has changed and is unstable. In other words, if a value falls outside the control limits, then you know that a special cause of variation has occurred or is occurring in your process.

Monitoring the process using an x-bar chart

Control charts for variables monitor the mean ($\bar{x}$-chart), also called an *x-bar chart,* and the range (*R-chart*) of the process.

When constructing an x-bar chart, you need to calculate the upper control limit (UCL) and the lower control limit (LCL). To do this, take a number of observations at the set time period (hour, shift, day, week, and so on) and plot the sample mean ($\bar{x}$) of those observations. Because of the central limit theorem, as the number of observations in a sample goes up, the mean becomes normal in its distribution. As a rule of thumb, you want a sample size large enough that the distribution of sample means is approximately normal. Thirty observations will do in most situations; oftentimes you can get by with less.

With a number of these sample means ($\bar{x}$) in hand, you can calculate the mean of the sample means ($\bar{\bar{x}}$) and the standard deviation of the sample means ($\sigma_{\bar{x}}$). Then calculate the UCL and LCL as follows:

$$UCL = \bar{\bar{x}} + 3\sigma_{\bar{x}}$$

$$LCL = \bar{\bar{x}} - 3\sigma_{\bar{x}}$$

Figure 12-6 shows a typical x-bar control chart. If a sample mean falls outside the control limits, then you know that the process has changed in some manner. This change can be attributed to a special cause and hopefully identified and eliminated.

X-bar Control Chart

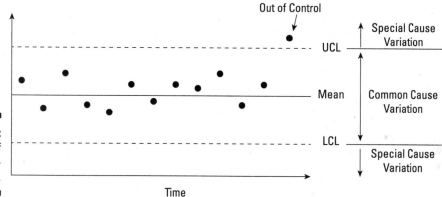

Figure 12-6: Example of a mean control chart.

The UCL and LCL are not the same as the USL and LSL described earlier in this chapter. The specification limits define where a defect occurs, and the control limits define the parameters within which a process naturally operates. A process can be in control, yet still produce a large percentage of defective products.

In general, if the specification limits are within the control limits, then the process has a high probability of producing defective products. If, however, specification limits are outside the control limits, then the process has a high probability of producing defect-free products. Figure 12-7 illustrates how the CL and the SL influence quality levels.

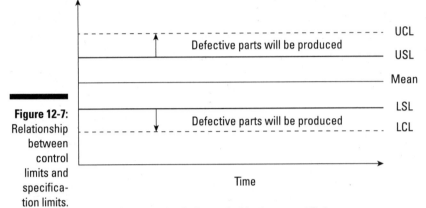

Figure 12-7: Relationship between control limits and specification limits.

Defective parts will be produced — UCL / USL

Mean

Defective parts will be produced — LSL / LCL

Time

Specification limits are inside the control limits

Illustration by Wiley, Composition Services Graphics

Often, the standard deviation of a process is not known. If this is the case, you can use the average of the sample ranges ($\bar{R}$) to calculate the UCL and LCL. Here are the formulas for these calculations:

$$UCL = \bar{\bar{x}} + A_2\bar{R}$$
$$LCL = \bar{\bar{x}} - A_2\bar{R}$$

Table 12-2 shows the value of A_2 for the different number of observations in the subgroup. As you notice from the table, the value of A_2 declines as the number of observations increases, which produces a smaller control range.

Table 12-2	Standard Control Chart Values		
Number of Observations in Subgroup, n	Factor for Chart, A_2	Lower Control Limit for R-Chart, D_3	Upper Control Limit for R-Chart, D_4
2	1.88	0	3.27
4	.73	0	2.28
6	.48	0	2.00
8	.37	.14	1.86
10	.31	.22	1.78
12	.27	.28	1.72
14	.24	.33	1.67
16	.21	.36	1.64
18	.19	.39	1.61
20	.18	.41	1.59

Constructing a range chart

The construction of a range chart is similar to the construct of a mean chart. Find control limits for a range chart by using the average sample range and the following equations:

$$UCL_R = D_4\bar{R}$$
$$LCL_R = D_3\bar{R}$$

The values of D_3 and D_4 are shown in Table 12-2.

Monitoring attributes

Attributes are counted. For example, you can count the number of products that have a defect in a sample or the number of scratches on the surface of a product. Two charts used to monitor attribute quality are the p-chart and the c-chart.

Constructing p-charts

A p-chart monitors the proportion of defective products. In a p-chart the product is inspected and is categorized as either good or bad. The underlying distribution of a p-chart is *binomial* (the discrete probability distribution of the number of successes given experiments with two outcomes, such as good/bad). However, the normal distribution provides a good approximation if the sample sizes are large enough.

The central line of a p-chart is the average fraction defective. You can calculate the standard deviation from the following equation when p is known:

$$\sigma_p = \sqrt{\frac{p(1-p)}{n}}$$

Calculate the control limits using the above standard deviation for a p-chart:

$$UCL_p = p + 3\sigma_p$$
$$LCL_p = p - 3\sigma_p$$

LCL may be negative. If it is, then be sure to set the LCL to zero.

If p is unknown, you can estimate it from samples. The estimate, $\bar{p}$, replaces p in the control limit formulas.

To use a p-chart, inspect a sample of products *(n)* and count the number of defective items. Calculate the proportion of defective items against total output and plot this ratio on the chart. If the ratio goes above the UCL, then something undesirable has happened to the process.

Just keep in mind that getting a ratio below the LCL is actually desirable. You want the proportion of defects to be low, so a number below the LCL indicates that the process may have improved. If it has improved, that's great, but you'll need to reestablish your p-bar and set up new control limits.

Constructing c-charts

In many cases more than one defect exists on a product. The c-chart monitors the number of defects on any one product. The underlying sampling distribution is known as *Poisson*.

In a c-chart, the center line is the average number of defects per product $(\bar{c})$, and the standard deviation is $\sqrt{\bar{c}}$. You can calculate the control limits with this equation:

$$UCL_c = \bar{c} + 3\sqrt{\bar{c}}$$
$$LCL_c = \bar{c} - 3\sqrt{\bar{c}}$$

Using control charts

Mean and range charts monitor different aspects of a process. Mean charts quickly reveal when shifts appear in the mean; range charts show a shift in the variability of the process.

In reality, using both types of charts is a very good idea. One chart by itself does not give the full picture. Fortunately, because most of the costs related to creating the charts are incurred by gathering the sample, both charts can be constructed from the same set of outputs. After you collect the sample, you might as well calculate the mean and the range with it.

When using control charts, you can experience two types of errors:

- ✔ **Type I errors** (or false positives) occur when you conclude a process is not in control when it actually is. Type I errors occur because a normal distribution always includes some occurrences in the tail (take a peek at Figure 12-5 to see what we're saying here).

- ✔ **Type II errors** (or false negatives) occur when you conclude a process is in control when it's actually out of control. That is, even if all values on your control charts are within the control limits, it's still possible that the process may be out of control. Figure 12-8 shows two examples of a process that can be out of control even though all values fall within the control limits.

Out of Control Process

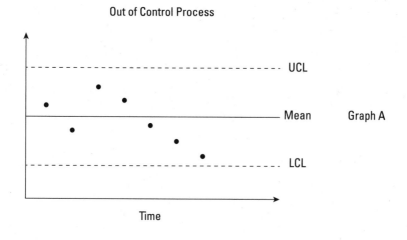

Graph A

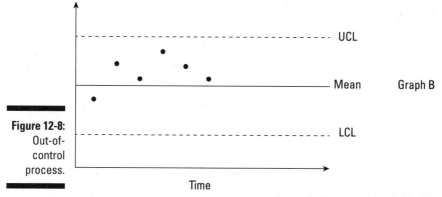

Graph B

Figure 12-8:
Out-of-
control
process.

Illustration by Wiley, Composition Services Graphics

Graph A in Figure 12-8 shows a *run* — a trend of five or more observations that are either going up or going down — which can indicate the process is out of control (even if all points are within the control limits). Tool wear and other machine-based functioning issues can cause performance to trend in one direction. In this case, an operations manager needs to take action to correct the trend.

If five or more observations are above or below the mean, which is the situation that's shown in Graph B of Figure 12-8, then this also indicates that the process may also be out of control; you should investigate to find out what in the process has changed to cause the mean to shift.

Chapter 13

Creating a Quality Organization

A quality mind-set must be part of the corporate culture for a company to produce true quality products. Planning for quality must begin in the executive suite, and the whole organization must embrace quality to really create it and deliver it to customers.

Not long ago, quality improvement efforts were the sole responsibility of a few selected individuals in an organization. Most manufacturing plants actually had what they called a quality control department, and many times those departments were located far from the factory floor. Unfortunately, those responsible for quality acted alone and at times were considered a nuisance to the personnel responsible for actually doing the work.

By now, most companies realize that the quality mentality must be part of what happens in every department — not just manufacturing. (See Chapter 12 for details on traditional quality-assessment tools.) In this chapter, we examine the evolution of a company becoming a quality organization. We introduce the tools necessary for building such an organization and highlight the obstacles that firms face on their journey toward quality central.

Reaching Beyond Traditional Improvement Programs

Quality improvement programs aren't a new concept or late-breaking fad in business. Companies have been using methods such as *total quality management* (TQM) and *statistical process control* (SPC) for decades; these methods are covered in Chapter 12. In this section, we examine how these traditional quality improvement initiatives have turned into what's become known as *Six Sigma* quality.

Multiplying failures

Most companies typically operate their process at a 3 sigma quality level. This means that the process mean is 3 standard deviations away from the nearest *specification limit,* which defines the boundaries of a good part (covered in Chapter 12).

Figure 13-1 shows a process operating at 2.6, 3, and 6 sigma. The figure reveals that 1 percent of the output of a 2.6 sigma process will be defective, assuming a normal distribution. By increasing the quality level to 3 sigma, you can reduce the defective rate to 0.3 percent. Even at this level, a company can lose a significant amount of profits, because 3 of every 1,000 products it makes have a defect.

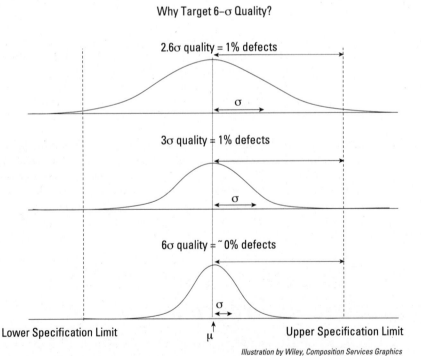

Why Target 6–σ Quality?

2.6σ quality = 1% defects

σ

3σ quality = 1% defects

σ

6σ quality = ˜0% defects

σ

Figure 13-1:
Six Sigma
quality.

Lower Specification Limit

μ

Upper Specification Limit

Illustration by Wiley, Composition Services Graphics

Realizing that 3 sigma just wasn't good enough, the Motorola Corporation embarked on a quality journey starting in 1985, which led to the birth of what's now called *Six Sigma*. Other companies picked up on the concept, and a quality revolution was launched in the world of business operations.

So you may be asking, if 6 sigma quality is so good, wouldn't 7, 8, or even 9 sigma be even better? Not necessarily. You start bumping into the point of diminishing returns. In other words, Figure 13-1 reveals that after you reach 6 sigma, the defect rate is very close to zero. Going beyond 6 sigma can get very expensive because you eliminate all the "easy" problems to get to this point; any gains you receive from further improvement are small — perhaps not worth the effort and cost required to achieve them.

For various obscure reasons, Motorola assumed that the mean could drift up to 1.5 standard deviations off center toward one side of the customer specifications or the other. So you may hear that a 6 sigma capability translates into a defect rate of 3.4 parts per million. In this book, we don't follow this assumption but instead assume that 6 sigma means that the process mean (average parameter value) is actually 6 standard deviations away from the nearest specification limit.

Because most products are assembled from multiple components, the quality level of each component is critical; each one has a compounding influence on the quality of the end product. This means that the expected quality of the end product diminishes as the number of components increases. You can calculate the expected quality of a product using this equation:

$$\% \text{ Defective products} = 1 - [1 - (\% \text{ Defective}/100)]^{\textit{Number of components}}$$

For example, operating at 3 sigma quality for each of 10 components that make up a final product may sound like a reasonable quality level, because only approximately 0.3 percent of each component will be defective. But the expected end quality of the final product when the 10 components are assembled is only 97 percent; 3 percent of the final products are defective. This only gets worse as the number of components increases, as shown in Table 13-1; here, each component is at a 3 sigma quality level.

Table 13-1	Final Product Quality
Number of Components	***Defective Rate of Final Product***
200 part DVR	45%
500 part laptop computer	78%
3,000 part automobile	Approximately 100%

Raising the bar

Six Sigma is similar to the quality initiatives described in Chapter 12. They all emphasize this set of values:

- ✓ Achieving quality improvement requires participation across the organization.
- ✓ The process characteristics must be measured, analyzed, improved, and controlled.
- ✓ To achieve high quality, a company must focus on continuous improvement.

Here are the fundamentals that separate Six Sigma from its predecessors and living relatives:

- ✓ Efforts to improve quality are prioritized by return on investment. Projects are selected based on a cost-benefit analysis.
- ✓ Decisions are made on concrete, verifiable data. Great attempts are made to remove qualitative assertions.
- ✓ Implementation is handled by experts of different degrees with formalized training (covered in the next section).
- ✓ An increased emphasis is placed on benchmarking competitive performance.

The Six Sigma concept applies an increased focus on concrete results that can be measured. Improvement projects are chosen based on the potential financial results the organization can achieve. All improvement is measured and documented. The firm's attention is squarely trained on actions that produce tangible results when Six Sigma is in action.

Varying skill levels

Perhaps one of the greatest differences that separates Six Sigma from other quality improvement programs is its emphasis on differentiated skill levels among employee training. Following the structure of martial arts training, Six Sigma uses a belt color system to designate the level of training the employee has received in the methods of Six Sigma:

- ✓ **Black belts:** At the top of the skill chain are the black belts. These employees are highly trained experts and are responsible for leading Six Sigma projects. In many organizations, the mission of implementing the projects and training others is their full-time position.

✔ **Green belts:** Next in line are the green belts. Although not experts, they're proficient in Six Sigma methodologies and are part-time participants in the implementation effort.

✔ **Yellow belts:** Yellow belts make up the majority of a Six Sigma project team. These are often the people who actually perform in the process being improved. The success of any project rests on the shoulders of these people because they not only work to improve the process but also maintain the gains after the others move on to their next project in the continuous improvement cycle.

Implementation of a Six Sigma initiative starts in the executive suite. Upper management must be fully committed to the program. Champions of the cause in upper management are usually tasked to oversee implementation of chosen projects. While upper management may not be black belts, they do require some understanding of the dedication required to successfully implement Six Sigma in their organization.

Adding to the Tool Box

At the foundation of Six Sigma quality lies a powerful tool box of techniques and methods that employees use throughout all phases of a successful project. In this section we introduce you to the must-have tools and explain how to best use them.

At the heart of any project is what has become known as DMAIC (define-measure-analyze-improve-control). DMAIC, pronounced "dah-*may*-ik," is a standardized process that's simply an extension of the Deming wheel (defined in Chapter 12). Employees follow a series of well-defined steps throughout the project and repeat the process repeatedly for continuous improvement.

Figure 13-2 shows the five phases of the DMAIC process:

✔ **Define:** Choose the project, determine what you'll accomplish in concrete terms, select the project team, and devise a plan for executing the next phases of the project.

✔ **Measure:** Document the current state of the process that you're targeting for improvement. After all, you need to know where you started in order to determine whether the process achieved improvements and met the objectives you established in the define phase.

✔ **Analyze:** Examine the current process to find out how it works. Identify the main process drivers and the causes of problems. In the "Analyzing the problem" section later in the chapter, we describe many of the tools you use during this phase.

✔ **Improve:** Implement solutions to the problems you've indentified. Be sure to measure and validate any improvements to find out whether your improvement efforts actually produced measurable results.

✔ **Control:** Establish a plan to monitor the ongoing performance of the changes. You can use statistical process controls (described in Chapter 12) to monitor and control the new process.

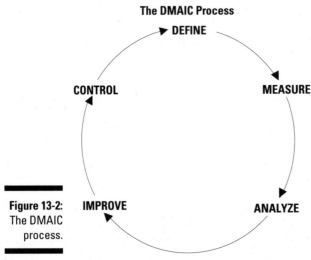

The DMAIC Process

Figure 13-2:
The DMAIC
process.

In addition to the DMAIC, Six Sigma utilizes DMADV (define, measure, analyze, design, and verify), particularly on new processes or when a process requires a radical change. The DMADV process mirrors DMAIC with one exception: A new process is designed instead of the improve step.

Defining the problem

All DMAIC projects start with a well-defined problem statement that states what the issue is and what needs to be improved. After you define the problem, you write an *objective statement,* which outlines the project's scope, defines its concrete and measurable goals, and provides a timeline for project completion. During the define phase of the project, you also identify all stakeholders and assemble the project team.

You can use *benchmarking* — comparing your performance to others — to set targets for your improvement goals. Find out who's "best in class," study what those companies do, and determine whether you can duplicate their attributes and habits in your organization.

When benchmarking, don't limit yourself to companies within your industry. Looking outside your immediate realm can offer new insights into the problems you're facing and possibly help you leapfrog the performance of your competition.

Measuring the process

After defining the project and establishing objectives, you must measure the current state of the process. Though many undisciplined firms want to skip this step and consider it a waste of time, documenting the status quo is critical for successful improvement projects. You must know where you started to claim improvement victory.

Start by creating an as-is process flow diagram and include metrics such as cycle time, flow time, process capacity, and current quality levels. (See Part I for full details on how to map, measure, and improve process metrics.)

Analyzing the problem

The output of any process is determined by the inputs into the process and the transformation activities that occur. Simply put, the output y is a function of the input x:

$$y = f(x)$$

In the analyze phase, find out which inputs influence the outcome and how they do it. Be vigilant about finding the root cause of your undesirable output. Several tools can help you do this; we describe them in the following sections.

Brainstorming

Brainstorming sessions can help extract possible causes of offending outcomes. By gathering a cross-functional array of employees, including management and line workers, you can get a wide assortment of ideas and often find the reasoning behind certain ideas.

Conduct a meeting in which you encourage everyone to voice his opinion about the problem's root causes. Place ideas on sticky notes and display them on a board. (Sticky notes allow for later rearranging.)

Companies often use *affinity diagrams* to organize possible causes into clusters. An affinity diagram is a tool that helps group ideas and concepts into similar sets. Affinity diagrams are useful because they make it easy to see how identified causes fit into a small number of categories, making the potential causes easier to analyze.

Brainstorming and the resulting affinity diagrams tend to open the door to meaningful discussions on the key issues influencing performance. In practice, a brainstorming session may begin with a high-level question, such as, "Why are our sales down?" Comments from employees might include "We don't have enough salespeople to service potential customers"; "Production can't deliver the products within the time the customer wants"; and "Our products have a bad quality reputation." You can probably imagine how discussions may proceed from there.

Determining cause and effect

Brainstorming usually results in several potential answers to the brainstorming question. From this information you can choose an area on which to focus your effort. Because this is a chapter on quality, we'll focus on the quality comments, which you'd probably group together on your affinity diagram.

The next step is to get to the root cause of the problem. There may be many possible reasons for poor quality, so to help quantify the important reasons, you can use the following tools.

Charting the causes

The *Pareto chart* is named after the Italian economist Vilfredo Pareto. In the early 1900s he observed that 80 percent of the land in Italy was held by 20 percent of the people. Further studies showed that this principle was true for many things, and it became known as the "80-20 rule" or "the law of the vital few." The principle states that 80 percent of the effects (problems, complaints, sales, and so on) come from 20 percent of the causes.

The Pareto chart is a bar graph in which the independent variables or events are on the horizontal axis, and the vertical axis is the number of occurrences. The values are plotted in decreasing order of frequency. For example, you can analyze customer product-return data and graph the reasons why customers return a product and the frequency that the product is returned for that reason. Figure 13-3 illustrates a Pareto chart.

Using the Pareto chart, you can quickly identify the vital few events that are causing most of your problems. You can then determine where you should focus improvement efforts.

Boning the fish

After you identify an event or events to address, use a cause-and-effect diagram to get to the root cause of an issue. One such tool is the *fishbone* or *Ishikawa* diagram. As the name implies, the diagram resembles the skeleton of a fish (see Figure 13-4).

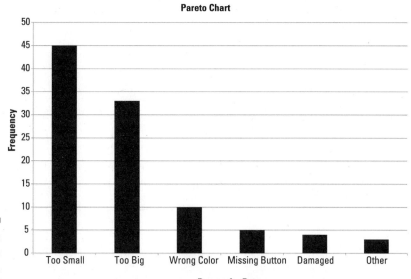

Figure 13-3:
A Pareto
chart.

Illustration by Wiley, Composition Services Graphics

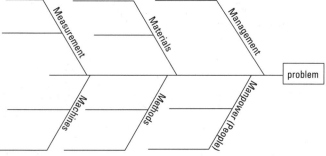

Figure 13-4:
A fishbone
diagram.

Illustration by Wiley, Composition Services Graphics

At the head of the diagram is a statement of the problem. If, for example, you discover from a Pareto chart that a top reason for customer returns is that parts are missing from the package, then "Missing Parts" would become the problem statement in the fishbone diagram.

Running along the central spine is a list of what could cause parts to be missing from the package. These causes are grouped into categories that make up sections, and each section can contain one or more specific causes.

Although the categories can vary, many companies use the six Ms to separate the causes:

- ✔ **Machines:** The state or characteristics of the equipment required to perform the operations.
- ✔ **Management:** The policies and procedures that govern the company.
- ✔ **Manpower:** The people performing the operation. This can also encompass the training or ability of the workers.
- ✔ **Materials:** The raw materials that go into the process and the tools or materials required to complete the operation.
- ✔ **Measurement:** The ways and accuracy of measuring the process.
- ✔ **Methods:** The hows of the process or the process steps necessary to complete the task.

When building a diagram, remember that these categories are flexible. You do, however, want to make sure that you cover everything. A good fishbone diagram contains many sections from the spine, and each section should contain its own cluster of bones projecting from it.

Analyzing failure modes

Cause-and-effect diagrams such as the fishbone provide a useful visual tool to identify the root cause of a problem. Another root cause determination tool is the *failure mode and effects analysis* (FMEA).

FMEA is a very structured approach to getting at root causes. FMEA begins by identifying all possible failure modes (what can go wrong) of your product or process. After you identify the failure modes, you assess what effect the failure mode would have if it occurred, as well as the likelihood that it may occur. You also consider the likelihood of the failure going undetected.

Rank each failure mode on three dimensions and give each dimension a value of 1 to 10. Here are the dimensions and the rating systems:

- ✔ **Severity (SEV):** How significantly does the failure affect the customer? A ranking of 1 indicates that the customer probably won't notice the effect or considers it insignificant; a ranking of 10 indicates a catastrophic event such as a customer injury.
- ✔ **Occurrence (OCC):** How likely is the cause of this failure to occur? A ranking of 1 indicates that it isn't likely; a ranking of 10 means that failures nearly always occur.
- ✔ **Detectability (DET):** What are the odds that the failure will be discovered? A ranking of 1 means that the defect will most certainly be detected before reaching the customer; a ranking of 10 indicates that the failure will most likely go out undetected.

After you determine the rankings, calculate a risk priority number (RPN), which is simply the product of the three rankings:

$$RPN = SEV \cdot OCC \cdot DET$$

The higher the RPN, the more critical the failure mode and the greater need for taking action. As a final step, after implementing corrective action, be sure to reevaluate the failure mode.

FMEA is a powerful tool for analyzing possible failure modes of products and processes. But take care when using the FMEA methodology. This ranking system is very subjective because it relies on the opinions of the employees taking part in the activity and results may be biased.

Correlating the variables

It's a safe bet to assume that every outcome will be the result of two or more factors. Therefore, you can't study variables in isolation. Analyzing the correlation among variables is a significant component of Six Sigma projects.

Correlation is the degree to which two or more attributes show a tendency to vary together. A positive correlation means that the attributes move in the same direction — up or down. A negative correlation means that the attributes move in opposite directions; one goes up and the other goes down.

Charting correlation

The simplest tool for looking at correlation between variables is the *correlation chart,* which plots two factors together and shows the visual relationship. Figure 13-5 shows a correlation chart with a positive correlation.

Designing experiments

Correlation charts are useful when looking at two variables, but a more powerful tool is necessary when multiple variables can interact. *Design of experiments* (DOE) is a methodology in which you change the levels of one or more factors according to a predesigned plan and then record the outcome of each experiment.

You can use a properly conducted DOE to identify the effect of the variables independently or the effect of the variables' interaction. In a typical DOE, you assign several levels of each variable and conduct experiments by changing the levels of each variable. Table 13-2 shows a DOE with three variables (X, Y, and Z) and two levels for each variable (H and L). When conducting the experiments, you want to randomize the order in which you test.

Correlation Chart

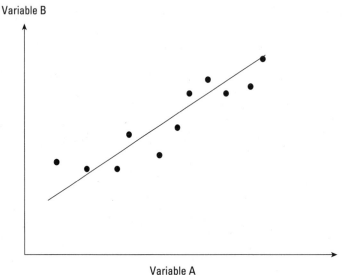

Variable B

Variable A

Figure 13-5:
A correlation chart.

Table 13-2	Design of Experiments		
Experiment Number	**X**	**Y**	**Z**
4	H	H	H
6	H	H	L
1	H	L	H
8	H	L	L
5	L	H	H
3	L	H	L
7	L	L	H
2	L	L	L

As shown in Table 13-2, eight experiments are required to capture all combinations of the variables and levels. You can then statistically analyze the data using a variety of methods to determine the effects of each variable and the interactions that exist among them. Details on how to do this are beyond the scope of this book. If you're interested in exploring this topic, check out *Statistics For Dummies,* 2nd Edition, by Deborah J. Rumsey (Wiley).

As the number of variables and levels that you want to test increases, the number of experiments required grows. For example, if you test three variables at three different levels, you'd have to run 27 experiments; four variables at two levels requires 16 experiments.

In general, the number of experiments in a full factorial design is equal to

Number of experiments = Number of levels$^{\text{number of variables}}$

Fractional factorial methods can help reduce the number of experiments without sacrificing statistical results. However, you must choose how you conduct these experiments carefully because they all carry some risk in accuracy; they do not account for all interactions of the variables.

Implementing a solution

After you identify the root cause of the problem, you need to select and implement a solution. Chances are the problem has many solutions. So a decision matrix can help you decide which solution to pursue.

A *decision matrix,* often called a *Pugh matrix,* evaluates alternative solutions by comparing each along a series of objectives. Often, the current method serves as a baseline.

Say your team comes up with three solutions (A, B, and C) to a problem. Follow these steps to construct a decision matrix (see example in Table 13-3):

1. **Select the solutions you want to evaluate.**

   Find out what improvement you can expect from each solution. The solutions are listed in the top row of the matrix in Table 13-3.

2. **Decide what the criteria for evaluation are.**

   Choose the most important criteria that relate to the issues that made you decide to focus your efforts on the project. The criteria are listed in the first column of the matrix in Table 13-3.

3. **Score each solution against each of the criteria.**

   Always give the baseline a score of 0. Typically, a 3-point scale is great for this, but if more differentiation among the solutions is desirable, you can use a 5-point scale (as shown in Table 13-3). In a 5-point scale, use the following numbers:

   +2 Much better than baseline

   +1 Better than baseline

    0 Equal to baseline

   −1 Worse than baseline

   −2 Much worse than baseline

4. **Rate the importance of the criteria if necessary.**

   If one or more of the decision criteria are considered more critical than the others, you can assign a weight to each. Then multiply the score from Step 3 by the criteria ranking, giving it a final score. The matrix in Table 13-3 omits this step.

5. **Sum the assigned scores.**

   Add together the scores for each solution along the criteria to get a net score.

6. **Choose your solution.**

   In most cases, you want to choose the solution with the highest score. (In Table 13-3, for example, solution B is best.) If all alternatives score less than zero, the baseline (current) process is considered the best option. You may want to consider other solutions if the current batch doesn't offer improvements worth the cost of implementation.

Keep in mind that rating the criteria, as described in Step 4, may have a great impact on your solution decision. For example, if you rate the importance of criteria 1 in Table 13-3 higher than the others, then solution C may well end up being the preferred solution.

Table 13-3	Decision Matrix			
Criteria	*Baseline*	*A*	*B*	*C*
1	0	+2	+1	+2
2	0	0	+1	+2
3	0	+1	+2	−1
4	0	−1	0	0
Total	0	+2	+4	+3

Maintaining the gain

After you analyze the situation, identify root causes, and implement the new process, you must continue to monitor the new process to assure that you maintain the improvements you've achieved. One statistical method you can use to do this is the *process control chart.* See Chapter 12 for a detailed description of how to set up and use these charts.

Two other tools, the run chart and the histogram, are also used to monitor the process. These tools are easy to set up and maintain and don't require the statistical calculations found in a control chart.

The *run chart* plots an individual metric over time and makes it easy to spot trends and patterns over time. Figure 13-6 shows a sample run chart.

<u>Run Chart</u>

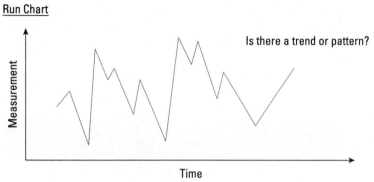

Illustration by Wiley, Composition Services Graphics

Figure 13-6: A sample run chart.

Here are some things to look for in a run chart that may indicate an unstable or problem process:

- ✔ **Cluster:** Several observations surrounding a certain value
- ✔ **Mean shift:** Several observations above or below the process average
- ✔ **Oscillations:** Observations that go up and down with recognizable frequency
- ✔ **Trends:** Several observations in a row that all go up or down

A *histogram* displays the frequency of different measurements. As shown in Figure 13-7, the histogram shows the distribution of the measurements and highlights measurements that are considered outliers from the rest. Histograms are useful to identify special cause variation (defined in Chapter 12).

Histogram

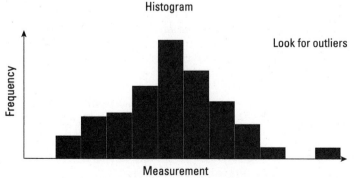

Figure 13-7: A sample histogram.

Illustration by Wiley, Composition Services Graphics

Overcoming Obstacles

Many things stand between a company and its quality-centered end game. Among the obstacles are the tendency to lose focus on the goal of quality improvement, get sidetracked by a seeming "silver bullet" that promises to solve all the quality issues, or simply give up when the gains don't come fast enough. In this section we explore common obstacles and pitfalls of quality improvement efforts and offer advice to help you avoid or overcome them.

Failing to focus

Implementing quality improvement requires a great deal of time and commitment. A mistake that many organizations make is to jump headfirst into too many projects. At the start of the journey, everyone is excited about the potential that quality improvement promises, and the firm may embark on several projects at a time. This reduces the focus on any one project and often stretches resources too thin.

Instead, we advise that you start by choosing a project that involves a process that employees have a lot of knowledge about and understand well. This helps ensure that the results are successful and encourages others to get behind future projects.

When adding projects, choose carefully. Tools such as the Pareto chart (see the "Charting the causes" section earlier in the chapter) can help you select the most important issues to address.

Prioritizing into paralysis

Some companies fall into the trap of spending so much time on prioritizing potential projects that they never get down to the real work. When selecting projects, companies typically rank them based on anticipated benefit, which is often the expected *return on investment* (ROI). This often leads to disagreement across the organization as to which project is the most important and should get first priority. And as you may know, benefits data — especially expected ROI — is easy to manipulate.

Don't get caught in this trap. If you must choose between two or more improvement projects that have roughly the same value, just choose one and get started. Completing any project that provides benefit to the business is much better than waiting to find the "perfect" project.

You may want to start with the project that's easiest and quickest to implement. A quick victory at the beginning of a quality improvement initiative can provide momentum to the organization on future projects.

Avoiding the lure of magical solutions

Falling victim to the "silver bullet" quality program happens to the best of 'em. Magical, fix-it-all, pain-free programs are usually touted as the program that is going to save the company, but easy, catch-all solutions often involve a consulting agency coming into the company with grand ideas and beautiful presentations that are likely to fail because they don't follow the proven methods (outlined in this chapter and Chapter 12). After a few months with few results, firms that embrace such programs often end up, moving on to the next program that promises quick and easy results.

This approach may ultimately sabotage your quality improvement efforts. Employees become tired and complacent about these programs, and they dismiss future programs as a waste of time; after all, none of the past programs ever panned out very well.

Lacking employee involvement

In order for quality improvement projects to be successful, all levels of an organization must commit to the effort. This means that all employees must understand the importance of the quality projects and contribute to their success.

Employees sometimes view improvement efforts as a threat to their job security or as an examination into whether they can do the job. Therefore, when identifying and implementing any process changes, be sure to consult with and educate the people involved with performing the process targeted for improvement. Often, just knowing why the change is being made is enough to earn buy-in from the employees.

Knowing what to do

One of the biggest obstacles to quality success is not knowing what to do if a process is discovered to be *out of control,* or unstable. Setting up and monitoring the control charts that are mentioned in this chapter and described in Chapter 12 require significant time and resources. Employees must take samples, perform the necessary observations and measurements, and record the results on the chart. That's the easy part.

What happens when a sample indicates that the process has changed and is now out of control? That's the hard part. A company must establish procedures and train employees to enact them to deal with an out-of-control situation. Failure to act or acting inappropriately won't lead to improved quality and may even make the situation worse.

Learning from the experience

Few firms make the effort to learn from past quality projects. After completing a project, companies often just move on to the next effort and lose what they learned from the last one. Projects should have a formal documentation process (often called *after-action* or *after-project review*) to record what happened, what the results were, and why.

Companies should also conduct after-project reviews to share project lessons. But don't limit these reviews to the project team; include personnel who may be working on other projects so they can duplicate successes and learn from mistakes.

Calling it a program

A *program* implies something that has a defined beginning and end. Quality improvement shouldn't be a program; it should occur naturally as part of the everyday job. Quality must become institutionalized and become an underlying foundation for the company. Without this shift in culture, true quality success is only a passing dream.

Giving up

Achieving improvement and implementing change is a slow, continuous process. It doesn't happen overnight. Expecting instant improvements is a recipe for disaster, and giving up too quickly because your first efforts don't produce the desired results only leads to failure. But with continual focus and a commitment to the methods and tools presented in this book, you *will* see improvement. Stick with it!

Part IV
Managing Projects

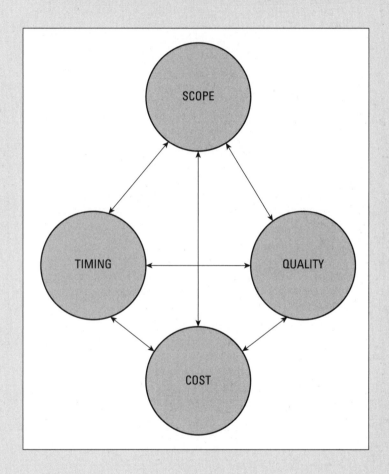

In this part . . .

✔ Develop a basic understanding of project management, including knowldege of what constitutes success and why many projects fail. Find out how to avoid failure with strong leadership and clear communication.

✔ Find out how to make accurate project estimates in order to avoid common pitfalls and potentially accelerate the pace of completing a project. Discover techniques for estimating cost and timing figuring out which activities you can delay safely and which you can't.

✔ Understand what it takes to manage project risks proactively in order to stay on time and on budget. Learn to establish a reliable tracking system and take a structured approach to identifying potential risk and how to deal with it.

Chapter 14

Using Communication and Leadership Skills When Managing Projects

In This Chapter

▶ Evaluating a project's success

▶ Understanding why projects fail

▶ Going through the steps of the project management process

▶ Communicating with stakeholders and the team

*P*rojects are initiatives that a firm undertakes as a one-time effort — a unique sequence of tasks such as building a bridge, designing a car, or developing a computer operating system. The circumstances and requirements to complete a particular project and how the activities interact with each other are, at least to some extent, different from any other project. This uniqueness means that the people involved in a project do not have prior experience that tells them what to do, when they need to do it, and whom to coordinate with to get the job done. Therefore, the first responsibility of managing a successful project is leadership and coordination.

Management must lead the project by communicating the overall goals of the project, what activities each person involved must do, the limits of their authority, and when they need to act. Coordinating all this activity so they come together successfully to achieve the desired result is a fundamental responsibility of project management, too.

Statistically, the odds of achieving a successful outcome at the conclusion of a project are slim. Most projects don't ultimately meet their objectives. Research in various industries — ranging from buildings and bridges to electronics and software — consistently reveals that about three of every four completed projects are late, over budget, or both. This dismal news doesn't even account for the fact that many projects are never even actually completed.

In this chapter, we describe what defines success for a project, point out why projects fail, and show you how disciplined management through documentation and strict adherence to standard project management processes can ensure that your project is on time, on budget, and meets its requirements. We then focus on two other pillars of good project management: defining explicit goals of the project and communicating with project stakeholders.

Defining Success

Unlike processes, you don't perform projects over and over again; they're usually one-time efforts. The metrics of success for any project depends on the objectives that the project is intended to meet. Yet many project leaders spend far too little time before launching a project figuring out what they want to achieve. In some cases, this failure is a matter of interest; other times it's due to a lack of tools and resources.

When initiating a project, you need to figure out ahead of time what needs to be done, how much it's likely to cost, what kind of time frame the effort requires, and how you can track the project's progress toward its goals. In this section, we present the most helpful criteria for launching a project plan.

Projects are generally evaluated against four criteria:

- ✔ **Scope:** What exactly is the project supposed to accomplish in terms of goals and deliverables? And, maybe more important, what is it not trying to accomplish?
- ✔ **Timing:** How long will it take to complete the project?
- ✔ **Cost:** How much money will it cost to finish the project?
- ✔ **Quality:** What does the project need to do well to achieve its goals?

Prioritizing criteria

How important each of these criteria is to a particular project depends on the project. If you're planning the construction of a new stadium for the Olympics, missing the deadline by a week is a disaster. If you're planning the construction of a new playground by volunteers in a neighborhood park, missing the deadline by a week isn't such a big deal. (After all, you get what you pay for!)

Similarly, missing the cost budget for an Olympic stadium by 50 percent may not be disastrous. For example, the Sydney Opera House is considered one of the great architectural wonders of the 20th century and is a UNESCO World Heritage Site. Its original budget was $7 million. When completed, it ended up costing approximately $100 million. Thus, it was over budget by a factor of 14 times. While many complained about the overruns at the time, there was no rioting in the streets. On the other hand, overshooting the budget of a playground by a factor of 14 times just couldn't happen because the project would be cut down or abandoned if costs ballooned to this degree. More important, you may never be invited to another neighborhood block party!

Quality is different from cost and timing. For starters, it's not as easy to measure (see Chapter 12). Yet its impression is usually longer lasting. For example, Australia has mostly forgotten its cost and timing issues with the Sydney Opera House, yet it constantly trumpets the quality of the structure in terms of beauty and acoustics.

Moreover, missing quality targets, such as falling masonry in a tunnel project, can literally kill people. Even smaller issues, like a persistent leaking in a roof, can sour clients on a project because, unlike late completion or cost overruns, poor quality continues to haunt the client on an ongoing basis — long after the project is completed.

The point is that people often worry about cost and timing more than quality in the short run, but in the long run, quality becomes much more important.

We're not suggesting that you plan on missing any of your project's goals or success criteria. But realistically, if you have to trade off one criterion for another, be very clear which of them is more important, and be aware that this answer may be different in the long term versus the short term.

Seeing the interaction of factors

Bear in mind that the four factors for success (scope, timing, cost, and quality) interact and trade off against one another. For example, you can usually speed up a project if you're willing to spend money on overtime and extra personnel. Similarly, you can always skimp on quality or scope to reduce cost or accelerate timing.

The project pyramid in Figure 14-1 shows the interrelationships among scope, cost, timing, and quality. For example, if you're willing to give up on building that third wing to your Hollywood mansion, your project costs are likely to go down.

One of the major jobs of the project manager is to juggle these four project success factors over the entire lifetime of the project.

At the start of a project, its cost, timing, and quality (and even scope — as that often changes during the project) are estimates. Some folks argue that the reason many projects are late or over budget is because upfront estimates are too optimistic. Though this is certainly true in many cases, a reason that estimates are done poorly in the first place is because not enough effort was spent planning out the goals of the project. Thus, planning and goals are tightly interlinked.

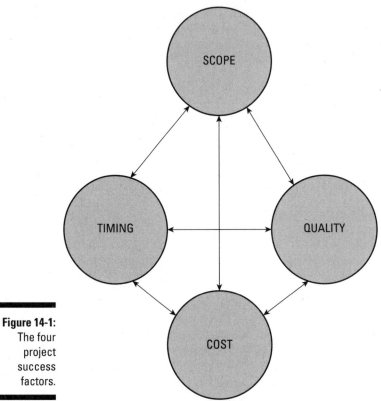

Illustration by Wiley, Composition Services Graphics

Figure 14-1:
The four
project
success
factors.

Figuring Out Why Projects Fail

There are literally dozens of studies on why projects fail. Most of them concentrate on why projects are late or over budget, because these factors are the easiest to measure. However, our own research indicates that failures in quality and scope seem to have the same root causes.

The root causes for most project failures come down to the following five issues:

✔ **Insufficient front-end planning:** Particular problems include poor project definition, unrealistic project plans, poor cost/timing/quality estimates, and insufficient contingency planning.

✔ **Poor scope control:** *Scope* is what the project includes and — just as important — what it doesn't. Scope problems are the great bane of project managers. Causes include poor project scope definition upfront and changes by the customer and/or the project management team.

✔ **Staffing problems:** Turnover of key individuals derails countless projects. If your project can't survive a member of your team dropping out, you have a problem. Another related issue is not bringing the right people with the right skills in on time.

✔ **Technology issues:** New technology can create uncertainty in any project. The worst case is if you have a number of technologies that all depend on one another to succeed. In that case, your project is almost certainly bound for trouble.

✔ **Weak progress monitoring:** This includes, among other causes, an inability to track progress or detect problems early. Often, this is as simple as not having any agreed-upon checkpoints with your client and your suppliers.

Some of these causes interact. For example, activities that a project requires are sometimes forgotten or improperly specified upfront. This guarantees that any status update regarding what percentage of the project has been completed is necessarily wrong because the number of activities being measured against is underestimated.

You can avoid many of these failure-makers by spending adequate time planning upfront in a disciplined manner using the tools described in this chapter and in Chapter 15.

Scope creep is as old as the pyramids — literally

Scope change has literally been going on since the time of the pharaohs. The first Egyptian pyramid (the great stepped pyramid of Pharaoh Djoser) was originally designed and built as a rectangular building about 25 feet high. However, Djoser wasn't happy with it and ordered his project manager (Imhotep, the first project manager's name to appear in history) to execute at least five major design changes. The end result was a pyramid 200 feet high, an increase of 8 times. And the poor construction workers didn't even have the wheel to work with!

Anticipating these sorts of scope changes upfront is difficult, and the attendant negotiations on adjustments to timing, cost, and quality result in most project managers keeping a large bottle of aspirin on their desks. (One wonders what Imhotep used to dull the pain.)

Laying Out the Project Management Life Cycle

Planning for a project can be a process, and like all processes, it benefits from standardization and discipline. A successful project rests on three legs, much like a stool (as shown in Figure 14-2). It needs

- ✔ Good processes to ensure that the appropriate actions are taken in the right sequence
- ✔ The right people working on the project
- ✔ Appropriate communication among project participants

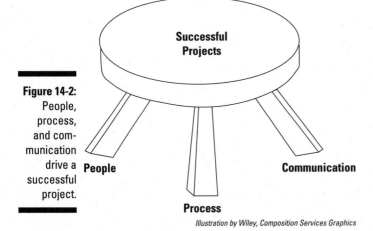

Figure 14-2: People, process, and communication drive a successful project.

Illustration by Wiley, Composition Services Graphics

Projects are, by definition, a one-time series of activities. But there's enough similarity among projects in terms of planning, communications, and coordination among the resources needed to complete them that a common process can help guide the planning and execution of a project through to a successful completion. This process is called the *project management life cycle.*

Detailing the phases of the cycle

The purpose of a project plan is to translate goals into objectives and results. Yet getting there requires adherence to a disciplined process. This process is laid out in Figure 14-3, which shows the four phases of the standard project management process. This same process is used for everything from developing space exploration projects to building bridges.

1. **Definition and scoping.** In this phase, you need to complete three primary tasks:

    - Identify the goals and stakeholders for the project

    - Write them up into a mission statement

    - Make a first pass at identifying the timing, cost, technologies, and organization that the project requires to be successful

2. **Planning.** This phase requires a great deal of work, including these specific tasks, to enable successful execution of the project:

    - Identify project specifications in detail (use quality function deployment, as described in Chapter 12, or some other method)

    - Review lessons learned from prior projects that are similar

    - Determine risks and opportunities and create contingency or mitigation plans as appropriate (see Chapter 16)

    - Create a work-breakdown structure (see Chapter 15) to identify what activities need to be done and who is responsible for them

    - Develop detailed scheduling and timing estimates (covered in Chapter 15) and establish progress milestones for later monitoring (see Chapter 16)

    - Develop detailed cost estimates (covered in Chapter 15) and establish progress milestones for later monitoring (see Chapter 16)

    - Assign resources, including suppliers to the project (see Chapter 10 for more on suppliers)

3. **Execution.** Now you need to actually do the project. In this phase, you handle these tasks:

    - Monitor progress, cost, and quality of the project

    - Activate contingency plans, if needed

    - Manage scope change and creep

4. **Handover and closeout.** This is when you finish up:

    - Hand over project deliverables to the client (this may involve some transition and training between you and your client)

    - Ramp up to normal operation, if applicable

    - Perform an after-action review to identify lessons learned

Figure 14-3:
The project
life cycle.

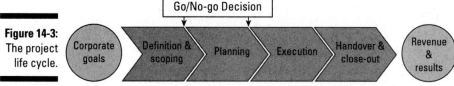

Illustration by Wiley, Composition Services Graphics

If you perform these four phases correctly, you should be able to achieve the desired results that were goals for your project.

Most project managers use the terms *scope change* and *scope creep* almost interchangeably. Scope change includes large, deliberate decisions about the extent of the project. Scope creep, however, indicates less conscious decision-making on the part of the project management team and the client. Successfully suppressing scope creep is one of the keys to achieving your cost and timing goals. On the other hand, if you're a consultant, you may want to encourage some scope creep. Just make sure you get paid for it!

Be aware that *scope growth* is a strategy for some companies. Under a very competitive bid, some companies will lowball the cost to win the business and then rely on customer scope changes to recoup the under bid. The classic example of scope change happens around the building of a custom home. The contractor is happy to accommodate that change from composite to natural granite countertops, at a substantial extra fee!

Your ability to make changes in your project decreases as you move through the process. Figure 14-4 shows that as you move from definition and scoping to handover, the cost and staff level of your project progressively increases. Moreover, the dependence of your future work on past decisions increases as well. This makes the cost of changes more expensive as you progress through the project life cycle, particularly for those decisions that you've already spent money on.

For the same reasons, the ability of management and stakeholders to make changes to the project decreases. Changes that you can make with a simple line on a piece of paper in the definition and scoping phase can literally cost millions of dollars in the execution phase. Getting it right early in the process is crucial.

Deciding to go or not to go

Go/no-go decisions occur between the defining/scoping, planning, and execution phases (as shown in Figure 14-3). In other words, after you complete the definition and scoping phase, you may decide that the project isn't likely to achieve its goals, which leads you to abandon the project. Companies often refer to these go/no-go decisions as *stage-gates* or *phase-gates*. Almost all companies use them.

Pulling the plug on a project may be a very good idea in some cases because you don't want to throw good money after bad. Energy companies are known to spend up to $3 billion on a $10 billion project in the planning phase and then cancel the entire project. And this is okay! It's much better to cancel a project after spending $3 billion than losing an additional $5 billion when your planning phase determines there isn't enough oil in the ground to make the project profitable.

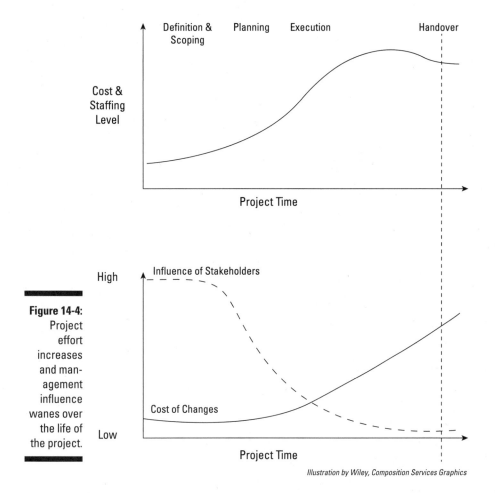

Figure 14-4:
Project
effort
increases
and man-
agement
influence
wanes over
the life of
the project.

Illustration by Wiley, Composition Services Graphics

Some companies have even expanded this idea to create competition in their planning process. For example, many electronic firms start 50 projects in the definition/scoping process each year, fully expecting to winnow that number down to 10 projects after the first stage-gate. After the planning phase, they expect to narrow that number down to 5 projects that they'll actually execute. This Darwinian-style competition is sometimes called the *project funnel;* it's used by firms in all kinds of industries — electronics, energy, movies, and many others.

Generally speaking, the likelihood that a project survives its next stage-gate is driven by its performance-to-date or by changes in the economic assumptions that made the project profitable. Thus, one would expect that many more high-way construction projects should survive go/no-go decisions than should high-tech projects. In many cases, the decision-makers and project managers need to guard against falling in love with the project; this is the phenomenon that occurs when project sponsors emotionally can't accept that assumptions and conditions have changed, and the project should be stopped.

Documenting the project

An important product of a well-executed project planning process is the set of documents that results from it. Formal documentation — so long as it's not just a fill-in-the-blank exercise — benefits the project in a number of ways:

- ✔ It promotes alignment with the client and team members (assuming they read the documents; more on this in a bit).

- ✔ It prevents rookie mistakes that occur because a project manager forgets to do something important in the process.

- ✔ It helps keep scope creep at bay by documenting exactly what is (or what isn't) in the scope of the project.

    One polite way to suppress scope creep from your client is to refer back to documentation showing that the new whiz-bang feature that your client now wants is indeed scope creep and can't be completed on schedule or within budget. (Or, if you're a consultant, documentation allows you to bill the client for these wonderful features with a minimum of fuss!)

Leading a Project

Successful projects require a leader who can coordinate a number of people from different organizations with different objectives and skill sets. Yet they need to work together toward the same goal to complete the project.

Have you ever watched a group of ants moving a piece of bread that's many times bigger than any one of them? They can do this by working together and pushing in the same direction. Imagine if the ants all moved in different directions; the bread certainly wouldn't make much headway.

Communication aligns the actions of the project team and coordinates the various project stakeholders. In this section, we describe tools you can use to manage project communication.

Developing a project proposal with a team

A common vision aligns the efforts of the people who are going to execute the project. One way of getting everyone on the same page is to develop a project proposal early on and refine it together over time. The project proposal should have the following elements:

✔ **Purpose statement:** This is a high-level description of the project and its goals. Think of it as the 30-second elevator pitch to sell your project. It should include these types of content:

- An explanation of the business opportunity — why you're doing this project

- Project objectives

- Expected benefits (both tangible and intangible) in rank order

✔ **Scope:** This encompasses what the project should *include* and *exclude*.

✔ **Final deliverables not mentioned in scope (other than paperwork!).**

✔ **Rough estimate of cost and timing:** A firm may require other specific metrics such as net present value, internal rate of return, payback period, and so on. (See Chapter 15 for details on how to estimate the cash flows necessary to calculate these common business metrics.)

✔ **Stakeholder analysis:** We cover this later in the chapter.

✔ **Chain of command for the project team and customer.**

✔ **Critical assumptions:** Potentially critical obstacles and the impacts of violated assumptions.

Write the proposal for the entire project as if you plan on actually completing it. And use a cross-functional team of experts to develop it. Locking the team in a room for a couple of days to write the initial pass often yields the best results. If that's not feasible, make sure you at least pass the proposal by all of your experts to get their input.

When writing a project proposal, always use ranges for any numerical estimates. Doing so helps convey the uncertainty inherent in any estimate, particularly for early passes such as that in a project proposal. For more information on making estimates for cost and timing, see Chapter 15.

Check out `www.dummies.com/extras/operationsmanagement` for a sample project proposal for constructing and operating a concentrated solar power plant.

Communicating with stakeholders

A *stakeholder* is anyone with a stake in the outcome of a project or initiative, including anyone who can stop a project. Stakeholders can be internal or external. Internal stakeholders can include your executive sponsors, your project team members, and those team members' functional managers. The customer and the customer's management are always stakeholders, but whether they're internal or external depends on whether they're part of the same organization as the providers of the project.

Key suppliers may also be considered internal or external for various purposes, depending on how essential their participation is and how close your inter-firm relationship is. External public stakeholders include nongovernmental organizations (such as environmental lobbies or consumer safety groups), communities, and various government agencies.

Identifying stakeholders and communicating with them on a regular basis is critical to successful project management. If you regularly communicate with stakeholders and they're satisfied with a project's performance, then they're less likely to riot when there are glitches, or when it's late or over budget.

One of the first jobs of a project manager is to establish a communications plan. To do this, list your stakeholders (by name), their organization, what you need to communicate to them, how frequently, and by what means (phone, e-mail, visit, and so on). Figure 14-5 shows an example of some entries in a communications plan.

Stakeholder	Organization	Needs	Frequency/Means
John Smith	GNB Corp. (Supplier)	Project proposal	On-site meeting plus sign-off
		Progress report to you	Weekly telephone call plus e-mailed document
Sandi Jones	Bluth Industries	Project proposal	On-site meeting plus sign-off
		Progress report to her	Weekly telephone call plus e-mailed document
David Williams	Veridian Inc. (Your boss)	Project proposal	On-site meeting plus sign-off
		Progress report to him	Daily meeting in person plus weekly e-mailed document
Rhiannon Price	Veridian Inc. (Your chief software architect)	Project proposal	On-site meeting plus sign-off
		Progress report to you	Daily meeting in person plus weekly e-mailed document
Jamie Evans	Veridian Inc. (Rhiannon's functional manager)	Progress report to him	Monthly telephone call plus e-mailed document
Tom Morgan	The Guardian Local newspaper	Press release	Monthly telephone call (along with firm publicist) and press release
James Pugh	Local mayor	Progress report to him	Monthly telephone call (along with firm publicist) and press release
Ed Longshanks	Wildlife protection agency (Regulatory power over project)	Environment Impact Reports	Monthly telephone call (along with firm attorney)

Figure 14-5:
Sample entries in a communications plan.

Illustration by Wiley, Composition Services Graphics

Keeping stakeholders in the loop

One of the biggest problems you face is managing your stakeholders and (if applicable) their managers. This is particularly true of your customers. So get them all involved early. These individuals *must* sign off on the project proposal. Otherwise, your chances to please the customer are essentially zero.

You also must communicate with stakeholders frequently to manage expectations and prevent misunderstandings. You need to exchange formal documentation because it leaves a paper trail if misunderstandings occur, particularly regarding scope creep.

But don't abandon phone and/or in-person communication because these traditional platforms allow you to highlight particular problems and to provide clarification that's difficult to achieve on the written page (or even via e-mail).

Frequent progress reports are also essential. The amount of detail in your status reports depends on the size of the project and the preferences of the stakeholders in question. Moreover, you may want to manage some external stakeholders (such as public pressure groups) differently from others.

In medium-sized consulting projects (about $200,000 to $1 million of work), a weekly report may contain four elements:

1. What did we accomplish the prior week?

2. What do we intend to accomplish the next week?

3. What obstacles are standing in the way of completing the project, particularly for this next week?

4. How far along are we in the project versus where we expected to be?

Typically, answering these four questions is sufficient to keep the client in the loop and to deal with the most pressing potential problems.

A useful data point for status reports is a numerical answer to the question, "How far along are we in the project?" Write "We're about 40 to 50 percent done." This objective measure of progress seems to comfort clients. For more details on progress metrics, see Chapter 16.

Managing the team

Managing a team of employees or other types of doers in a project is much like managing other kinds of stakeholders. Upfront participation and frequent communication go a long way on the road to successful outcomes. And it's crucially important to establish crystal-clear responsibilities upfront.

With an approved project proposal in hand, you can get the project rolling by distributing the proposal to all prospective team members along with a *responsibility assignment matrix* (RAM). Assign deliverables to people according to these four categories:

✓ **Responsible:** These people do the work to complete the activity. At least one *R* needs to be assigned to each activity. Often, you'll have more.

✓ **Accountable:** These people need to sign off on the work of the people who are responsible for completing it. You should have exactly one *A* per task. A person can be both an *R* and an *A* on a task.

✓ **Consulted:** These are people who should be consulted. Typically, they're sought out for expert advice on the activity or they're responsible for related activities in the project.

✓ **Informed:** These are people who need to be informed on an ongoing basis about the project.

Project managers sometimes call a RAM a *RACI matrix* because of the initials used to fill in the matrix.

See an example RAM in Figure 14-6, and keep in mind that RAMs only work if the team members can actually see them! Be sure to distribute these documents to at least the people with an *R, A,* or *C* next to their names. No individual should have more than one letter next to his or her name for a particular task, except possibly *RA.*

There should also be a tight correspondence among the stakeholders, the communications matrix (as described in the preceding section), and the RAM matrix. In other words, if the stakeholders show up on one chart, they ought to show up on both of them.

You can modify the RAM chart later to make it much more detailed, after you create the work breakdown structure to identify all the activities in a project, as described in Chapter 15.

Activity Code	Activity Name	Victoria Project Sponsor	Marshall Business Analyst	Ted Project Manager	Lilly Software Architect	Robin Supplier Manager
A	Study market	A	R	I		
B	Prepare project proposal	A	C	R	C	
C	Sell to client	I	I	RA		
D	Architect project	C		A	R	
E	Outsource coding	I		RA	C	R
F	Perform coding	I		A	C	R
G	Integrate	I		A	R	C
H	Handover to client	A	I	R	C	C
I	After action review	RA	C	C	C	C

Figure 14-6: Example responsibility assignment matrix (RAM).

Illustration by Wiley, Composition Services Graphics

Chapter 15

Estimating and Scheduling Projects

In This Chapter

▶ Projecting time and cost from the bottom up

▶ Reducing the uncertainty of your estimates

▶ Accelerating a project or reducing its scope

*W*hen projects are late, over budget, or both, the problems are often a result of faulty estimates for the work involved and the related costs at the beginning of the effort. A vital part of project management improvement is finding a way to gather accurate estimates.

Estimating how long a project or task will take seems to be particularly difficult. Many students find that the initial timing estimates used for their projects (such as starting up new businesses) are gross underestimates. Some of this is because people have not systematically thought through all the activities needed to complete their project and have missed a number of them. Some of it arises from project managers being overly optimistic in their estimates.

A major, but subtle, problem with estimations is that you can delay some activities in a project without delaying the entire project. But this doesn't apply to all activities. Telling the difference between the two types of activities is extremely difficult without the proper tools and techniques.

This chapter presents the basics of making accurate project estimates. We describe techniques for estimating cost and timing for the project from the bottom up and figuring out which activities can be delayed safely and which can't. We tell you how to work with uncertain aspects of a project. We also point out how to avoid estimation pitfalls and accelerate the pace of completing a project.

Estimating Time and Cost

Somewhere between two-thirds and three-quarters of all projects are late, over budget, or both (see Chapter 14) — usually because of poor planning.

But that's not the whole story. Too often, estimates related to timing and cost are faulty from the beginning, which makes hitting the estimates nearly impossible.

Unlike processes, which occur over and over (and over), projects are one-time gigs. Estimating the time and cost of a process that has tons of backstory is pretty simple because you can just look at the historical data and work it out with math. But building accurate estimates for a project — work that has never been done before — is challenging. There's little data to guide the predictions.

Grasping for context or boundaries, people often make estimates based on how much time and money is available. They fail to put enough consideration into the specific tasks involved in the work. This approach generates nearly useless estimates.

So what's the answer? Where do accurate estimates come from? The first step is planning — from the bottom up. In this section, we tell you how to break down a project into the tasks it requires and then use that information to connect the dots of costs and timing to reveal a clear picture of the project at hand.

Compiling a list of tasks

Building estimates from the bottom up is better than working from the top down because it's so easy to forget key things that need to be done when working from the top down. Similar to the process of building physical structures, you want to start conceptualizing a project by developing a solid foundation and gathering the components you'll need for construction — before you start building. List all the activities, or operations, that the project requires, using as much detail as possible.

You can do this in a spreadsheet, but the task of compiling the individual components of a project is usually done in a *work breakdown structure* (WBS). Figure 15-1 shows a classic table version of a typical WBS. This example describes the activities required to host a business banquet — by category.

Here are some guidelines for creating a WBS:

🖈 A WBS is hierarchical. At the top is a description of the entire project, and each category of activities is identified under the project title. Under each category is a lineup of specific tasks.

Name each task or activity and category with a verb and an object to ensure the item is descriptive and easy to take in at a glance. Don't worry too much about using any specific wording. The important thing is to provide a quick and easy reference.

✔ To estimate the time it takes to complete an activity, determine how many hours or minutes it would likely take one person (or other appropriate resource) to complete the activity if he were working 100 percent of the available time on that activity. This is not calendar time. If you think it will take 40 hours of work to complete an activity over a two-month period, write down 40 hours on the WBS, not one week or two months.

✔ Break down the project into enough detail that allows you to present activities that each take somewhere between 8 and 80 hours to complete. If any single operation requires more than 80 hours, further segment it into two or more smaller activities. Note that this rule works best for middle-sized projects. If your project is huge, like designing a new jumbo jet, you'll have to aggregate more.

✔ List activities in chronological order, if possible and appropriate, but don't obsess over this. Often, activities overlap or occur as possible; sequencing isn't that important for a WBS.

Be sure that your WBS includes a category that contains all the upfront and ongoing planning and supervisory activities for the project. These operations require time and money, too! In fact, planning can take up to a quarter of a project's budget. And that's okay. What's not okay is skimping on these tasks because you fail to budget for them or simply forget them during the madness of executing the project.

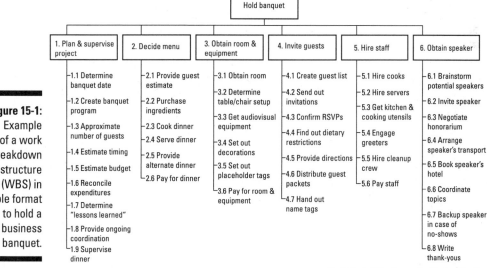

Figure 15-1: Example of a work breakdown structure (WBS) in table format to hold a business banquet.

Illustration by Wiley, Composition Services Graphics

Getting stakeholder input

Forgetting to account for an activity in work-breakdown structures is a common and potentially painful mistake. To ensure that you include all the operations that a project requires, gather appropriate stakeholders (such as representatives for each of the activity categories; see more on stakeholders in Chapter 14) and ask each person in the group to name a task that needs to be done to complete the project. Use a white board to record this information. Often, a suggestion by one person triggers a cascade of ideas from others. Continue this process until the group is out of new ideas. When a list of tasks is complete, ask the project stakeholders to cluster the activities into groups of five to eight tasks and then name the categories.

If you can't hold such a group meeting, you can create the document and route it by e-mail for input from the category representatives. In fact, even if you do have the meeting, one of the first things you need to do after you create an initial WBS document is to ask stakeholders to review it and provide feedback. No question, stakeholders will identify activities that you haven't thought of, and you need to add these activities to the WBS.

Formatting the WBS

For some projects, using a list format (instead of a table) for the WBS makes it easier to present the details of the operations (see Figure 15-2). You can create a list format with a standard word-processing program and include notes for individual items if needed.

Just keep in mind that the WBS is a living document and will likely change over time as a project evolves.

The Project Management Institute, an international standards organization for promoting good project management, calls individual activities *work packages* and groups of activities *summary tasks.* In Figure 15-2, *Decide menu* is a summary task and *Provide guest estimate* is a work package.

The WBS has a natural hierarchy associated with it. It's customary to number each of the activities and titles to show a sequential order. In other words, *Send out invitations* in Figure 15-2 has a two-level number, 4.2, because it's the second task of the fourth category in the hierarchy. It's important to point out that the numbers are simply used for reference; 4.2 is not more important than, or doesn't necessarily need to happen before, 4.3 or 6.3.

For really complex projects, like building an offshore oil extraction platform, the number of levels in the hierarchy can get quite high. A not-so-complex example of deepening the hierarchy is to consider all the actual steps of creating a guest list for a wedding. For example, you need to secure names and addresses from the bride and the groom, as well as names and addresses for guests that the bride's parents want to invite and the same for the groom's parents. Then the primary stakeholders (that's the bride and groom and their parents) must negotiate to create a final list of guests.

Hold banquet WBS

1. Plan & supervise project

1.1. Determine banquet date
1.2. Create banquet program
1.3. Approximate number of guests
1.4. Estimate timing
1.5. Estimate budget
1.6. Reconcile expenditures
1.7. Determine "lessons learned"
1.8. Provide ongoing coordination
1.9. Supervise dinner

2. Decide menu

2.1. Provide guest estimate
2.2. Purchase ingredients
2.3. Cook dinner
2.4. Serve dinner
2.5. Provide alternate dinner for dietary restrictions
2.6. Pay for dinner

3. Obtain room & equipment

3.1. Obtain room
3.2. Determine table/chair setup
3.3. Get audiovisual equipment
3.4. Set out decorations
3.5. Set out placeholder tags
3.6. Pay for room & equipment

4. Invite guests

4.1. Create guest list
4.2. Send out invitations
4.3. Confirm RSVPs
4.4. Find out dietary restrictions
4.5. Provide directions
4.6. Distribute guest packets
4.7. Hand out name tags

5. Hire staff

5.1. Hire cooks
5.2. Hire servers
5.3. Get kitchen & cooking utensils
5.4. Engage greeters
5.5. Hire cleanup crew
5.6. Pay staff

6. Obtain speaker

6.1. Brainstorm potential speakers
6.2. Invite speaker
6.3. Negotiate honorarium
6.4. Arrange speaker's transport
6.5. Book speaker's hotel
6.6. Coordinate topics
6.7. Backup speaker in case of no-shows
6.8. Write thank-you's

Figure 15-2:
Paragraph
(or list)
version
of a work
breakdown
structure
(WBS)
to hold a
business
banquet.

Illustration by Wiley, Composition Services Graphics

If *Create guest list* is a 4.1 operation that's comparable to the item 4.1 in Figure 15-2, then here's how this additional layer to the WBS for a project titled *Host Wedding* may look:

- 4.1.1 Create bride's guest list

- 4.1.2 Create groom's guest list

- 4.1.3 Create bride's parents' guest list

- 4.1.4 Create groom's parents' guest list

- 4.1.5 Combine all guest lists

- 4.1.6 Figure out how many guests the budget can accommodate

- 4.1.7 Adjust guest list to hit target number

In short, if estimating the timing and/or cost of an activity is easier by breaking it down into finer details, then break it down. If aggregating two or more activities makes estimating easier, then aggregate. Ultimately, the purpose of the WBS is to account for all the activities in a project and to generate accurate estimates for the project's timing and cost.

Adding up the project costs

For each activity in the work breakdown structure, you need to calculate a cost. For example, *Get audiovisual equipment* may simply be a cash transaction with the banquet venue. Or you may need to bring in a computer and rent a projector. In that case, you need to consider the cost of renting a projector as well as costs to pay someone to acquire the audiovisual equipment, transport it to the venue, hook it up, and make sure it works.

A reality is that the bulk of the budget for many business projects goes to paying for the time people spend working on the project. Even if you're already paying these people a salary, if their work time is devoted to one project, then they're not available for other operations.

Calculating the probable cost of a project is vital, and the pivotal tool is a good WBS. With a comprehensive list of activities that a project requires, you can begin identifying what resources (both people and equipment) you need to accomplish each task — and then how much the resource costs.

For example, say that the rental fee for audiovisual equipment for the banquet illustrated in Figure 15-1 is $500. On top of that, you need someone to pick up the equipment, transport it, set it up, and monitor it during the banquet. If these tasks require 12 hours of work and the cost of labor is $25 per hour, then the cost for this activity increases by $300. This brings the total cost for *Get audiovisual equipment* to $800 — and don't forget that there's probably a cost for someone to make sure that this person completes the audiovisual work, which needs to be budgeted as part of the ongoing coordination activity.

Go through this type of process to develop a cost estimate for each of the other activities in the WBS — and then add them to get the total project estimate up!

Large projects with very long time horizons may experience inflation (or in some cases, deflation) for supplies and labor during the life of the project. Estimating inflation and deflation incorrectly contributes to costing error.

Figure 15-3 shows a cost estimate for an electronics-module development project. The salary per person for each month of work on each operation on this project is $4,000 (except activities 1.1 and 3.3). This means that activity 2.1, *Internal design,* costs $20,000 for five months ($4,000 · 5).

Note that Eamonn, the internal design resource, may take eight calendar months (not five) to complete the internal design operation because he gets interrupted by other projects, training classes, and so forth. But this project is only charged for the actual time this resource spends working on it.

Activity	Description	Duration (months)	Cost per Person-Month	Total Personnel Cost	Equipment Cost	Total Activity Cost	Allocated Resource(s)
1.1	Architecture	2	$7,000	$14,000	$0	$14,000	Albert
2.1	Internal design	5	$4,000	$20,000	$0	$20,000	Eamonn
2.2	Internal build	2.5	$4,000	$10,000	$0	$10,000	Eamonn
2.3	External design	4	$4,000	$16,000	$0	$16,000	Michelle
2.4	External build	3	$4,000	$12,000	$0	$12,000	Michelle
3.1	Integration I	1.5	$4,000	$6,000	$0	$6,000	Sid
3.2	Self-test	4	$4,000	$16,000	$5,000	$21,000	Tania
3.3	Assembly	1.6	$3,500	$5,600	$12,000	$17,600	Guido
3.4	Integration II	2.3	$4,000	$9,200	$0	$9,200	Sid
4.1	Acceptance test	3	$4,000	$12,000	$10,000	$22,000	Diana
4.2	Final test	1.8	$4,000	$14,400	$5,000	$19,400	Petra, Roberto

Figure 15-3: Cost worksheet for an electronics development project.

Illustration by Wiley, Composition Services Graphics

Activity 3.3, *Assembly,* requires a bit more calculation. Guido spends 1.6 months working to complete the activity at $3,500 per month. Equipment costs are also associated with assembly. So the total cost for activity 3.3 is $5,600 (1.6 · $3,500) plus $12,000 = $17,600.

Watch out for activities that require multiple employees. For example, activity 4.2, *Final test,* uses Petra and Roberto; both need to be paid, so the total cost for this activity is 2 · $4,000 = $8,000 · 1.8 months = $19,400.

To get the estimated cost for the entire project, just add up all the activity costs. Doing this in Figure 15-3 results in a total cost for the project of $167,200.

Timing: The critical path

Unlike estimating cost for a project, timing estimates aren't a matter of simple addition — chiefly because some activities can happen at the same time. Figuring out how much time you need for various activities and what can happen when is tough to do in your head. So don't try.

Instead, develop a critical path diagram. A *critical path diagram* identifies which activities need to be completed before other activities begin. These activities are also called *predecessors* and must be carried out before the subsequent dependent activities can begin. The critical path diagram is an important reference for determining which operations can happen at the same time and which can be scheduled independently. It also tells you which activities can be delayed without delaying the entire project — and which ones can't.

Activities that can't be delayed without jeopardizing the project schedule overall are called *critical path activities;* their sequence is called the *critical path.* The critical path determines the shortest possible timing of the project. A project always has a critical path. It's neither good nor bad. What's important is that you identify it correctly.

Consider a volunteer project to build an outdoor sitting area with several benches. The activities related to this project are described in Table 15-1. Sometimes, you may see activities labeled with letter identifiers instead of numbers, so we use letters here.

Table 15-1	Description of Activities for an Outdoor Sitting Area Project		
Label	*Tasks*	*Predecessors*	*Days*
A	Select site with client	None	1
B	Recruit volunteers	None	21
C	Get landscaping tools	B	7
D	Secure donations	None	30
E	Build park benches	B	2
F	Clear sitting area of trees and debris	B, C	0.5
G	Buy materials	A, D	0.25
H	Transport materials to work site	G	0.25
I	Landscape sitting area with crushed limestone	B, C, F, H	0.25
J	Situate benches in sitting area	E, I	0.15
K	Clean up	J	0.3

To begin the process of determining timing requirements for this project, look for activities without predecessors — activities that can begin without any other activity being completed beforehand. In Table 15-1, activities A, B, and D qualify; they can start before any other activities are complete.

Next, identify activities that do have predecessors. In the outdoor sitting area project, volunteers supply the landscaping tools, so activity C is dependent on activity B. Activity E is also dependent on activity B for the labor. Activity G needs to be preceded by both Activity A (because the size of the site determines how much material is required) and D (because you need money to buy materials). Activity I requires completion of activities B, C, F, and H.

If you have any doubt about whether an activity is a predecessor, go ahead and list it as one. Adding a predecessor unnecessarily won't affect your timing calculations, but missing a necessary dependence will almost always mess up your calculations.

Now you're ready to draw a critical path diagram. Follow these steps to create a diagram for the outdoor sitting area project:

1. **Put each activity with no predecessors in a circle.**

    Arrange these circles in a vertical line if you can, although this isn't critical. In Figure 15-4, these activities are A, B, and D.

    If you don't have enough space in the circles (called *nodes*) to list the title of an activity, use its label.

2. **Label each activity with an estimated duration inside the circle.**

    In Figure 15-4, time is presented in units of days.

3. **Draw a new circle to the left of the circles showing activities with no predecessors.**

    Label it *Start,* with a duration of 0.

4. **Connect the start node to the initial activities with an arrow.**

    The direction of the arrows indicates which activities are predecessors and which are successors.

5. **Then, working sequentially, find the activities that follow the existing activity circles and add them to the diagram, placing them to the right of their predecessor(s).**

6. **Continue this process until no more activities remain.**

7. **Add a final node and label it *End,* with a duration of 0.**

    Connect all the activities with no successors to the End activity. You now have a complete critical path diagram, also sometimes called a critical path method (or CPM) diagram.

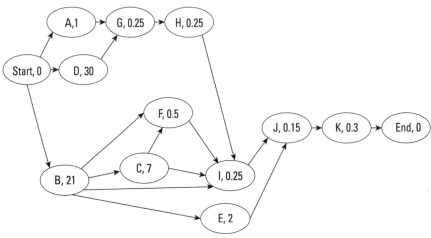

Illustration by Wiley, Composition Services Graphics

Figure 15-4:
Critical path diagram for an outside sitting area project.

Performing a forward pass

With a critical path diagram complete, you can calculate a timing estimate for your project. Follow these steps to perform a *forward pass analysis,* which defines the earliest start times and earliest finish times for each activity. This also identifies the earliest finish time for the project as a whole:

1. **Begin by writing the earliest start (ES) time (which is customarily 0) in the upper-left corner of the start node.**

2. **Add the duration of the start node (0 days) to determine the earliest finish (EF) time for the start node and mark it in the upper-right corner of the node.**

   That is, *EF = ES + Duration.*

3. **All the activities that can begin right away (activities with no predecessors) have an ES time of 0 because they are successors to the start node.**

   In Figure 15-5, B's ES time is 0, as noted in the upper-left corner. The duration of this activity is 21, which means that B's EF Time = ES Time + Duration = 0 + 21 days = 21 days. This information is noted in the upper-right corner of the activity's node.

4. **Subsequent activities, operations with a predecessor, have an ES time that's equal to the earliest finish time of its predecessor.**

   In Figure 15-5, this means that Activity C's ES is 21. Its duration is 7, so C's EF time is 28.

5. **If an activity has two predecessors, then its ES is the later of the two predecessor's EF times.**

   In Figure 15-5, Activity F has two predecessors, B and C, with earliest finish times of 21 and 28, respectively. So F's ES is 28. Its EF time is 28 + 0.5 = 28.5 days.

6. **Continue noting the ES and EF times for all the activities on the diagram.**

   Note an EF time on the End node. In Figure 15-5, the EF time, 31.2 days, is the minimum time needed to complete the project.

Working backward

When you've finished entering timing data for a forward pass analysis, you can create the *backward pass analysis,* which determines the latest times an activity can be started and finished without compromising the timing of the project as a whole. Follow these steps to complete this part of the diagram:

1. **Set the latest finish (LF) time for the project by setting the LF of the END note equal to its EF time.**

   Mark this time in the lower-right corner of the End node.

2. **Subtract the duration of the End node (0 days) from the latest finish time to get the latest start (LS) time.**

   That is, LS = LF minus Duration. Mark the LS in the lower-left corner of the node.

3. **The LF time for all the activities in the diagram is equal to the LS time of its successor activity.**

   In Figure 15-5, for example, the LF time of activity J is the LS time of activity K, which is 30.9 days. J's duration is 0.15, so its LS time is 30.9 minus 0.15 = 30.75.

4. **If an activity has several successors, its EF time is the earliest of the successors' LS times.**

   In Figure 15-5, Activity C has two successors, F and I. F's LS time is 30, and I's is 30.5. So C's LF time is 30.

5. **Repeat this process until you get back to the start node.**

   If the start node's LS time is something other than 0, you've made a mistake.

Pointing out slack

Now you need to calculate *slacks.* The slack for each activity is the amount of time that its finish can be delayed without lengthening the completion time of the entire project. Find slack by subtracting the EF time from the LF time. That is, Slack = LF minus EF. For example, in Figure 15-5, activity B's slack is 23 minus 21 = 2.0 days. Note the slack for each activity somewhere convenient.

Finding and using the critical path

The project's *critical path* is the sequence of activities with zero slack and is the longest possible path through the CPM diagram in terms of timing. The critical path is what determines the timing of the project. Note that it's possible to have more than one critical path if the two (or more) longest paths through the CPM diagram have the same duration.

Figure 15-5 shows a completed critical path diagram of the project defined in Figure 15-4.

Ensuring that none of the activities on the critical path is delayed ensures that the work is completed according to time estimates. For this reason, it helps prioritize a project manager's time by identifying what activities need the most attention at specific periods in the process.

Keep in mind that the critical path diagram, like all other project management documents and tools, is a living thing. If the actual completion time of an activity exceeds your estimates by more than its slack, then you need to recalculate the critical path.

Use the critical path to determine timing. Never use it to determine cost because the critical path does not include all the activities related to a project. And you need to account for all activities when calculating cost. For example, in Table 15-1, activity E *(Building park benches)* is not on the critical path; it doesn't affect timing. But if you have to hire someone to complete that activity, you still need to pay the person two days of labor, which must be included in the project cost estimate.

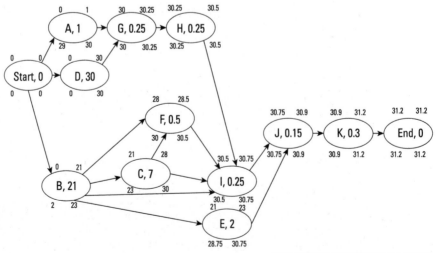

Figure 15-5:
Critical path diagram with timing data.

Illustration by Wiley, Composition Services Graphics

Assigning tasks

You must assign someone to be responsible for each activity in a project. Otherwise, it's unlikely to be completed. Making this assignment through the work breakdown structure (WBS) is a popular technique.

Be sure to watch out for resource conflicts (covered in Chapter 4) when you assign an individual to handle certain activities. A critical job for the project manager is finding and removing *hidden dependencies,* which are situations when one task is delayed because it shares a resource with another activity.

For example, in Figure 15-6, the critical path seems to be Start-A-B-D-End, which appears to take an estimated 46 days (0 + 14 + 20 + 12 + 0).

Figure 15-6:
Critical path
diagram
showing a
resource
conflict.

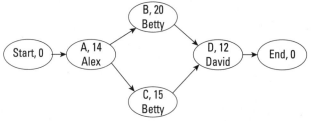

Illustration by Wiley, Composition Services Graphics

But a closer look reveals that Betty is working on Activity B and Activity C. Time estimates in project management generally assume that a resource is working on an activity 100 percent of the time, so Betty can't work on both B and C simultaneously without stretching out their duration. There is a hidden dependency between B and C!

The actual critical path (because of the shared resource for B and C) is Start-A-B-C-D-End (or Start-A-C-B-D-End), which means the duration of the project is 0 + 14 + 20 + 15 + 12 + 0 = 61 days. The only way to get activity C off the critical path and reduce the timing back down to 46 days is to assign someone other than Betty to perform either B or C.

Presenting the schedule

As discussed in Chapter 14, keeping the client and other stakeholders for your project in the loop with schedules and other project information is critical. However, critical path method diagrams are not useful tools for communicating or visualizing schedules. Something else is needed.

Most project managers use a Gantt chart (developed by Henry Gantt, an early operations management guru) for this purpose. A simplified version of the outdoor sitting area project, which you might present to potential donors or your client, is shown in Figure 15-7. The bars to the right of each activity indicate when the activity will take place. The right side of the rightmost bar in the Gantt chart indicates when the project will be completed.

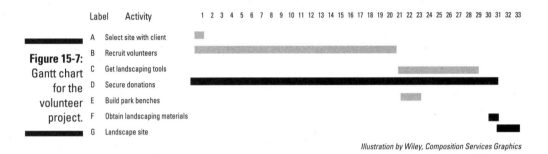

Figure 15-7: Gantt chart for the volunteer project.

Label	Activity
A	Select site with client
B	Recruit volunteers
C	Get landscaping tools
D	Secure donations
E	Build park benches
F	Obtain landscaping materials
G	Landscape site

Illustration by Wiley, Composition Services Graphics

Indicating dependencies in a Gantt chart is difficult. Many people show the activities that belong to the critical chain (and hence have no slack) in a different color. In Figure 15-7, this is black. While it doesn't give any direct information on dependencies, one can get some indication of an activity's slack from a Gantt chart. So while it is excellent for visualization and communication, it hides much critical information. So it needs to be used in conjunction with a critical path analysis, not instead of it.

Working with Uncertainty

Estimates are uncertain. One wit once commented that "the only certain thing about estimates is that they will be wrong." So, you may be wondering how you can communicate this uncertainty (and how big it is) to others and how you can reduce the uncertainty in your estimates. In this section, we address these puzzling questions.

Estimating with ranges

All *point estimates* — estimates that center on a single point, such as 145 days for a project duration as opposed to a range estimate of 140 to 170 days — will almost certainly be wrong. If you say a project is going to be completed in 12 days, you may be done in 12 days, but in most cases, you'll be much more likely to finish the project in 9, 10, 11, 13, 14, 15, or some other number of days.

Another problem with point estimates is that they imply much more certainty about the completion time than you probably want. The reality is that 12 days — even if calculated with great care — is a guess, and being able to convey the uncertainty inherent in this estimate can set up more realistic expectations among the project stakeholders.

If you use a range estimate, such as "between 10 and 15 days," then you have a better chance of being correct. And the mere fact that you're using a range conveys a more appropriate level of uncertainty than a specific number of days. The gap between the lower and upper end conveys how uncertain the estimate is — a 20-day spread is far less certain than a 4-day range.

In the project management world, percentiles are expressed by *P* followed by the percentile. A *P95* estimate of 15 days means that the project has a 95 percent chance of being completed in 15 days or fewer. A *P05* or *P5* estimate of 8 days means that a project has a 5 percent chance of being completed in 8 days or fewer.

So how do you set the range? The most popular options for timing and cost estimates are ranges defined by the P5 and P95 estimates. Using a P5–P95 range means that your actual timing or cost has a 95 percent – 5 percent = 90 percent chance of falling within the estimate range.

Using historical data

The best way to calculate the end-points of an estimate range, particularly if you're using a P5–P95 range, is to use any cost or duration data you have on similar activities that you've done on other projects in the past. You may have written or computer records. Ideally, if you can find a number of similar activities that would be best, because from this data, you need to find the *mean* (representing the expected value) and the *standard deviation* (to determine the range of error) for each activity. Then you can calculate cost and timing estimates for the entire project, as we show later in this section.

The expected value is the mean average of a number of observations. Mathematically, the expected value for a number of observations $X_1, X_2 \ldots X_n$, is

$$\frac{X_1 + X_2 + \ldots + X_n}{n}$$

A major pitfall when using historical data is assuming that the nature of the activity has stayed the same over time. For example, drilling oil wells now is much more complicated than it was even ten years ago, because drills need to go to much greater depths to extract oil; this raises both cost and duration.

Similarly, creating the artistic renderings for videogames on newer platforms is much more expensive and time consuming than it was in the past because the platforms can render almost photorealistic animation. In contrast, paving roads has not changed much in terms of timing over the past several decades, although the labor cost per hour of work has increased.

The standard deviation is the square root of the variance. Mathematically, the variance for a number of observations $X_1, X_2, \ldots X_n$, is

$$\frac{(X_1 - \mu)^2 + (X_2 - \mu)^2 + \ldots + (X_n - \mu)^2}{n-1}$$

where the μ is the expected value (mean) of X. You can think of the standard deviation as roughly speaking the average distance an observation is from the mean. People often confuse the variance and the standard deviation.

Standard deviations are often easier to work with to develop timing and cost estimates because they can be in the same units (days, months, dollars) as the factor you're trying to estimate, but you can't add them together. You can, however, add variances.

Figure 15-8 shows the historical data for an electronics project. Use it first to calculate cost of the project. To find the expected cost (mean) for the entire project, add together the mean costs for all the activities in the project. This gives you a sum of $122,800, which is the expected cost of the project.

Getting the standard deviation is trickier because you can't directly add standard deviations together. You need to square each activity's standard deviation to get a variance. Then you can add up the activity variances to get the variance for the cost of the entire project, $3200^2 + $12,000^2 + \ldots + $1600^2 = 588,640,000. The square root of 588,640,000 is $24,262, which is the standard deviation of the estimated cost for the project.

So the estimated cost of the project has a mean of $122,800 and a standard deviation of $24,262. With this information, you can calculate the P05, P10, and so forth.

If you add up enough activities, you can obtain a normal distribution for the estimate thanks to the *central limit theorem* from statistics, which says that if you add up more and more independent random variables, the sum will look more and more like a normal distribution (also called a bell curve).

How many activities is enough depends on the shape of their own historical distributions. A rough rule of thumb is that 30 usually is enough, but if the individual activities have normal distributions themselves, then you can get by with a lot fewer. For purposes of estimation, most real-world projects that are complicated enough to detailed estimation have enough activities to get an approximately normal distribution.

Activity	Description	Predecessors	Mean Duration (months)	Std. Deviation (months)	Mean Cost (dollars)	Std. Deviation (dollars)	Allocated Resource(s)
A	Architecture	none	2	0.8	$8,000	$3,200	Alice
B	Internal design	A	5	3	$20,000	$12,000	Edmond
C	Internal build	B	2.5	1	$10,000	$4,000	Edmond
D	External design	A	4	4	$16,000	$16,000	Mikayla
E	External build	D	3	2	$12,000	$8,000	Mikayla
F	Integration I	C, E, G	1.5	0.5	$6,000	$2,000	Sam
G	Self-test	A	4	2	$16,000	$8,000	Toni
H	Assembly	F	1.6	0.5	$6,400	$2,000	George
J	Integration II	H	2.3	0.7	$9,200	$2,800	Sam
K	Acceptance test	B, D	3	1	$12,000	$4,000	Dolly
L	Final test	J, K	1.8	0.4	$7,200	$1,600	Paula

Figure 15-8: Historical timing and cost data for example project.

Illustration by Wiley, Composition Services Graphics

With a normal distribution, you can figure out a particular percentile. Use the following equation, where PXX represents the P5, P50, P90, or other percentile:

$$PXX = \mu + z\sigma$$

The μ is the expected value (mean), σ is the standard deviation, and z is the number of standard deviations that the estimate is above (or, if z is negative, below) the mean.

Because the estimates are normally distributed, you can find the value for z in any standard z-chart for the normal distribution. Figure 15-9 presents a table of the z's for the most commonly used values of P.

Figure 15-9: Z values for the most commonly encountered values of P.

P-value	Z
P05	−1.64
P10	−1.28
P50	0
P90	1.28
P95	1.64

Illustration by Wiley, Composition Services Graphics

In the example in Figure 15-9, the P90 estimate for cost is

$$P90 = \mu + 1.28\sigma = \$122,800 + 1.28(\$24,262) = \$153,855$$

The P10 estimate is

$$P10 = \mu + (-1.28)\sigma = \$122,800 - 1.28(\$18,859) = \$91,745$$

When you communicate with your colleagues about the cost of the project, you can just say, "It has a P10 to P90 range of $92 thousand to $154 thousand." It's a good idea to round off your figures so that you don't give the impression that your estimate is more accurate than it really is.

To calculate the time estimate for the project, you need to adjust the critical path method a bit. This adjustment is called the *program evaluation and review technique* (better known as PERT). The technique was developed originally by the U.S. Navy to manage the building of nuclear submarines.

Here's the PERT process:

1. **Get the mean and standard deviation estimates for each activity.**

2. **Use the mean timing estimates for each activity to draw a critical path diagram.**

3. **Identify the critical path.**

4. **Add up the means of all the activities on the critical path.**

   This is the mean for your project's duration.

5. **Add up the variances of all the activities on the critical path.**

   This sum is the variance for your project's duration; the square root of that variance is the project's standard deviation.

6. **Then you can find the values for P10, P50, and P90 (or alternately P5, P50, and P95) using P = $\mu + z\sigma$.**

Make sure to use the means as the durations in the PERT critical path diagram! If you use a P50, median, or mode for individual activity durations instead, you'll underestimate the project mean, because activity durations typically are *not* normally distributed.

Figure 15-10 shows the PERT version of the critical path diagram for the example electronics project. The critical path is Start-A-B-C-F-H-J-L-End. Adding up the expected (mean) durations for each activity on the critical path yields an expected duration for the project of 16.7 months.

Adding up the variances for each activity on the critical path yields a project timing variance of 11.79. The square root of this variance reveals a standard deviation for the project timing of 3.43 months.

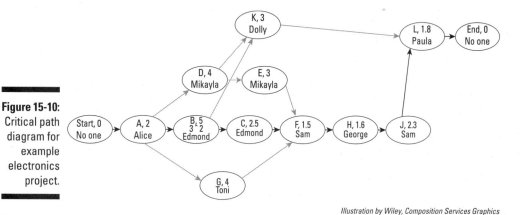

Figure 15-10:
Critical path
diagram for
example
electronics
project.

From this, the P90 estimate is

$$\mu + 1.28\sigma = 16.7 \text{ months} + 1.28(3.43 \text{ months}) = 21.1 \text{ months.}$$

The P10 estimate is

$$\mu + (-1.28)\sigma = 16.7 \text{ months} - 1.28(3.43 \text{ months}) = 12.3 \text{ months.}$$

This tells you that the project has a 90 percent chance of being completed within 21.1 months or less and only a 10 percent chance of being completed within 12.3 months or less. Now you have your range: The project will be complete in 12.3 to 21.1 months according to your P10–P90 range estimate.

Sometimes the PERT assumption that the P90 (or P95, if you use that instead) of the critical path is approximately equal to the P90 of the project as a whole can lead you astray. This, which could result in a significant underestimate, happens most often if a very high-risk activity — one with a large standard deviation — is on a path that's almost as long as the critical path. To avoid this, calculate the P90 for each path in the project, and use the biggest P90 path estimate as the P90 estimate for the entire project.

For example, the expected duration of the Start-A-D-E-F-H-J-L-End path is 16.2 months (which is a little less than that of the critical path), and the standard deviation is 4.67 months (which is significantly higher than the critical path). Using these numbers yields a P90 for this near-critical path of

$$P90 = \mu + 1.28\sigma = 16.2 \text{ months} + 1.28(4.67 \text{ months}) = 22.2 \text{ months.}$$

Because 22.2 months is greater than the critical path's P90 of 21.1 months, use 22.2 months as your P90 estimate of the project as a whole.

Relying on expert knowledge

Sometimes data for a particular activity doesn't exist. What do you do then? The rule of thumb that the U.S. Navy developed as part of the PERT methodology is to find the industry expert who is most familiar with the activity. Then have him or her make the following three estimates related to the activity's time to completion.

- ✔ **Minimum:** Estimate the minimum time that it will take to complete the activity. Tell the expert that only a 5 percent chance of completing the activity in less time than this minimum estimate (or 1 chance in 20) should exist. This is the equivalent to a P5 estimate.

- ✔ **Most likely:** Estimate the most likely duration for the activity. This is the mode (not the median or mean). In practice, this is the estimate people usually give anyway. They are unlikely to provide the mean, because this isn't an intuitive number to calculate in your head. But the expert might give you a P50 (median). If this happens, don't worry because the median usually results in only a slight overestimate, and overestimates are generally much less problematic for project managers than underestimates!

- ✔ **Maximum:** Estimate the maximum amount of time that it will take to complete the activity. Tell the expert that only a 5 percent chance of the project duration exceeding this maximum estimate (or 1 chance in 20) should exist. This is the equivalent to a P95 estimate.

After you have these three estimates, use the following two equations to get the PERT 3-point estimates for the expected value (mean) for the activity's duration and the corresponding standard deviation:

$$Mean = \frac{minimum + (4 \bullet most\ likely) + maximum}{6}$$

$$Std.\ Deviation = \frac{maximum - minimum}{6}$$

For example, assume that you are trying to calculate the mean and standard deviation to remodel a kitchen. The project manager gives you minimum, most likely, and maximum estimates of 2 weeks, 4 weeks, and 10 weeks.

Do you notice that the most likely estimate is significantly closer to the minimum than it is to the maximum? This is typical of most activities. If this isn't true in your estimates, be suspicious.

In this case, the expected value (mean) estimate of the activity's duration is (2 weeks + 4 · (4 weeks) + 10 weeks)/6 = 4.67 weeks. The standard deviation is (10 weeks – 2 weeks)/6 = 1.33 weeks. The expected value of 4.67 weeks is greater than the most likely estimate for the activity. This is normal because many things in an activity are much more likely to go wrong than right. (Yes, the great project manager in the sky is a pessimist.) In fact, the gap might be much larger.

With the estimates, you can use them to replace the historical estimates you used in the PERT method. Then calculate the critical path and duration of the project as a whole — just as if you're working with historical data.

Use the same approach to estimate cost. For example, if your kitchen remodeling has minimum, most likely, and maximum estimates of $13,000, $25,000, and $65,000, then your expected cost is $29,700, and the standard deviation is $8670. You then replace the historical data with your numbers to determine overall project cost estimates.

The PERT 3-point estimates assume that you're getting the actual minimum and maximum estimate of an activity's duration (or cost). But research shows that people (even experts) can't accurately determine these end points very well; they often give you a P5 and P95 when you ask for the minimum and maximum (even if you ask them not to). This causes the mean and the standard deviation to be underestimated.

To address this issue, statisticians often use these formulas instead:

- ✔ Mean = (0.185 · minimum + 0.63 · P50 + 0.185 · maximum)
- ✔ Standard deviation = (maximum – minimum)/3.25

Note that the P50 is really the P50 estimate (the median) in this formula, not the most likely estimate (the mode).

Putting It All Together

As you make all your calculations for a project, bear in mind that they aren't set in stone just because they crank out a number. You also have to cope with meeting the expectations of management, which may differ from your estimates. However, you can often adjust the assumptions behind the estimates by adding resources to the project to accelerate it or by reducing the scope of the project, which reduces the number of required activities.

Avoiding the estimation dance

Good project managers are pessimists. Things go wrong much more often than they go right in a project because of unforeseen circumstances. And every estimate is a contract. When estimates are exceeded — because of scope creep or other common issues — clients tend to punish the providers who developed the estimate. Padding estimates with additional time or money is usually much less problematic for contractors than being punished for being late. Many people and companies pad their project estimates to avoid exceeding them.

Here's how it may go: A well-respected consultant spends a great deal of time setting up his WBS and laboriously works through the critical path to get a timing estimate for a project. Then he multiplies the estimate by 2 before giving it to his client. He says he does this for two reasons: No project ever has the same scope at the end as it does at the start, and clients always want a little more and don't want to pay for it. So that's why he multiplies the initial estimate by 2. However, he says that even this doesn't provide enough padding in case things go wrong, so he multiplies the initial estimate by 3 to provide some padding and give him something like a P90 level of protection.

Padding (also known as sandbagging), however, sabotages the effort of making good project estimates. To avoid the near-endless back-and-forth negotiation process that fake estimates spark, try to keep your estimates clean. Use range estimates; they have some padding already built in. And be very careful about punishing employees for missing their targets if they create a good-faith, workmanlike estimate for their activity.

Accelerating the project

Sometimes a project manager needs to speed up a project. Fortunately, you can often do this by spending money on overtime, extra work crews, and other investments to shrink project duration. Spending money on an activity to accelerate its completion is called *crashing* the project. The trick is figuring out which activities to crash.

The traditional way to accelerate timing is to hit the cheapest activity to crash on the critical path. This works well in a lot of cases, but the critical path is defined by the expected estimate, not the worst-case estimate, which is probably more important for you to manage in an acceleration situation. So look at high-risk activities that are not on the critical path as candidates for crashing. Almost anything that has to do with the government or technology tends to be high-risk with respect to timing.

One PC manufacturer had a significant technology risk developing a portable with a new type of lithium battery. This was not on the critical path if the technology worked, but if the technology failed, it would have delayed the project. The company's solution was to spend some extra money developing a more standard old-technology nickel-cadmium battery in parallel to the lithium battery. If the lithium batter failed, the firm would just substitute in the nickel-cadmium battery, preventing a late completion of the project.

Chapter 16

Responding to Risks That Threaten Your Project

· ·

· ·

Responding to risk in the cost, quality, scope, and especially timing of your project can only be done well if you can identify and prepare for those risks beforehand. Trying to correct for those risks without preparation delays your response time, letting things only get more out of control as you try to develop response plans on the fly. One of the marks of a superb project manager is his ability to anticipate, plan for, and successfully manage project risks.

In this chapter, we explore the two key tools needed to manage risk effectively. One is a good tracking system so that you know whether your project is on schedule and budget. In practice, this is trickier than it sounds. However, there are some common methods that work well.

The other main tool is a structured approach to identifying and preparing for risk ahead of time. By identifying cost, quality, scope, and especially timing risks ahead of time, sometimes you can eliminate them entirely at the beginning of the project at relatively low cost. For other risks, you may take a wait-and-see approach. However, if the worst does happen, having a contingency plan in place can make the difference between successfully coping with a problem and having that problem sink your project.

Finally, sometimes you fall behind despite your best efforts to anticipate and manage obstacles. What do you do? The answers are not intuitive. For example, adding lots of extra employees often can sink your project because the resources you need to get them up to speed must be stolen from completing the project. We finish the chapter by discussing these problems and how best to cope with them.

Tracking Project Progress

One of the major causes of project failure is poor tracking of project progress. The reason for this is that it's almost always easier and more effective to make corrective actions earlier rather than later in a project's execution. If you can't or don't track project progress on an ongoing basis, you're going to find out you're in trouble far too late to do anything effective. To avoid this, project managers have a number of options to track progress effectively.

Assessing earned value

There are a number of ways to track project progress. One of the simplest is to set up milestones during the project planning phase of the project life cycle (see Chapter 14). If there are enough milestones and they are spaced relatively evenly, you can get a good idea of where you are in the project by tracking which milestones have been completed on a regular basis.

A more sophisticated method is the earned value (EV) analysis approach. To use this approach, list all the activities in your project, along with their estimated costs. (Find out how to estimate costs in Chapter 15.)

Figure 16-1 shows an example of earned value analysis tracking at the end of week 8 for an example project. To perform the analysis, find these four metrics for each activity:

- ✔ **Budgeted cost:** In the planning phase of the project, determine how much it will cost to complete each activity. For activity B in Figure 16-1, the budgeted cost is $2,000. For activity D, it's $6,000. These values don't change over time.

- ✔ **Planned value:** This is estimated from the planning phase upfront about how much you'll spend on completing an activity. During the planning phase of the project depicted in Figure 16-1, activity B was expected to be complete by the end of week 8. So 100 percent of the budgeted cost of $2,000 yields a "planned value" of $2,000. In contrast, activity D was planned to be only 30 percent complete by end of week 8, so its planned value is 30 percent of the budgeted cost of $6,000, which yields a planned value of $1,800.

- ✔ **Actual cost:** This is what you actually end up spending on completing an activity. In the example, this is $1,900 for activity B and $2,100 for activity D. Usually, the actual cost won't equal the planned value (although hopefully it's close).

✔ **Earned value:** This is the actual percent complete for an activity times its budgeted cost. For activity B in Figure 16-1, 100 percent of the project was actually complete by the end of week 8; 100 percent of the budgeted cost for activity B of $2,000 is $2,000. Thus, though it cost only $1,900 to complete activity B, the earned value for project monitoring purposes is $2,000. Activity D is only actually 25 percent complete at the end of week 8, so its earned value is 25 percent of its budgeted cost of $6,000, or $1,500. Note that activity D's earned value will increase in subsequent weeks (at least we hope so!).

Activity	Budget When Complete (Budgeted Cost)	Percent of Activity Complete at End of Week 8 (Planned)	Planned Value	Actual Money Spent at End of Week 8 (Actual Cost)	Percent of Activity Complete at End of Week 8 (Actual)	Earned Value
A	$3,000	100	$3,000	$4,000	100	$3,000
B	$2,000	100	$2,000	$1,900	100	$2,000
C	$2,500	50	$1,250	$3,000	75	$1,875
D	$6,000	30	$1,800	$2,100	25	$1,500
E	$4,000	0	$0	$0	0	$0
Total	$17,500	–	$8,050	$11,000	–	$8,375

Figure 16-1: Example earned value analysis.

Note: At the end of week 8, according to plan, $8,050 should have been spent (in other words, the planned value is $8,050). In actuality, $11,000 has been spent (in other words, the actual cost).

Illustration by Wiley, Composition Services Graphics

Now you need to find the planned value (PV), actual cost (AC), and earned value (EV) of the entire project. To do this, you'll figure out what activities you planned to complete by now in the project versus what you actually have completed. You'll also need to figure out what you planned to spend versus what you actually have spent.

To find the PV for the project described in Figure 16-1, sum up the PVs for all the activities at the end of week 8. This gives you a total of $8,050. Adding up the ACs of all the activities totals $11,000. Finally, summing the EVs totals $8,375 at the end of week 8. This means that the PV is $8,050, the AC $11,000, and the EV is $8,375 for this example project.

Now calculate these four measures of progress for the earned value method:

✔ **Cost variance (CV):** CV = EV – AC

This is how much less than you've spent by this point in the project than what you planned to. It's measured in dollars. Counterintuitively, a positive variance is good, and a negative variance is bad.

✔ **Schedule variance (SV):** SV = EV – PV

This is how much more of the project you've completed by this point in the project than you planned to. It's measured in dollars. Again, a positive variance is good; a negative variance is bad.

✔ **Cost performance index (CPI):** EV/AC

This is the ratio of how much you've spent on the project by this point over what you had planned to. It's measured as a percentage. Counterintuitively, a value above 100 percent is good, and a value below 100 percent is bad.

✔ **Schedule performance index (SPI):** EV/PV

This is the ratio of how much of the project you've completed by this point over what you had planned to. It's measured as a percentage. A value above 100 percent is good, and a value below 100 percent is bad.

In all four of these measures, higher is better. For example, a cost performance index (CPI) of 110 percent means that the project is not 10 percent over budget, but 9.09 percent under budget (1 – 1/1.10 = 0.909).

The example described in Figure 16-1 has these tracking measures:

✔ Cost variance is EV – AC = $8,375 – $11,000 = –$2,625. This means the project is $2,625 over budget at the end of week 8. Yes, negative does mean it's over budget. A positive value would actually be under budget.

✔ Schedule variance is EV – PV = $8,375 – $8,050 = $325. So the project is $325 ahead of schedule at the end of week 8. (Yes, this method does use dollars to measure time!)

✔ Cost performance index is EV/AC = $8,375/$11,000 = 76.1 percent. This means the project is significantly over budget. (1/0.761 – 1 = 31.3 percent over budget, to be precise.) Frankly, for project management purposes, saying that the project is about 100 percent – 76 percent = 34 percent over budget is close enough.

✔ Schedule performance index is EV/PV = $8,375/$8,050 = 104 percent, which means that you are 4 percent ahead of schedule at the end of week 8.

Based on this earned value analysis, your project at week 8 is a little ahead of schedule. Unfortunately, it is way over budget.

Earning value over time

It is common to graph the three values, planned value, actual cost, and earned value for a project over time. However, they are all typically divided by the budgeted cost for the entire project to form percentages as shown in Figure 16-2. For example, if you have an actual cost (AC) of $2.5 million in December 2012, you would divide it by the total budgeted cost for the project (at the planned time of completion) of $3.3 million to get 76 percent. This is what you would graph on the project progress chart in Figure 16.2.

Looking at the chart in Figure 16-2, you can deduce three things rather quickly:

✔ The earned value is lagging the planned value, which means that the project is behind schedule.

✔ The other is that the actual cost is significantly ahead of the earned value. This means that the project is seriously over budget. Note that you don't want to compare the actual cost to the planned value. If you do, the project looks over budget, but it doesn't seem nearly as over budget as it really is, because the planned value assumes that you have completed more work than you actually have!

✔ These variances are not improving over time. If anything, they appear to be getting slightly worse. So unless some intervention occurs, the project is going to be late and very over budget.

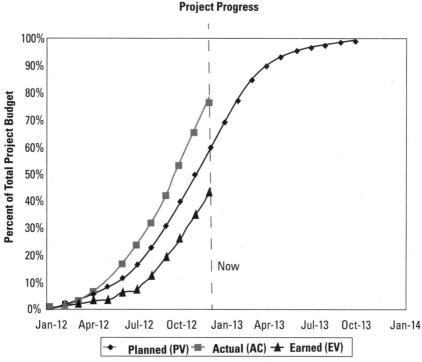

Project Progress

Figure 16-2:
Project progress chart.

Finally, the S-shapes of the curves in Figure 16-2 are typical. In fact, any shape other than an at least approximately S-shaped curve is a hint that there may be something wrong with your either your planning or your calculations.

Sometimes, project managers and their clients simplify reporting earned value progress by using one of these approaches:

- ✔ **The 0/100 rule:** Counting an activity for purposes of earned value only when it's 100 percent complete (0–100 method). Otherwise, it is considered 0 percent complete. For example, an activity with a budgeted cost of $800,000 that's 75 percent complete would have an earned value of $0 (zip, nada, nothing!). This method is typically used for short duration tasks, less than a month.

- ✔ **The 0/50/100 rule:** If an activity is between 0 and 49 percent complete, its earned value is $0. If an activity is between 50 and 99 percent complete, its earned value is half its budgeted cost. For example, if an activity has a budgeted cost of $2 million and is 88 percent complete, then its earned value is 50 · $2 million = $1 million. If an activity is 100 percent complete, only then does it get 100 percent of its earned value. For example, a $3 million dollar activity that is 100 percent complete has an earned value of $3 million.

- ✔ **The progress per unit method:** For activities that consist of performing a number of identical sub-tasks, you divide how many subtasks you've completed by the total number of sub-tasks. For example, if an activity for a project is to install 300 wind turbines for a wind farm project, one natural way is to count progress by the number of wind turbines installed. In this case, if 100 of the 300 turbines have been installed, then that activity's progress would be 100/300 = 33 percent.

The purpose of using these rules is to take some of the subjectivity out of determining progress completion. But a project needs to have a very large number of activities for the 0/100 or the 0/50/100 rules to work well. Otherwise, measuring the project progress becomes too granular. The progress per unit method, on the other hand, can be applied to many different types of projects because it is so easy to calculate.

Monitoring the metrics: Who's responsible?

Someone must be responsible for tracking project progress. Otherwise, it may not get done. If it's a small project, you — as the project manager — can do it yourself. On the other hand, if you're managing a big project, progress monitoring might itself turn into a full-time job. In that case, you'll need to appoint someone to do this who (1) understands the project's technical aspects (so he or she can't be fooled so easily); (2) is extremely detail-oriented; and (3) you trust implicitly. After the project manager, the person who monitors progress has arguably the most important job within the project. Get someone good!

An interesting aspect to consider is that suppliers might be performing some of your activities. If it's a big activity, you'll have to pay them for it, and — unless you're in the charity business — you'll only want to pay them for what progress they've actually made. The problem is: Who determines the progress that a supplier has made? If you do it, the supplier might very well accuse you of underestimating their work. If the supplier reports their own progress, they very well might exaggerate it, even if unintentionally.

There's no perfect solution to this problem. But one option is to hire a third-party vendor to monitor the progress of suppliers. Just be sure that you and the supplier agree on who is to do the monitoring upfront. The last time you want to argue over a third-party monitor is when you're already having an argument over progress!

Realizing your project's in trouble

While it's nice to know that your project is ahead of schedule and under budget, the actions you'll take are probably minimal (other than patting everyone on the back!). What you are really concerned about is whether your project is in trouble. What would be even nicer is to figure out whether the project looks like it's headed in trouble before it actually is!

There are a number of ways to accomplish this kind of foresight. All of them involve visual charts that reveal trends. The earned value progress chart is the most popular option; it is shown in Figure 16-2. Other options are the project run chart and the buffer penetration chart.

Using a project run chart

The next most common way also uses earned value, but also incorporates some of the ideas from a process control chart, as shown in Chapter 13. However, this version, which is called a *project run chart,* is simpler. As shown in Figure 16-3, the idea is to graph the schedule progress index (SPI) and cost progress index (CPI) over time.

If your CPI and SPI are equal to or greater than 100 percent, you're in the "green" zone and in good shape. If either your SPI or CPI index falls below 100 percent but remains above 90 percent, you're in the "yellow" zone and caution is advised. Make sure that you have plans in place in case things get worse, particularly if either index dips below 90 percent.

If either of your indices drops below 90 percent, you are in the "red" zone. Performance is poor, and you probably need to execute any correction plans you have in place. (Hopefully, you made these while you were in the "caution" zone!)

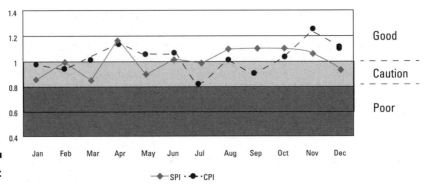

Figure 16-3:
Project run
chart.

SPI ◆ CPI •◆•

Note: In color, the shaded region from 0.4 to 0.8 would be red, and from
0.8 to 1.0 would be yellow. Above 1.0 would be green.

Illustration by Wiley, Composition Services Graphics

The progress of your CPI and SPI is going to have statistical fluctuations, just like everything else in operations management (or in life, if you are in a more philosophical mood). Sometimes things are going to go better, sometimes worse. So just because you are in the yellow zone does not mean that you need to panic. It just means that you should be watchful and be prepared.

Utilizing slack with a buffer penetration chart

Another version of the run chart is used sometimes to watch the progress of the critical path. The critical path contains all those activities that, if delayed, will delay the project as a whole. They have no "slack" in them. See Chapter 15 for more on how to determine the critical path.

The central idea is to establish a project time reserve or "buffer," which accounts for the fact that there is going to be some statistical variation in completing your project's critical path, just like for everything else in operations management. (If we sound like a broken record about this, it's strictly intentional!) The schedule buffer accounts for the fact that — even if your estimates are perfectly correct — at times you are going to be behind schedule. The question is how much of this is normal statistical happenstance and how much means that your project is in trouble.

The typical approach is to establish an expected (mean) time estimate to complete the project and a maximum time estimate that would be expected under normal statistical circumstances. There are a number of ways to do this. One way that works well is to make the P50 estimate (you have a 50 percent chance of equaling or beating this estimate based on your initial planning) the expected time estimate, and to make the P95 (you have a 95 percent chance of equaling or beating this estimate) estimate the maximum time estimate.

For example, your project's critical path may have a P50 of 8 months and a P95 of 12.5 months. You set these to be expected and maximum estimates. Then, your Buffer = Maximum – Expected = 12.5 months – 8 months = 4.5 months. Each month you determine how many of the critical path activities you have completed. You'll need to determine the planned completion date of this last critical path activity. Once you have determined that, just subtract it from the time into the project.

In the project depicted in Figure 16-4, the last activity completed in the critical chain during September was supposed to be completed 6.9 months into the project according to plan. However, by September, 9.0 months have elapsed since the beginning of the project. So your buffer penetration is 6.9 months – 9.0 months = –2.1 months of buffer penetration. (For reasons unknown to the authors, the convention has grown to use a – to indicate buffer penetration.) You can see this graphed in Figure 16-4. If instead, you were ahead of schedule on the critical path, the convention is to graph a zero for buffer penetration. For example, in February, the last completed activity of the critical chain was planned to be completed in 2.5 months. Yet two months have elapsed. Because 2.5 months – 2 months = 0.5 months is a positive number, you graph it as having zero buffer penetration.

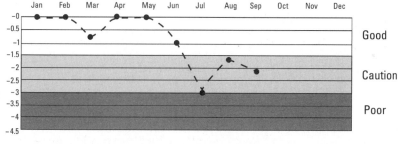

Figure 16-4:
Buffer
penetration
chart.

Note: In color, the shaded region from –4.5 to –3 would be red, and from –3 to –1.5 would be yellow. Above –1.5 would be green.

Illustration by Wiley, Composition Services Graphics

Otherwise, the buffer penetration chart works like the project run chart for SPI and CPI shown earlier. Green is okay. Yellow means caution. This is when you want to figure out any contingency plans. Red means it's time to activate these contingency plans.

Planning Ahead with Risk Registers

Identifying the risks that threaten your project and planning early for how you can minimize impacts to your outcomes shortens your actual response time when one of those risks occurs and improves the effectiveness of the response. In some cases, by planning ahead for risks, you may even be able to take actions that prevent certain risks from occurring.

The risk management process is a cycle with four phases (as shown in Figure 16-5): Identify, prioritize, respond, and track. Keep in mind that risk management begins in the planning stage of the project, and it continues through project execution and into the handover phase. In other words, the wheel of the risk management cycle never stops.

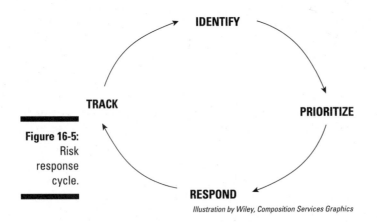

Figure 16-5:
Risk
response
cycle.

Illustration by Wiley, Composition Services Graphics

Knowing what can go wrong

The first and possibly most important risk management activity for a project is to brainstorm all the things that can go wrong. Do this during the planning phase — well before you begin actually executing the project. The most common tool for managing risk is a risk register.

To begin developing a risk register, consider the critical assumptions from the original project proposal that will harm the project if they are violated (see Chapter 14 for details). Then put together a cross-functional team of experts and use the project proposal plus any other information your experts have at their disposal to brainstorm an initial list of risks.

- ✔ **Technology:** If your project depends on any new technologies, whether these are information, engineering, or service technologies, these may pose significant risk to positive outcomes because they may not work, they may cost more than you expect, or they may take too long to complete. The likelihood of these risks occurring and their potential harm to the project increase if there are multiple technologies that depend on each other.

- ✔ **Financials:** If the financial assumptions such as resource or material costs (or possibly cost of capital or inflation rates) are wrong, then core cost estimates for the overall project profitability might be off. For example, labor or important materials may cost more than you expect, which sets up the potential for going over-budget. A different type of financial risk occurs if the project may end up late. Being late can create problems such as contract penalties or — in the case of product development — lost market share. Again, these impact profit assumptions. For international projects, another financial problem is the rate of currency exchange, which fluctuates continuously.

✔ **Market demand:** If your project involves building a plant or developing a new product or service, the demand for your product may not be as strong as you originally predict. If demand is less than expected, then so too will revenue, again impacting the profitability of the project. Note that there is a bit of overlap with financial risks because late projects may result in less market share if the project is developing a new service or project.

✔ **Organizational:** The majority of organizational problems are the result of turnover. If there is somebody on your project who is irreplaceable, then establish a backup and a transition plan in case she leaves for greener pastures. Turnover happens, so be sure to plan for it.

Another organizational-based risk to some projects involves opposition to the project from inside a stakeholder organization. Hopefully, you identify roadblocks, or sources of opposition, during your stakeholder analysis process as described in Chapter 14.

✔ **Government or legal:** The government regulates many kinds of project from new drug development to building bridges. If permission from the government for a project activity is not forthcoming, great harm can be done to the project. For example, the great nightmare for people managing construction projects is running afoul of some government agency or organization or a legal restriction of some kind. The number of projects derailed by environmental concerns is legion. One gas drilling project was delayed because the noise from it interfered with the breeding activities of gray whales *700 miles away.*

The second greatest fear of people managing construction projects is upsetting some non-governmental lobby or pressure group, such as environmental advocacy groups, community activists and so on. For project managers in other industries, these problems are not so prevalent, but they are still a problem. For example, the laptop computer lithium battery fires of the early 2000s were a big problem for computer manufacturers.

✔ **Safety:** No one wants workers to get injured on a project, but every major bridge that's ever been built has had fatalities. Some industries are inherently less exposed to safety and health risks, but this is a primary area of concern for major construction and industrial projects. That said, at least one videogaming software company was sued successfully by the spouses of their engineers and programmers for overwork-induced stress resulting in heart attacks and the like. (To be fair, said company was alleged to work their employees up to 100 hours per week.) So no project is entirely free of safety concerns.

Prioritizing risks

Risk registers prioritize risks by likelihood of occurring and severity of impact if it does occur. In an ideal world, a project manager has access to a numerical probability of a risk occurring and the expected value (mean) of its impact in terms of cost or timing. Usually, however, this information is not available, so you want to qualitatively rank the likelihood of experiencing the risk from 1 to 5, with 1 representing a "very low" probability to 5 representing a "very high" probability.

The expected impact of the risk is also ranked from 1 ("very low") to 5 ("very high"). The two numbers are multiplied to create an unmitigated risk score ranging from 1 to 25. You can then use the risk scores to prioritize the risks.

To see this tool in practice, consider an example of the Melville Island tar sands project, whose risk register is shown in Figure 16-6. When oil prices were approximately $125 per barrel, there was some thought given to processing tar sands on Melville Island in Canada for oil. The logistical hurdles would have been immense. The distance to the nearest port, Churchill in Manitoba, Canada, on Hudson Bay, is 1,200 miles. (And Churchill is another 1,100 miles from Winnipeg, but at least there's a rail link to it.) Melville Island and Hudson Bay are both icebound six months of the year. Finally, there is no permanent human habitation on Melville Island. Any settlement or port would have to be built from scratch with materials sent from Churchill. There is no vegetation except for lichens, moss, and some woody vines that grow along the ground. However, there are a lot of polar bears!

Figure 16-6 shows the risks for a disguised oil exploration company ExploriCo. At the top of the chart is an organizational risk, which is the risk that not enough skilled labor is willing to relocate to Melville Island. (We can't imagine why. Think of the polar bears romping in your backyard.) The expert group (and again, you should use a group, just like when brainstorming risks) decides that the unmitigated likelihood of this being a problem is medium, so they give it an unmitigated likelihood score of 3 (we'll get to the mitigated scores in a minute). However, if it does happen: no workers, no project. So they give the risk an unmitigated impact score of 5 (very high). This gives you an unmitigated risk score of $3 \cdot 5 = 15$.

Let's consider another risk, not enough icebreakers available for rent. The risk is that you could lose 6 months of port usability per year. This might very well double the time to complete the project. While the experts think the likelihood score is a 2 (low), the potential impact is a 5 (very high). This creates a risk score for the icebreakers of $2 \cdot 5 = 10$.

Event	Risk	Unmitigated Likelihood**	Unmitigated Impact**	Unmitigated Risk Score (Likelihood x Impact)
Lack of skilled labor willing to relocate	Operation becomes infeasible	Medium (3)	Very High (5)	15
Cannot find another oil company to partner with	Entire risk borne by ExploriCo if failure	Medium (3)	High (4)	12
Environmental impact statement unfavorable	Extra cost to ensure low impact	High (4)	Medium (3)	12
Cannot acquire land from Canadian government	Project untenable	Low (2)	Very High (5)	10
No good natural harbor	Delay of one year	Low (2)	Very High (5)	10
Not enough icebreakers available for rent	Lose 6 months of port usability per year	Low (2)	Very High (5)	10
Environmental advocacy group protests	Some bad publicity	High (4)	Very Low (1)	4

Figure 16-6:
Risk register for example Melville Island tar sands project.

Risk Score Colors: Red → Risk Score>10; Yellow → 5<Risk Score<=10; Green → Risk Score <5

Illustration by Wiley, Composition Services Graphics

You then continue brainstorming risks and assigning them risk scores. This continues until you can't think of any more risks. However, the identification process does not end with the planning phase. It continues throughout the life cycle of the project until its completion. The risk register is a living document. Likelihood and impact scores change as a project progresses, and new potential risks emerge. All must be continuously tracked.

Developing a contingency plan

After you identify risks, you need to figure out a way to handle them. The best way to handle risks for a given project depends on the nature of the risk and the specifics of the project.

Here are the three basic varieties of risk:

✔ **Variance risk:** Some risks look like Figure 16-7 in that they have a probabilistic distribution resulting from uncertainties from concerning knowledge, materials, labor productivity, etc. The best way to respond to this type of risk is upfront by doing things like additional research, switching suppliers, and assigning additional resources. Oftentimes, mitigation plans such as using more reliable suppliers may reduce the variance of a risk but increase cost as shown in Figure 16-8. Even so, most project managers prefer the variance risk after response (the dashed line) because it's more predictable. Because most project managers are risk-averse — they have enough uncertainty in their lives and there is only so much aspirin can do — they prefer to mitigate the risk even if it costs some money.

✔ **Contingency risk:** Some risks look like Figure 16-9. Here, if a contingency risk occurs, the base cost variance shifts to the right. Sources of contingency risk are things that are predominantly either/or in nature. For example, you either get a building permit, or you don't. The new battery technology either works, or it doesn't. Oftentimes, it makes sense to not mitigate a contingency risk upfront, but put in place a contingency plan, should the contingency risk actually occur. One rather drastic contingency plan that sometimes makes sense is simply to terminate the project if the risk occurs.

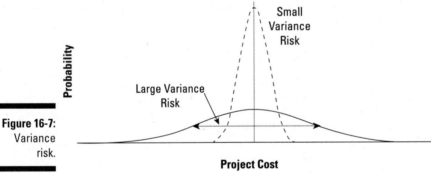

Figure 16-7:
Variance
risk.

Illustration by Wiley, Composition Services Graphics

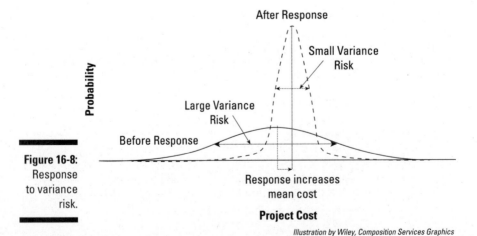

Figure 16-8:
Response
to variance
risk.

Illustration by Wiley, Composition Services Graphics

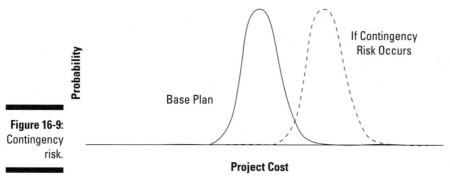

Figure 16-9:
Contingency
risk.

Illustration by Wiley, Composition Services Graphics

✓ **Unknown unknowns (often referred to as *black swans*):** These are the risks that you know exist but can't identify. The only way to respond to these risks is to cope with them when you encounter them. One of the goals of the risk identification process in the planning stage is to uncover as many potential black swans as possible so they can be responded to ahead of time.

Black swan risks take their name because, since Roman times, it was proverbial in Europe to refer to something being rare "as a black swan." As far as Europeans knew, there was no such thing as a black swan because there are no black swans in Europe (or Asia or Africa). However, Dutch Captain Willem de Vlamingh's explorations around western Australia in 1697 sighted a whole species of — you guessed it — black swans.

Let's look at the Melville Island example filled out with response plans in Figure 16-10. One risk is "cannot acquire land from the Canadian government." The experts during the planning phase judged this to have an unmitigated likelihood of 2 (low) but an impact of 5 (very high). This creates an unmitigated risk score of 10.

The policy at ExploriCo is to create response plans for all risks with scores over 5 and particularly for those with risk scores over 10. The mitigation plan the firm comes up with is to treat it upfront by hiring lobbyists to work with the Canadian government to sell the project and allow them to buy up the necessary land rights in Ottawa. Additionally, if the lobbyists don't succeed, ExploriCo makes a contingency plan to abandon the project early before much money is spent. Importantly, note the mix of upfront and contingency approaches in the response plan.

After they've developed the response plan, the experts decide the mitigated likelihood with the response plan in place is a 1 (very low), though the mitigated impact is only reduced slightly to a 4 (high). The resulting risk score is 1 · 4 = 4, which is considered acceptable by ExploriCo.

Event	Risk	Unmitigated Likelihood**	Unmitigated Impact**	Unmitigated Risk Score (Likelihood x Impact)	Mitigation/ Contingency Plan, if Risk Score >8	Mitigated Likelihood**	Mitigated Likelihood**	Unmitigated Impact**
Lack of skilled labor willing to relocate	Operation becomes infeasible	Medium (3)	Very High (5)	15	Combination of incentives, plus on-site education	Low (2)	High (4)	8
Cannot find another oil company to partner with	Entire risk borne by ExploriCo if failure	Medium (3)	High (4)	12	Terminate	Very Low (1)	Very Low (1)	1
Environmental impact statement unfavorable	Extra cost to ensure low impact on wildlife	High (4)	Medium (3)	12	Hire lobbyists	Low (2)	Medium (3)	6
Cannot acquire land from Canadian government	Project untenable	Low (2)	Very High (5)	10	Lobbyists + early terminate	Very Low (1)	High (4)	4
No good natural harbor	Delay of one year	Low (2)	Very High (5)	10	Start scouting now, and terminate depending on findings	Low (2)	Medium (3)	6
Not enough icebreakers available for rent	Lose 6 months of port usability per year	Low (2)	Very High (5)	10	Purchase own icebreakers	Very Low (1)	High (4)	4
Environmental advocacy group protests	Some bad publicity	High (4)	Very Low (1)	4	No need for response plan	High (4)	Very Low (1)	4

Figure 16-10:
Melville Island risk register with contingency risks.

Risk Score Colors: Red → Risk Score>10; Yellow → <5 Risk Score<=10; Green → Risk Score <5

Illustration by Wiley, Composition Services Graphics

ExploriCo then proceeds with all the other risks with risk scores above 5. It can't mitigate all risks to a 5 or below through response plans. However, the risk profile of the project is overall much better than prior to the development of response plans.

Response plans, as part of a project's risk register, need to be continuously tracked and updated over the entire project. As time wears on, some risks can be deleted from the register because they don't happen and the time period for them to occur passes. Other risks are discovered and need to be added to the register. As this happens, risk management shifts from tracking and identification back to prioritization and response, continuing the risk management cycle until the end of the project.

In any project, opportunities exist as well as risks. Contingency plans for emerging opportunities, if they arise, make it more likely that you can take advantage of them.

Responding Productively to Risk

Responding to risks when they occur is one of the great tests of a project manager. This is particularly complicated by three "laws" that work against efficiently completing the project. One law, Parkinson's law, applies to times when things are going well. The other two, Brook's law and Homer's law, kick you when you're already down.

Staying productive: Parkinson's law

Cyril Northcote Parkinson observed in 1955 that "Work expands to fill the time available for its completion." He based this observation on years of working with the civil service, yet engineers and programmers are often accused of "gold plating" or "over-engineering" (these are both terms meaning that the engineers have developed the project far beyond what the customer requires or cares about) when left with excess time. Yet tightening deadlines too much to prevent "gold-plating" can also be counterproductive. Research consistently shows that employees, when faced with clearly unrealistic deadlines, simply give up trying to meet them and make progress very slowly.

The best approach to avoid Parkinson's law without driving employees to despair is to establish moderately aggressive timelines.

Recovering from delays: Brook's law and Homer's law

When a project falls behind schedule, getting the project back on track is surprisingly difficult. Typically, managers resort to one of four methods:

- ✔ Adding resources (typically, extra employees)
- ✔ Working employees overtime
- ✔ Delaying the project
- ✔ Reducing project scope

The first two methods are both problematic, because of the rework cycle. Research also shows that rework — work that you thought was complete but turns out to be defective and needs to be redone — is a large part of all projects. Rework is prevalent in every project from building airports, to remodeling houses, to developing new services, to writing software. In some complex electronics projects, for example, rework increases expected completion time by a factor of four or more.

Figure 16-11 shows a diagram of the rework cycle. In any project, there are a number of tasks to complete. The *remaining tasks* in the project are completed by *personnel* at an *apparent task completion rate*. Some of these are indeed actually completed. However, many of them only appear completed. In reality, they become *undiscovered rework,* which will need to be done over again once it is discovered. As this rework is discovered, it increases the *remaining tasks* that need to be completed.

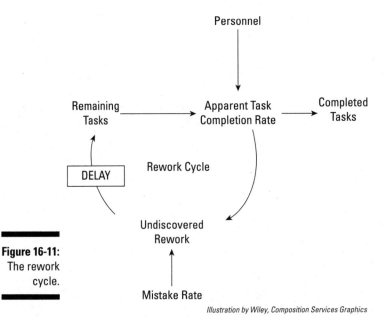

Figure 16-11:
The rework
cycle.

Illustration by Wiley, Composition Services Graphics

The rework cycle interferes with project completion because adding personnel only increases effective personnel after a delay as the new employees learn enough about the project to be useful. However, in the short term, until the new employees come up to speed, the average experience of personnel is reduced (at least with this project). This increases the mistake rate, which drives up undiscovered rework, thus delaying the project.

Brook's law

Adding workers to a project late in its life cycle usually results in mistakes and delays. This is the reason behind Brook's law, which is "adding workers to a late project makes it still later." The implication is that if you need to add resources, then you really need to do it before you actually need them in order to properly train and prepare them to help. This also means that you'll have to vigorously monitor your project (see "realizing your project's in trouble") so that you can add resources at the first sniff of trouble.

One alternative to adding new workers is to work existing workers overtime. This usually works as long as you don't work them overtime for too long. Otherwise, Homer's law comes into play.

Homer's law

If you make overtime a fact of life for employees for too long, you'll end up stretching out the timetable for your project, according to Homer's law. Working overtime increases productivity in the short run. In the long run, however, it increases fatigue, which in turn increases the mistake rate, setting the rework cycle off again, this time with a vengeance.

Delay the project

Adding employees to a late project often doesn't work, and working employees overtime has limited usefulness, so sometimes the best approach for managing risks related to productivity is to revise the schedule to reflect a delay. While this may seem defeatist, it may actually get the project done faster than adding new people or working your current personnel overtime for too long because it won't kick off the rework cycle.

Sacrificing functionality

Another approach that works well is to sacrifice functionality, also known as reducing scope.

Sacrificing functionality is often a successful strategy for managing a delayed project. One way to implement this approach is to design "sacrificial" functionality into the project in the planning phase. If the project runs over budget or is delayed, then this functionality can be sacrificed.

The advantages of this approach are twofold. Early in the project, while it is still on time, all the employees are fully occupied so that they don't waste time on over-engineering the project. Later on, if the project timing does go awry, you have already identified what functionality can be dropped with the least impact on the customer's satisfaction.

For example, one software provider delivered 85 percent of its software project to a client on time, and the client was reasonably happy. However, the provider made sure that the 85 percent delivered contained the functionality that was most important to the client. At a more prosaic level, we've all turned in papers in school in which we've sacrificed some content in order not to be late!

Part V
Scaling and Globalizing Your Operations

Checklist: Is outsourcing this portion of the product going to be a problem?		Yes	No
Strategic Risks			
Hostage-taking	Can the supplier hold you up by withholding delivery?		
Forgetting capabilities	Are you at risk (from turnover or technology change) for forgetting how to specify the outsourced product or service or bid it?		
Leakage	Can your intellectual property leak out through the supplier?		
Creating your own competitor	Can another firm backwards integrate your suppliers' components so as to compete with your firm?		
Cost Risks			
Logistics	Are the total logistics costs (including timing) prohibitive?		
Travel	Have you figured in travel costs?		
Employee co-location	What about co-locating your employees on site or vice versa?		
Telecommunications	Any extra communications costs such as web meeting software?		
Secure data transfer	Any costs arising from securing the transfer of data to protect your intellectual property and corporate strategy?		
Managerial costs	Are the costs to manage the outsourced supplier prohibitive, particularly as you are likely to need specialized integration personnel?		
Product/Service Design Risks			
Modularity	Does the outsourced portion of your product have poorly defined interfaces with the rest of the product?		
Standards	Are the interfaces between the outsourced portion and the rest of your product not defined by common industry standards?		
Tribal knowledge	Does the outsourced portion of your product have critical relevant tribal knowledge (such as info that is not easily written down)?		
Legal issues	Does the outsourced portion have any prohibitive legal issues such as offshoring prohibited technologies?		

Want to know more about protecting a company's technology intelligence? Check out an article on this topic at www.dummies.com/extras/operations management.

In this part . . .

- ✒ Understand the pros and cons of outsourcing and know the three most important decisions you have to make for successful outsourcing.

- ✒ Walk through a product's life cyle and discover how each life stage influences operating requirements. Find out how to nuture new companies and prolong the life of established products and businesses.

Chapter 17

Considering Outsourcing

A tidal wave of *outsourcing* — a term meaning that a company hires another firm or firms to perform specific operations — has been hitting businesses throughout the United States since the 1990s. Before, firms typically only outsourced support tasks such as human resources management or janitorial services. Then came call centers and technical support. Nowadays, companies are even outsourcing the production and delivery of the products and services that make up their core business. If these production and delivery operations aren't performed well, a firm's costs can increase, customer service can suffer, brand reputation can be harmed, and market share can decline — sometimes fatally.

This chapter describes the pros and cons of outsourcing and highlights the three most important decisions for successful outsourcing. We also point out some critical factors of outsourcing, including product design and management.

Seeing the Upsides and Downsides of Outsourcing

Hiring a separate company to build a product or provide a service can make sense for some companies because outsourcing may be cheaper, provide higher component quality, or reduce capital costs. But sometimes it's better to just do it yourself. Outsourcing the wrong process, product, or service can, over the long run, end up increasing costs, harming overall product quality, and even leaking core technology. Some firms have spent billions of dollars reversing outsourcing mistakes.

In this section we describe the potential benefits as well as the risks of outsourcing.

Outsourcing versus offshoring

Outsourcing means having another firm produce a product or provide a service for you. This isn't the same as *offshoring,* which just means that a product or service is produced in a different country. If a company manufactures or develops a product at one of its divisions that's located in a country different from its headquarters' location, that's offshoring, not outsourcing. Location of a partner company isn't a factor in the definition of the term outsourcing. The term refers only to a situation in which one company hires another to do some of its work.

Benefiting from the pros

Outsourcing has continued to be a popular business tool since the turn of the 21st century. Here are some of the most compelling benefits of outsourcing:

- **Better quality:** Sometimes another company is just better at building a product or delivering a service than your firm is. And do you really want your company to produce its own pens and paper? Most automotive firms outsource the production of tires. Ultimately, that's a pens and paper kind of decision. When the part or service to be outsourced, like tires, has a standard, easily defined interface with the overall product, the quality benefit rules. To buy a tire, even in the aftermarket, all you need to know are three measurements. If the tire matches those three measurements, you can put it on your car.

  In contrast, very few automotive firms outsource transmissions because most transmissions are tailored to individual engines and automobiles.

- **Improved return on investment:** A mainstay of outsourcing is its ability to reduce the investment in plant and equipment needed to produce a product, which must be booked as an asset. If you can retain the bulk of the profits for the product and not lose too much to supplier markups, then your return on investment should increase.

- **Lower costs:** Some suppliers have economics in their favor. Generally speaking, outsourcing to low-cost labor means a company can reduce the labor cost that goes into the outsourced components. For example, labor costs in China are lower than in Western nations, so some firms hire Chinese companies to perform labor-intensive, low-skill activities, like cutting and sewing clothing. This also has a reinforcing effect. If a number of companies outsource to a common low-cost supplier, then that supplier can obtain economies of scale from specialization. Sometimes, it just doesn't make financial sense for a company to set up facilities and hire employees to produce an item that another company is already making efficiently.

✔ **A transfer of fixed cost to variable cost:** If you produce a product or component yourself, you incur a number of investment costs that you need to recoup before you can make a profit. If a supplier provides the part, you may be able to purchase it on a per-unit basis before repackaging and selling it. This transforms the fixed cost (investment and other costs that do not vary by unit) you incur into a variable cost (per-unit costs).

The upshot is that the number of product units you have to sell before you make a profit drops. Even if the product doesn't sell well, you're still likely to make a profit when you outsource.

Avoiding the cons

If the goal of outsourcing is to gain a competitive advantage in the marketplace, companies need to seriously weigh the outsourcing option. For some businesses, sharing intellectual property with partners is basically an invitation for trouble. This trouble, often referred to as an *outsourcing trap*, can manifest itself in a number of ways:

✔ **Creating your own competitor:** If you outsource enough of the parts of your product to suppliers, another firm may be able to buy those parts (or ones very similar) and put them together to create a competitive product. This happened most notoriously in the U.S. television industry in the 1960s and 1970s.

✔ **Disconnecting with the customer:** This is more of an issue with services than manufacturing. If a supplier is dealing with your customers, you may have a problem. The supplier's personnel are representing your firm to the customer. They are effectively the face of your company! And those personnel may not have the same investment in your firm's success that your own personnel do. (Witness this with call centers!) Another problem is that suppliers may subtly try to steer your customers to deal directly with their own business.

✔ **Experiencing leakage:** The supplier who works for you also works for a number of other firms. Anything the supplier learns from you can be (and, historically, often has been) leaked to their other customers so that they can improve their products. This is true of suppliers in all regions of the world, but regions that traditionally provide less intellectual property protection (patents, trade secrets, and so on) pose a greater risk.

✔ **Forgetting your capabilities:** Some firms successfully outsource all or part of the manufacturing of their products. Over time, when technology changes or people who understand the technology move on to other jobs, two problems emerge. One, you may not be able to specify to the supplier exactly what you want, so you may end up with a product or component that isn't as well adapted to your needs as it could be. The other issue is that you'll have less information on what the product or component should cost. This weakens your negotiating position with the supplier.

One way to get around this problem is to design and produce a small percentage of the components in-house, while outsourcing the remainder. What you produce in-house may be relatively expensive on a per-unit basis, but by improving your knowledge of component level design and manufacturing, you may improve your bargaining position enough to make in-house component production worthwhile.

✔ **Getting taken hostage by your supplier:** If you outsource a key component to your supplier and divest yourself of the means to make it, you may create a problem. If no one else makes it (or, worse, knows how to make it), then you become dependent on your supplier. Losing the leverage that comes with the option of taking your business elsewhere can become expensive.

Outsourcing to multiple suppliers may help, but this too can get expensive because of managerial overhead.

Related to hostage-taking (but a bit different) is depending on only one supplier (known as *sole-sourcing*). It is good practice to develop a second source for critical or high-cost parts. This fosters competition and holds costs down. It also minimizes problems if the supplier goes out of business or is disrupted by earthquakes or other natural disasters.

Another downside to outsourcing centers is *linkage costs,* which are the costs to administer an outsourcing relationship that you wouldn't need to spend in-house. These costs can be very high, averaging as much as 60 percent of the expected savings from an outsourcing relationship. Because linkage costs can actually overwhelm any projected savings, some companies determine that bringing outsourced work back in-house is less expensive.

Here are some common types of linkage costs:

✔ **Co-location:** Many firms send one or two of their employees to be present at the supplier plant to facilitate communication or vice versa. Such co-location usually costs much more than just the salaries of the employees involved — you need to consider housing and relocation expenses. You may also have to pay a premium to induce your employees to work offshore if an offshoring relationship is involved.

✔ **Logistics:** If you ship components very far from the supplier to your firm, you incur significant logistics costs. You also experience a significant delay. Shipping components by sea to the United States from Asia takes several weeks. In contrast, air shipping is fast, but it's very expensive for large components. We know of at least one firm that, because it had to use air shipping so often to expedite orders, burned up all its savings from outsourcing to an Asian supplier. Because most companies today run with very lean inventories (see Chapter 8 for more on inventory), they don't have a buffer against any disruption of the supply chain connecting the supplier to their firm.

- **Management:** We discuss management linkage costs in detail in the later section "Developing a lasting relationship." However, for various reasons, the number of potential miscommunications and disagreements increases in an outsourcing situation, which can be very expensive. Specialized managers can reduce these costs, but the managers themselves are expensive.

- **Secure data transfer:** You don't want your data to leak to other firms that may use it against you. Securing your data necessitates the use of appropriate software and training employees at both your firm and the supplier to use the software properly.

- **Telecommunications:** You can significantly improve virtual conferences with appropriate virtual meeting software. The software, however, isn't cheap.

- **Travel:** Because most outsourcing involves suppliers at some geographical distance from your firm, your employees have to do a lot of traveling between your firm and the supplier. Virtual meetings can only do so much.

Getting Down to the Basics

When you're developing an outsourcing plan, three critical questions exist. Successful planning requires you to know what, who, and how. In most cases, you answer the questions in that order. Companies first decide what to outsource. Outsourcing the wrong part of your product or service can result in poor quality, increased costs, and other mishaps. A poor outsourcing decision can result in key intellectual property being leaked or, worse, the creation of a new and fierce competitor.

Finding the right partner for outsourcing is also vital to a successful outcome. Much like a marriage, the choice of partner can make or break the outsourcing relationship. A particularly poor choice can harm or even destroy your firm.

The third decision is how to structure the outsourcing relationship to get the most out of it. This is more difficult than it looks. It involves questions of incentives, information sharing, and governance. Perhaps most important is the choice of the personnel to make the relationship work. People are the glue that holds the outsourcing relationship together.

Figuring out what to outsource

An important part of product design is the manufacturing process. You need to consider how an item will be made when designing it. You can't just design a product, throw it over a wall, and hope that the manufacturing people can figure out how to produce it.

Outsourcing creates the same issue. If you outsource, you have to design your supply chain at the same time. You also have to design the components of your product that you want to outsource so that they're easy to outsource.

Most of the factors that make a component or product easier to outsource reduce the amount of communication necessary between your firm and the supplier. We list a number of them here:

- ✔ **Legality:** You can't legally offshore certain things, such as certain defense-related technologies. This limits the choice of outsourcing partners to domestic suppliers. If you design your product to avoid such legal restrictions, the pool of firms you can outsource to is much larger.

- ✔ **Modularity:** A component is *modular* if it has very few interconnections (electrical, physical, or informational) with the rest of the product. The more modular a component is, the easier it is to outsource. Tires are a great example of modularity because they have only three physical specifications. If they meet those specifications, they'll fit the automobile. Everything else about tires is standardized (see the next bullet). Stereo speakers are similar. They typically have a single pair of wires that carries an electrical signal from an amplifier (or, these days, from a computer) that is turned into sound. Speakers don't need to be produced along with an amplifier and don't need any electronics or software connectivity. Speakers can be designed pretty much independently of the amplifiers that provide the sound signal. The design doesn't have any physical constraints other than the plug at the end of the wire.

- ✔ **Standards:** A *standard* is an agreement by a number of firms to create an interface to the same technical published specifications. Examples of standards include the USB connector that people use to connect peripherals to computers and the electrical outlets in your house that you plug things into. Standards make components easier to outsource because component makers don't have to communicate or work with the outsourcing firm much because what they're making is designed to universal specifications.

  The beauty of standards is that it allows relatively complex interfaces between components to be agreed on without going into all the detail necessary to specify those interfaces (electrical, physical, information, and so on) that would be necessary if those standards did not exist. The use of standards combined with reducing the number of interfaces through modular design reduces the necessary information flow between your firm and the supplier, which makes components much easier to outsource.

- ✔ **Tribal knowledge:** A lot of knowledge about how to produce a product never gets written down. The more of this *tribal knowledge* that a product or component has, the more difficult it is to outsource. One way to design for outsourcing is to try to include as much of this knowledge as possible in the specifications you send to your supplier. Another way is to substitute some standard for that tribal knowledge. Using standards is the better path if you can do it.

Figure 17-1 lists the risks commonly associated with outsourcing. If you can't answer no to these risks (or have a plan to deal with problem areas), you need to rethink any plan to outsource your product or service.

Checklist: Is outsourcing this portion of the product going to be a problem?		Yes	No
Strategic Risks			
Hostage-taking	Can the supplier hold you up by withholding delivery?		
Forgetting capabilities	Are you at risk (from turnover or technology change) for forgetting how to specify the outsourced product or service or bid it?		
Leakage	Can your intellectual property leak out through the supplier?		
Creating your own competitor	Can another firm backwards integrate your suppliers' components so as to compete with your firm?		
Cost Risks			
Logistics	Are the total logistics costs (including timing) prohibitive?		
Travel	Have you figured in travel costs?		
Employee co-location	What about co-locating your employees on site or vice versa?		
Telecommunications	Any extra communications costs such as web meeting software?		
Secure data transfer	Any costs arising from securing the transfer of data to protect your intellectual property and corporate strategy?		
Managerial costs	Are the costs to manage the outsourced supplier prohibitive, particularly as you are likely to need specialized integration personnel?		
Product/Service Design Risks			
Modularity	Does the outsourced portion of your product have poorly defined interfaces with the rest of the product?		
Standards	Are the interfaces between the outsourced portion and the rest of your product not defined by common industry standards?		
Tribal knowledge	Does the outsourced portion of your product have critical relevant tribal knowledge (such as info that is not easily written down)?		
Legal issues	Does the outsourced portion have any prohibitive legal issues such as offshoring prohibited technologies?		

Figure 17-1: Outsourcing checklist.

Illustration by Wiley, Composition Services Graphics

Choosing the right partner

Getting the most out of your outsourcing relationship depends on a number of factors. One obvious one is that the supplier needs to be financially stable so that it does not go out of business while working with you. A less obvious but no less important issue is a candidate supplier's familiarity with serving firms similar to yours in terms of geography, product requirements, and sales volume. Lack of familiarity can create miscommunication. Sometimes, suppliers from one industry simply don't have the technical capabilities to produce components for another industry.

An ideal outsourcing partner has some familiarity with your industry. Otherwise, you'll likely spend a long time training the manufacturer about how to make your product properly. For example, imagine that a medical equipment company decides to outsource the production of a relatively uncomplicated measurement device to a toy manufacturer with significant experience in plastic injection molding. The firm makes a mock-up of the device it wants the supplier to produce, and the supplier creates a product that looks exactly like it's supposed to, only to discover that the device can't perform its main function, which is precision measurement of air exhaled by a patient. Toy companies are all about a product's external appearance, and our fictional supplier is unfamiliar with how to make precision measurement products. Eventually, the toy company does a stellar job, but it takes literally thousands of hours of work by employees in both the buyer and supplier firms to overcome these issues. A supplier that's familiar with the medical equipment industry wouldn't need this time.

If a supplier firm needs to ramp up its volume significantly (see Chapter 18), then adjusting production levels takes time and investment to buy new equipment and hire new personnel.

When you find the right supplier, you want to stick with that supplier for the long haul. Switching from partner to partner to develop sophisticated products for your business is a recipe for disaster.

Developing a lasting relationship

Managing outsourced projects is almost always more difficult than people expect. The learning curve — for your firm and the supplier — that goes into the making of a smooth, successful relationship is often very difficult.

The following sections discuss ways to get to the facts about what outsourcing can and can't do and how to overcome some common hurdles.

Using a matchmaker

The outsourcing relationship is more like a marriage than speed dating, so you may need a matchmaker to find the right partner. A growing number of firms specialize in facilitating outsourcing relationships throughout the world. These firms (sometimes called *supply chain*

orchestrators) tend to be region-specific. They know the territory, the best local firms, and the capabilities of each. Supply chain orchestrators can also act as eyes on the ground for their clients to ensure that requirements are met.

Busting some common myths about outsourcing

The conventional wisdom about managing outsourcing relationships involves a number of misconceptions, particularly that outsourcing makes managing the outsourced component easier and cheaper and doable with less management and personnel.

The following are some particularly common outsourcing myths:

- ✓ **External suppliers reduce the number of personnel working on your project.** This is patently false. You will indeed have fewer people working directly for you, but you'll have to hire a number of employees to coordinate the outsourced work from your end. The supplier has to do the same at his end. And there are still the people who need to do the actual work. So, in the end, the number of people working on the project will increase.

- ✓ **Managing an external supplier is easier than managing internal suppliers.** You may think this at first, when the supplier wants your business. But, after the initial honeymoon, you'll soon realize that your firms may not have the same goals and that you don't have the same control over people in other firms that you do in your own firm. There's no common boss that can resolve disagreements short of the CEOs of both firms.

  Of course, you can always fire the supplier, but you'll end up harming your own firm because you won't have anyone to supply your component. The end result is that you have to manage external suppliers much more by persuasion than you would within your own firm.

- ✓ **You need fewer middle managers and can flatten your organization.** It's only going to look like your organization is flattening. The people who will manage these outsourced products, components, or services need to manage uncertainty, persuade and cajole, and hold perhaps hundreds of people accountable. This sounds very much like the job description for a middle manager. The only difference is that the people being managed aren't at your firm but at the supplier. Moreover, there are counterparts to your supplier management personnel at the supplier. So rather than flattening the organization, you'll probably add at least one layer of management!

Going into a partnership believing that everything will be easy is a recipe for failure. But take heart; we've worked with dozens of firms that have great outsourcing partnerships. How did they do it? By taking the time, being patient, and setting realistic expectations.

Bridging gaps

A number of issues can make managing an outsourcing partner especially difficult. Here are some of the challenges you need to address when developing an outsourcing relationship:

- **Culture:** Nations have their own distinct cultures. Initially, this can lead to many mistaken assumptions and crossed signals. A yes answer from a person from some nations may not indicate agreement but merely that she hears you and understands what you're saying. Some cultures like to solve problems themselves rather than communicate to you that they're having problems. Other cultures tend to be very abrupt and blunt (relative to North Americans), which can be interpreted as anger or frustration when it's nothing of the sort. In short, expect to be surprised at the number and variety of misunderstandings that occur when working with different cultures. The one bright side to this is that you'll get better at intercultural communication after a while, especially if you continue working with the same counterpart. And learning about new people, places, and customs can be one of the joys of working across national borders.

- **Geography:** Studies confirm that trying to coordinate with people in different time zones is difficult. For example, you're likely to have only a one- to two-hour window of overlapping work time each day to communicate by phone between North America and Asia. E-mails aren't any different because they just sit overnight before you can read them. In such situations, they may experience up to a 12-hour time lag each way, so resolving even a simple problem by e-mail often takes a day.

- **Industry:** Different industries have different cultures as well. For example, one automotive firm tried to outsource some of its electronic control modules to a well-respected consumer electronics contract manufacturer. However, the contract manufacturer came from an industry in which high quality for its products was 99 percent good. The supplier had difficulty reaching automotive standards of reliability, which are much higher, especially considering that a typical car has about 3,000 parts, and even if only 1 percent of the parts are defective, that means that 30 parts aren't working, which is likely to cripple the machine. In short, if your suppliers come from a different industry, don't make the assumption that they understand your requirements.

- **Language:** If you're reading this book, you'll most likely be communicating with your suppliers in one language (such as English). Fortunately, most suppliers have this capability. However, if the supplier's first language is not the same as yours, communication will be hard. Remember, you're probably having a discussion with your counterpart at the supplier in the first place because of some misunderstanding or technical difficulty. Communicating technical information across languages can be particularly challenging.

One helpful trick in these situations is double-confirmation. When you finish communicating something or giving an instruction, ask your counterpart to repeat to you in his own words what he thought you were trying to tell him. This catches a lot of potential miscommunications.

Integrating the product

Outsourcing a product is much like smashing Humpty Dumpty. After its components have been scattered to dozens of suppliers all over the world, all the king's men may have a very difficult job putting Humpty Dumpty back together again. Still, it can be done.

Figure 17-2 highlights several ways to span the boundaries between your firm and the supplier to solve the Humpty Dumpty problem. We discuss how to use them in the following list:

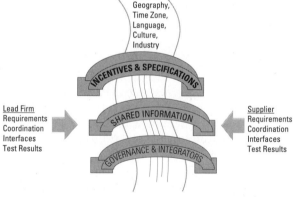

Figure 17-2: Integrating the project by spanning the boundaries.

Illustration by Wiley, Composition Services Graphics

✔ **Incentives:** Einstein said that physics models should be as simple as possible, but no simpler. Research suggests that incentives should follow the same formula. When incentives become overly complicated, they tend not to achieve their goals because they're difficult to properly spell out beforehand to cover all situations, they're prone to gaming and abuse, and they promote a contractual relationship as opposed to one based on trust and goodwill.

When developing incentives, you don't want to only reward what's easy to measure. Firms often incentivize suppliers based on cost. However, one way to save money is to shave on quality, which is hard to measure until the warranties and recalls come in. You also want to resist the temptation to nickel-and-dime suppliers. If you shave every possible cent from your suppliers, don't be surprised if they take that out of the product in some way.

✔ **Specifications:** Specifying what you actually want from your outsourced product, component, or service is surprisingly hard. Some of this difficulty is due to language and cultural assumptions. For example, an oil services project manager told us the following story:

"We make oil service equipment that involves literally miles of wires, as we put fiber optic cables down oil and gas wells. A couple of years ago, I was speaking with a client engineer in Malaysia on the phone. He asked me whether we had 'monkey-proofed' our equipment. We had big, colored, ergonomic buttons, user-friendly menus, and what not. It would be pretty hard to mess up the measurements. So I said, 'Sure, we've monkey-proofed it.'

"Fast-forward six months and we're in the jungle. Everywhere I look, there are hundreds of monkeys swinging on our wires and chewing on them. What our client really wanted was equipment that wasn't *foolproof* but literally monkey-proofed."

To give another perspective, consider the following. The U.S. Constitution is about 10 pages long as it was originally written. *The Federalist Papers,* written by proponents of the then-proposed Constitution, took 500 pages to explain it. This is approximately a 50:1 ratio. Even after that, there are still questions as to what the writers meant. Unfortunately, they are all dead, so it is difficult to give them a phone call.

One thing that research suggests helps in these situations is to explain not only what you want done but also why you want it done. This enables the supplier to figure out how to achieve your goals and make appropriate trade-offs. The supplier will probably arrive at better solutions than if you try to specify how to achieve these solutions yourself.

✔ **Modes of communication:** Remember the 60/30/10 principle. Some researchers argue that your body language conveys about 60 percent of your meaning, your tone conveys another 30 percent, and your actual words convey only 10 percent. Therefore, you should use the phone whenever possible if you have a tricky misunderstanding to resolve. If you can set up a good-quality video conference, that's even better (especially one that permits sharing drawings). However, if the video's resolution is poor, don't bother; it will just confuse the participants. A side effect of this principle is that you (or someone in your firm) is likely to do a lot of traveling to bridge the information gap because many things (such as brainstorming or negotiations) can be communicated much more effectively in person than over a phone, much less an e-mail.

✔ **Governance:** Make sure that you set up the governance issues to resolve any disagreements upfront. The last thing you want to do is negotiate both the disagreement and the resolution mechanism for that disagreement at the same time.

Related to this, one interesting recent research finding is that assigning some of the purchasing department's traditional functions for acquisition, negotiation, and quality assurance to the project managers responsible for the outsourced project can be beneficial for the project. However, this is only true if there are different first languages between your firm and the supplier. Apparently, the benefit of a single point of contact in such situations overbalances the additional leverage of a separate purchasing department conducting parallel negotiations with the supplier. If the supplier's first language is the same as yours, however, the purchasing function should perform its normal role.

✔ **Co-located personnel:** Many firms co-locate personnel from their firm at the supplier or vice-versa. Studies have shown that these personnel are quite helpful when there's either a big time-zone difference (see the earlier "Bridging gaps" section) between the lead firm and supplier, probably because it reduces the time-lag issue, or a difference in first languages between personnel at the lead firm and the supplier, probably because the 60/30/10 principle (see the earlier bullet) is particularly important when bridging languages. However, don't co-locate just to co-locate. Co-location seems to actually be counterproductive if there's no time-zone or first-language difference because it inserts another layer of management without any of the benefits of time-zone or language bridging.

✔ **Supply chain integrators:** These are the personnel that manage the outsourced project for your firm. Several things are helpful here. One is to realize that these are essentially middle managers because they're effectively managing potentially hundreds of people at a supplier. So using a rookie engineer with raw people skills to save on personnel costs isn't a good idea.

In fact, this job is even more difficult than a typical middle manager's job because of the need to be persuasive at a long distance while bridging all the language and cultural gaps involved. Simply put, managing by walking around may work very well in a firm that makes everything in house, but it doesn't work in an outsourced environment.

Your best bet are middle managers from vertically integrated firms that have experience in all the major aspects of the industry (in manufacturing, for example, they should have both product design and manufacturing experience). If you can't find such managers, people with hybrid backgrounds in business and engineering in college tend to do particularly well in these positions, probably because hybrid backgrounds tend to emphasize the following skills, which are essential to managing outsourced projects:

- **Decision-making:** Backgrounds in systems engineering (which teaches how to evaluate the business benefits of engineering trade-offs) are quite beneficial. So is experience in business case evaluation.

- **Project management:** Both the hard skills (cost and timing estimation, and risk identification and mitigation) and soft skills (communication, persuasion, and negotiation) are quite important.

  Research suggests that one- or two-day training courses in hard skills such as project cost and timing estimation work fairly well. However, one- or two-day classes in soft skills such as negotiation can be detrimental, probably because they train people just enough to be dangerous!

- **Domain knowledge:** The personnel can benefit from a broad (but not necessarily deep) knowledge of operations management (obviously!), product development (if appropriate), finance/budgeting, and information technology.

Integrators tend to get better with experience managing outsourced projects. But because of long hours talking to the other side of the world, extensive traveling, low pay relative to their skill set, and often unrealistic expectations by higher management, integrators burn out quickly. Given that they have steep learning curves, this is very bad news indeed. You may need to pay integrators more than you expect if you want to attract people with the strong skill sets you need and the tolerance for travel and odd work hours that the job requires.

Chapter 18

Scaling Operations throughout the Product Life Cycle

· ·

In This Chapter

▶ Implementing strategies for new products and those in the growth stage

▶ Meeting the challenges of maturing and dying products

▶ Preventing the decline of a product

▶ Heeding special considerations for new businesses

· ·

*P*roducts and services, like living organisms, have a natural life cycle. Products are conceived and nurtured, they mature, and eventually, they decline and fade away. Each phase of the cycle requires a different operating strategy.

In this chapter we take you on a journey through a product's life and describe how each life stage influences operating requirements. We start by introducing the common life stages that products typically evolve through and describe how best to manage each stage. We look at ways to prolong product life, and we also describe the special operating considerations of new companies.

Managing Operations Age-Appropriately

A product goes through four distinct stages as it evolves. These stages (illustrated in Figure 18-1) are quite similar to those of the human life cycle. For instance, at birth, a new product is much like a baby; it needs constant care and nurturing. For a product, this stage of existence is called *incubation*. After the product starts to get some traction in the marketplace, it enters a growth phase, where it can experience a tremendous sales explosion. Eventually, the product may experience a slower growth rate as it matures, saturates the market, and then enters a state of decline as newer products enter the market and take away market share.

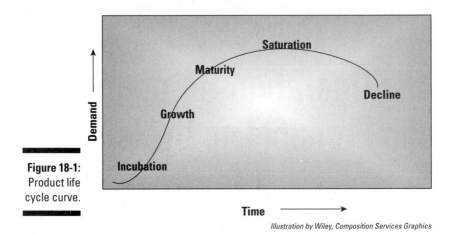

Figure 18-1:
Product life
cycle curve.

Different products move through this cycle at varying speeds. Some products, such as fashion apparel, move through the life cycle so quickly that you may miss them entirely if you blink. Other commodities, such as refrigerators and tax return preparation, may spend many years on the journey.

Table 18-1 highlights the operations strategy differences that exist in each stage of life for a product.

Table 18-1	Comparison of Product Life Stages			
Operating Decision	*Incubation*	*Growth*	*Maturity/ Saturation*	*Declining*
Demand forecasting	Unpredictable	Rapidly changing	Predictable	Declining and possibly more unpredictable
Production volume	Low	Increasing	Steady	Decreasing
Capacity	Flexible; mostly variable cost	Expanding to meet demand; may transition to fixed cost	Focus on efficiency and utilizations to reduce costs	Continued focus on efficiency and possible reallocation of capacity
Inventory	Minimal	May be used to smooth capacity	May be used to reduce needed peak capacity	Reduce as demand decreases

Operating Decision	Incubation	Growth	Maturity/ Saturation	Declining
Pricing	Generally high to maintain profit margins	Generally decreases as the product moves along the growth curve	Product becomes a commodity and price becomes a competitive advantage	Generally declining but in some cases can increase as the product becomes scarce
Supply chain	Flexible to produce low volumes quickly; usually single-sourced	Expanding to accommodate growth in demand; multiple sources may be required	Stable with an emphasis on efficiency	Decreasing; may benefit from single source within lower volumes
Competitors	Very few if any	Increasing	Established	Exiting
Quality	Emphasis on improving functionality of product	Focus on standardizing and improving processes for efficiency	Intensify focus on process improvement to reduce costs	Maintain process improvement but may shift focus to other products and processes

Swooning Over the Baby

New products are like babies — they need constant attention and they change rapidly. New products are said to be in the *incubation phase* and are typically prototypes; their design can change quickly in response to market reception. You must be flexible and responsive when managing a product in this phase.

The characteristics and operation strategies for a product in the incubation phase include low and unpredictable demand requiring minimal inventory and flexible capacity. These products tend to command a higher price because competition is scarce and the products are often considered novel.

Dealing with low demand

The market for products in the incubation stage is generally nonexistent or very small, and the demand for such products is highly unpredictable. Typically, these products are revolutionary and totally new to the market, which makes demand forecasting more difficult than it is for more established products. When attempting to forecast demand, you must rely on data that's often unreliable and on feedback from marketing efforts. (See Chapter 6 for more forecasting details.)

Because the market in the incubation phase is small or nonexistent, significant investment in marketing is required. You should focus this marketing effort on better defining the customer and on creating awareness of the product. You can often create demand by using lead customers to promote the product. Using this strategy, you can distribute the product at little or no cost to "beta" customers who can create a buzz surrounding the product and provide sources for product reviews. Apple has used this strategy to promote new products such as the iPod. No matter what strategy you use, it often takes significant time and energy to gain traction in the market.

Keeping capacity flexible

Because demand for new products is small and unpredictable, you must minimize your production costs. The incubation phase is characterized by high development and marketing expenses, which can drain cash flow, making it important to minimize fixed investments in production to preserve cash.

In the incubation phase, you should focus on producing products using a variable cost model. This may involve forgoing automation and using more manual labor until sales increase and you reach economies of scale. This is especially critical for a start-up company. Though an established company may be able to convert some of its existing capacity from an older product to the new one, a new company doesn't have this luxury. (See the section "Managing Start-up Operations" later in the chapter for info on the special needs of new companies.)

In addition, flexibility is key to driving down production costs, particularly if the design is still evolving. Outsourcing and using flexible labor to perform more than one task helps keep overhead and employment levels low. For a detailed discussion of capacity, turn to Chapter 7.

Minimizing inventory

Inventory decisions are especially difficult for new products with very low sales. You can use capacity levels and inventory to help maneuver the low and variable demand you face in the incubation phase. You need to keep capacity costs low, not maintain excess capacity, and minimize inventory to avoid being stuck with product that you may not be able to sell. So what should you do?

If possible, you want to produce only when you receive an order (called *make to order*). This policy, however, requires that you have very low production and delivery lead times because potential customers typically won't wait for a product, especially a new and unproven one. Few companies, particularly those who sell directly to consumers, have the privilege that Apple has earned to be able to sell everything it makes on pre-order before the product's release.

Instead, for most consumer products, you often must build inventory in advance so that you can instantaneously make it available to a potential customer. To be successful you must rely on your forecasting methods (see Chapter 6) and your marketing efforts to make sure you place the inventory where your customers are most likely to be.

You need to make the inventory and capacity decisions in concert because trade-offs exist in both. Developing flexible capacity allows you to be more nimble in production and possibly reduce the need for inventory. Outsourcing capacity may help you control production costs, but doing so may also require you to carry a greater quantity of inventory because of possible minimum production requirements of the supplier. If you do choose to outsource, you must make sure that your supply chain can support your needs, and if your product contains innovative technology or processes, you must make sure you properly protect your intellectual property.

Starting off with high pricing

During the incubation phase, you can often charge higher prices. With the proper marketing buzz surrounding a product, lead customers are often willing to pay a higher price to get the product first. You saw this phenomenon in consumer products when high-definition TVs first came out; they commanded a high price because of their novelty and their limited availability. Now this is being repeated for 3D TVs.

Many companies rely on higher pricing during the incubation phase to offset the initial development and marketing costs. Because of the upfront costs of introducing a new product, many products experience significant losses in this early stage. A high initial price allows firms to generate more cash to invest in marketing and in producing the product, and this can get the product to profitability quicker.

Although the high-price scenario seems to be the most common, you may sometimes benefit from starting a product at a relatively low price, which could more rapidly increase sales, allowing quicker market penetration and thus visibility to potential customers. After demand has increased, you may be able to raise the price point. However, this strategy can be dangerous because you may lose potential customers because of the price increase.

Designing a supply chain for a new product

Designing a supply chain for a new product can be challenging. Because of the low demand and required production volumes, getting favorable contract terms with a supplier can be difficult. Though pricing is always a priority, flexibility should be at the top of the list in the incubation phase.

Building a supply chain that can produce low volumes with small lead times is critical for new products. One incentive you can offer suppliers to get them to agree to producing smaller quantities while keeping costs low is to offer long-term contracts for the current product and engage the same suppliers on subsequent products. If you've successfully worked with a supplier before and have experienced mutual success with a past product, the supplier may be more willing to take a chance on any new product offerings. As lean manufacturers have learned, nothing is more advantageous than a lasting relationship with suppliers.

Defining a market with no competitors

New and innovative products face little or no competition when they're introduced. This lack of competition allows the *first-to-market* product to define the market and establish a customer base before competitors can enter, giving such products a commanding market share lead and advantage. Having no competition also allows you to charge the characteristically high price, as discussed earlier.

How long you're able to maintain your sole hold on the market depends on many industry and technological factors. Factors such as the ease (or lack thereof) of replicating the product and entering the market determine how fast competitors will enter.

Proper intellectual property protection can often hinder competition and allow you more time to establish your lead in the market.

Even if you are introducing a product with a competitor in the incubation stage, you are still in a position typically to charge a high price. You also have some leverage over defining the market as market tastes are not fully set yet, although less than if you were the first to come out with the product.

Avoiding failure in incubation

Almost any misstep in the incubation phase can kill a product. A primary mistake is a product with no sustainable market. Many times a product may catch on with a small niche market but quickly die as other new products capture the eye of the consumer. In most cases, the anticipated market never materializes beyond the initial niche market. This could be because of poor market research or because the product didn't perform as expected. For more information on how to effectively capture the needs of the customer and translate them into product functionality, flip to Chapter 12.

Another reason why products fail in incubation is because continuing to market and produce them becomes too expensive. New products are characterized by upfront losses. If these losses are too big or the time to profit is too long, you may have to pull the plug on the product before it can enter the growth phase. In extremely competitive industries, similar new products can hit the market at roughly the same time, requiring even more investment in marketing to gain sales. This competition also quickly drives down price, removing the expected higher revenue. The extent to which you are affected depends on how fast you can introduce or improve your products features versus how fast potential competitors can produce copycat products.

To avoid this painful and extremely expensive death, you can benefit from an agile product development process. Focusing efforts on product development facilitates a faster time to market with a superior product. Though product development is outside the scope of this book, see Chapter 12 to discover the *house of quality,* which successful firms often use in their product development process. Also see Part I for information on how to design efficient processes, because you can apply many of these techniques to the product development process.

Surviving the Awkward Stage of Quick Growth

You may think that after you make it through infancy, you have a clear path to success. This is anything but true; many products that make it out of the incubator fail in the growth phase. Just like the teenage years, the growth phase is almost always turbulent. The product faces both internal and external obstacles. Demand, market forces, and the competition are rapidly evolving.

The characteristics and operation strategies for a product in the growth phase include rapidly increasing and unpredictable demand, gradual increases in competition and decreases in product price, expanding your supply chain, and investing in developing standard processes to improve scalability and begin to reduce defects.

Adjusting to growing demand

Demand rapidly changes in the growth phase, making traditional forecasting methods especially unreliable (check out Chapter 6 for the lowdown on forecasting). You must observe the trend and adjust your inventory and capacity to meet this changing demand.

Another factor influencing demand is that the customer profile may be changing as the product penetrates the market. For example, in the incubation phase of a high-tech product, the primary customer is usually technically sophisticated, but later buyers may be less so. This change in customer may require product changes to make the product desirable to a larger market. In addition, you may introduce new features, increasing the product variety to appeal to a greater customer base. These changes may make inventory and capacity decisions more difficult.

Increasing capacity

When demand is unpredictable, producing enough product to meet it is difficult. Because bringing new capacity on-line by adding facilities, purchasing equipment, or hiring and training workers often requires time, you may find your capacity levels lagging behind demand.

During this growth phase, many companies transition to fixed capacity and make investments in automation and equipment. These assets allow you to increase production in an efficient manner at a lower cost structure, taking advantage of economies of scale.

Product proliferation often occurs during the growth phase. This increase in product variety requires that you maintain focus on keeping your capacity flexible to accommodate producing smaller volumes of more variations. You can benefit by designing products to be as similar as possible while at the same time maintaining product differentiation. This enables you to use the same manufacturing facilities to produce all varieties as much as possible.

During the growth phase, an emphasis on process improvement is vital to increase production and reduce costs out of the system. Production lead time takes on a critical role in your organization. By reducing the time it takes to produce a product, you can increase capacity and reduce the amount of inventory required to keep up with increasing demand. Part I takes an in-depth look at process design and reducing lead times.

Maintaining enough inventory

In the growth phase, inventory takes on a significant role in improving market position. Competition is usually fierce, and if you don't have your product on the shelf when the customer wants it, the customer will probably buy a competitor's product. Not only will you lose that sale, but it may cost you future sales and customer goodwill. (Turn to Chapter 8 for all you need to know about inventory.)

Most companies adapt some form of *make-to-stock* process (see Chapter 5 for details), producing to a forecast in anticipation of future demand. However, you can counterbalance the amount of inventory that you need to hold with effective capacity management and lead time reduction.

Slowly decreasing your pricing

Falling prices is a normal condition for most products in the growth phase due to the increase of competition in the marketplace. Many firms try to get around this decrease in price by introducing incremental changes to the product. When the new feature is released, the product is usually sold at a premium over the price of the older product. The new and improved product can either replace the existing one or be sold in tandem, offering multiple models with varying prices.

You can often turn a very nice profit at the lower price if you pay attention to reducing your costs and taking advantage of growing market opportunities.

Growing your supply chain

Just as the product is going through a growth spurt, so must the supply chain. As cutting costs to maintain profits becomes necessary, you should start looking at ways to make your supply chain more efficient. Though you don't want to alienate the suppliers that helped you through the incubation phase (you never know when you may need them again for your next new product), they need to grow with you and provide the levels of efficiency and service that you need in a growing market.

During the growth phase, you may consider offshoring or globalizing your supply chain. This is a complex decision, and you must consider many factors. Check out Chapter 17 for a detailed discussion of outsourcing. One benefit of globalizing your supply chain is that doing so can get you into new markets and expand the demand for your product.

Distinguishing your product from competitors' products

During the growth phase, the market size grows, and more and more competitors enter. This increased competition pushes prices down and puts a premium on quality products that are available on the shelf (or online) when the customer wants to purchase them. At the same time that you're focusing on quality, functionality, and availability, you must also continually look for ways to reduce costs.

Your marketing of the product can change during this phase as it becomes important to distinguish your product from the pack. The growth phase is when you build your brand, which requires establishing a product image and promoting the product to a mass market, usually through extensive advertising. The key is to place your product above the others in the eye of the customer and make it the one everyone must have.

Upping production to meet increased demand

Although a firm failing in the growth phase may seem implausible — after all, who could possibly fail with increasing demand? — companies often face their greatest challenges during this phase. In the incubation phase firms face little if any competition, and the entrance of competitors into the market often catches them off guard and unprepared to actually compete.

Perhaps the greatest cause of death in this phase is an inability to grow with the market. You may not have the capacity or the managing ability to keep up with the increasing demand. This results in lost sales because product isn't available, disappointing potential customers and sending them into the welcoming arms of entering competitors.

In an effort to increase production, be careful not to lose your focus on quality. This can have devastating results if you're trying to build a reputation in the market. A reputation for poor quality spreads through the marketplace very quickly and is often difficult to repair.

Getting Comfortable with Market Maturity

As a product matures, its sales usually level off as the market becomes saturated. This saturation phase is usually a relatively calm period in which the demand, products, and competition are stable. Despite the stability, this can be a challenging time for a company. Because the total market size is generally already determined, firms start looking for new ways to get a bigger slice of the existing pie by stealing market share from competitors.

The characteristics and operation strategies for a product in the saturation phase include steady customer demand, increasingly competitive pricing, and reducing costs and defects to gain market share.

Staying the course with steady demand

In the saturation phase, demand is fairly constant and predictable, and sales may be just to replace an existing product. The needs of the customer base are well known, and the rate of introduction of improvements decreases.

To increase sales in a market of constant size, you must find ways to increase market share at the expense of your competitors. You can accomplish this by continuing to reduce costs so you can reduce prices, focusing on ways to differentiate the product from the competition, and increasing marketing efforts. For more on ways to prolong entering the saturation phase before eventually entering decline, see the "Emerging Anew" section later in the chapter.

Exploiting predictable capacity

In the saturation phase, capacity is established, required levels are available, and reducing costs takes center stage. Production volumes peak during the saturation phase (refer to Figure 18-1), and these volumes allow you to take advantage of economies of scale. The predictable sales also allow you to better utilize automation equipment and to schedule production.

Reducing your inventory

The stable demand and efficient production characteristics of the saturation phase enable you to better manage inventory. Variability in demand often requires you to hold larger quantities of inventory to meet surges in customer demand. Because this variability is reduced in the saturation phase, you can reduce inventory levels while maintaining customer service levels. If you're curious about how variability influences required inventory levels, flip to Chapter 8.

Stable demand also reduces the risks of not being able to sell inventory. This reduced risk associated with inventory may allow you to use inventory to reduce the needed peak capacity, resulting in reduced capacity costs.

Offering competitive pricing

Products often become commodities in the saturation phase, meaning that customers have many substitute choices. At this point, price becomes a competitive advantage. Faced with similar products with equal quality levels, a customer typically purchases the lowest-priced product, leading to decreasing prices.

To gain market share and possibly force competitors out of business, you may have to force pricing wars, offering aggressive pricing at or even below cost to eliminate competition with the hope of increasing prices as you corner the market.

One way to counteract this pricing pressure without putting yourself on the verge of bankruptcy is to continue to market and build a brand where your product is considered superior to the others. Doing so can prevent your product from becoming a commodity and can protect it from the increasing price pressure.

Balancing a mature supply chain

By the time a product reaches the saturation phase, the supply chain should also be relatively mature. Chances are good that you've built solid relationships and that the supply chain runs smoothly. At this point, however, you may consider outsourcing some processes or even bringing some of the work back in-house to consolidate operations and maintain economies of scale, especially if demand could soon be in decline.

Gaining market share over your competitors

By the saturation phase, the competitors are usually established, and competition is fierce. Gaining market share becomes critical, and because the market as a whole is saturated, the only way to gain market share is to "steal" sales from the competitors. During this phase, some competitors may transition out of the market or, in some cases, may buy operations from or sell operations to, or merge with, a former competitor.

Foreseeing the market's decline

In the saturation phase, firms usually leave of their own volition as they see the decline of the market and the squeezing of profit margins. This may create a temporary advantage for those products remaining as they capture market share from those products exiting the market.

Preparing for the End

Most products reach a point at which sales start to decrease. This declining phase requires many important end-of-life decisions, such as when to permanently retire the product, how to handle the repair of existing products in the market, and what to do with current capacity.

The characteristics and operation strategies for a product in the decline phase include decreasing demand and prices, an emphasis on reducing costs through efficiency and reduction of inventory, shrinking your supply chain, and beginning to reallocate resources.

Adapting to decreasing demand

Demand for the product decreases during the decline phase. As it decreases, it often becomes less predictable. Just as it's important to capture the upward trend of the growth phase, it's equally important to capture the rate of the decline so that you can adjust capacity and inventory levels.

The decline phase may have an upside if you choose to stay in the market while competitors exit, leaving their market share behind. You may be able to increase sales. The pie is shrinking, but you can get a bigger piece, although this increase may be short-lived, depending on the rate of market decline.

Repurposing capacity

An important decision that you must make in this phase is if and when to exit the market. Declining sales may make it unprofitable to continue production. What to do with existing capacity that you no longer need is an important decision. You may look to repurpose the capacity to make other products, sell the resources (some companies may sell the product line entirely to a competitor), or just scrap the resources altogether.

One consideration in this decision is how to handle servicing existing products still in use by customers. This is an important concern, especially in durable consumer goods. You have several choices. You can cease production and stop servicing the product, although doing so may have serious repercussions on customer satisfaction and affect future sales of other products as customers fear not getting full use out of a product. To get around this, you may offer incentives for the customer to upgrade to a next-generation product if one is available.

You can also maintain a small capacity to make replacement parts as needed, carry a stockpile of parts in inventory for future replacement demand, or outsource the product entirely to a supplier that would take responsibility for the outgoing product.

Reducing inventory

As with capacity, you want to make efforts to reduce your inventory costs. However, if you choose to stop production altogether, you may want to build an inventory to serve the remaining market.

Making the most of lower pricing

Product prices tend to also decline in this phase. However, in some cases, prices may actually increase as the product and competing products become hard to find. Often, when a firm announces a product's exit from the market, consumers purchase the product before it becomes extinct. This buy-it-before-it's-gone mentality may temporarily raise the product's price.

Consolidating the supply chain

You'll probably be looking for ways to reallocate the supply chain to other products you're making or developing. You may consolidate suppliers to produce the lower volumes and to reduce costs.

Increasing sales as competitors exit

Competitors exit as the market declines. This may be an opportunity to increase sales for a brief period.

Emerging Anew

Some products, such as baking soda or refrigerators, are fortunate enough to never reach the decline phase; they remain in the saturation phase for eternity, usually at a lower sales level than they reached at their peak. This section covers a few strategies you can take to help prevent the decline of a product or to avoid it stalling out in the saturation phase.

Repositioning

One tried-and-true method of breathing new life into a product is to find alternate uses for it. Take baking soda. When sales for the product were in the saturation phase, manufacturer Arm & Hammer came up with a brilliant idea to take advantage of the product's odor-absorbing properties and started an advertising campaign suggesting that customers place whole boxes of the product in their refrigerator to keep it smelling fresh. Arm & Hammer even put a spot on the box where customers could record the date they placed it in the refrigerator, and the company recommended a regular replacement schedule. To exploit the advantages even further, the firm advised customers to dispose of the contents of the old box down the garbage disposal to keep their drains smelling fresh as well. (Basically saying, buy our product, take it home, and dump it down the drain!) Now you can find baking soda in a wide range of cleaning products.

Another familiar example that probably happened initially by accident is the wide use of duct tape. Initially created to be used on heating ducts, the tape is now the universal "go-to" for holding anything together. If you look around most homes, you're sure to find a roll or two, and most likely it isn't used for its intended purpose. In fact, you can probably find duct tape in almost any color. The array of alternate uses for duct tape took a product with a very limited market and made it a household product.

Making improvements

Companies have become wise to the fact that, by introducing even small improvements to their product, they can entice consumers to abandon the old product even though it still provides good service and to purchase a new one. The iPhone is a familiar example.

A classic example of how incremental improvements breathed new life into a product that was in its saturation phase is the refrigerator. Although the refrigerator will probably never enter a total decline, it had certainly reached a saturation point where most sales, especially in the United States, were replacement sales. Manufacturers have found that by continually introducing new features, they can persuade some consumers to replace their refrigerator long before it stops working and actually needs replacement.

The first major feature that sent consumers back to the store was the addition of the automatic ice maker. This was followed by the side-by-side door design that facilitated putting the ice and water dispensers on the outside. The newest design is the French-door model that fixes a major flaw of the side-by-side, which is that you can't fit a pizza box in without significant rearranging of shelves and contents. Making these incremental improvements is a creative way to get more revenue out of a product because the improvements continuously reset the product's position on the life cycle curve.

Changing the product portfolio

Rapidly changing technology has sped up the product life cycle and created the need for companies to introduce new products much more quickly. The computer industry has experienced these dynamics. The technology changed so rapidly at one point that a device could become obsolete within months of being purchased.

Figure 18-2 illustrates the introduction of a new product in its incubation phase, before the old one has completed its cycle. Two major risks are involved with the introduction of the new. If you introduce the new product too early, you'll cut off sales of the old, often before full profit materializes. On the other hand, if you wait too long, a competitor may beat you to market with a new product that steals sales from your existing product (and may hurt the introduction or your new product). These risks are why the timing of a new product that provides a replacement/alternative for an exiting product is such an important decision for companies in rapidly changing environments.

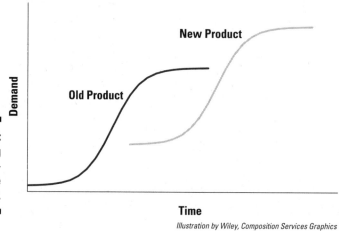

Figure 18-2:
Introducing
new prod-
ucts into the
market.

Illustration by Wiley, Composition Services Graphics

A key to success in this environment is to make sure that design and operations are well coordinated around the introduction of the new product. Operations employees must be well informed of the timing of new introductions because they may need to make process changes to make the new product and to reduce inventory levels of the old product before the new one hits the market.

Managing Start-up Operations

Managing the incubation phase and entering the growth phase is much easier for a company with multiple products in different phases of the curve than for one that has only one product that it's trying to commercialize. Not only does the multiple-product company already have a reputation, but also, the products in the growth phase can help fund and fuel those products trying to survive incubation. The products in saturation can also provide a base upon which to introduce new products. A new company trying to get its first product into the market doesn't have these advantages. In this section we present the special challenges facing a new company trying to get footing in the marketplace.

Operating on a shoestring

Though all businesses face financial constraints, the situation is often more critical in a new business attempting to introduce a new product into the market. Unlike established companies, a start-up doesn't have a recurring source of revenue upon which to support its development efforts. New companies typically operate on money raised directly from investors or on their own personal cash. Because more cash is flowing out than in, the firm must find ways to do more with less.

Above all it's important for a new company to stay flexible. Because of the inability to afford a large staff, the company's founders often have to take on multiple roles. They must handle not only the financials but also the design, production, and marketing of their product. This requires workers to be flexible and have a wide breadth of knowledge.

In terms of operations management in a new company, you must produce the product with as minimal an amount of cash outflow as possible. Doing so often involves outsourcing much of the initial production to keep costs variable rather than fixed to preserve cash.

Outsourcing is often a difficult decision for many companies that are worried about protecting their technologies from potential competitors. Proper intellectual property protection through the attainment of patents can protect you from these issues. However, the patent process can be very expensive and can take considerable time, eating up valuable resources.

Whether you produce in-house or outsource, maintaining flexibility in your capacity is important. For details on flexible capacity, see Chapter 7. For information on how to establish a flexible supply chain, visit Chapter 10, and for suggestions on how to protect core competencies and outsource, turn to Chapter 17.

Transitioning to growth

If you're a start-up, perhaps one of the greatest challenges you face is the transition to the growth phase of your product. This transition requires you to meet several needs:

- ✔ **Documented processes:** As the complexity of your organization increases, so does the need for defined and documented processes. These processes are necessary to promote smooth operations and planning. See Part I for more on designing processes to meet your organizational and product needs.

- ✔ **Organizational structure:** While in the incubation phase, you probably didn't have any policies or procedures in place. You may not have needed them because your staff was small, and everyone was up to speed on what was going on. However, with growth comes the need to add staff, giving rise to the organization chart, complete with a need for a reporting structure.

- ✔ **Systematic planning:** In the beginning of your new venture, you may have done things by the seat of your pants. Your staff may have acted on any opportunity that came along as quickly as possible. But as your enterprise matures and grows, planning becomes essential because coordinating the organization becomes more difficult.

- ✔ **Task specialization:** As you grow, the need for specialized individuals increases. Dedicated resources to such tasks as operations, marketing, and sales become increasingly important, and your firm may establish separate departments. This task specialization makes seeing the big picture more difficult and requires more coordination across the organization.

These changes can be difficult for those involved with a start-up. Larger companies often have different groups that take over product management as a product transitions from one phase to another. This is often necessary because the skills required in each phase tend to be different. Because the introduction of a new product is so unpredictable and fast-paced, individuals who thrive in such an environment don't often perform well in an environment that requires more structure, monitoring, and control.

Finally, as your firm grows, more control of the company must be delegated. This loss of control may be difficult for those involved in starting up a business, but without some delegation, the firm's growth may be stalled.

Part VI

The Part of Tens

Head to www.dummies.com/extras/operationsmanagement for ten questions to ask if you're considering a career in operations management.

In this part . . .

- Discover ten pivotal developments in operations management.
- Avoid ten mistakes that new operations managers often make.
- Explore ten common traits of successful operations.

Chapter 19

Ten Pivotal Operations Management Developments

In This Chapter

▶ Tracing the innovations that led to modern-day operations management

▶ Recognizing some pioneers who changed production and manufacturing methods

*W*hat's currently called *operations management* evolved from a long line of discoveries, inventions, and revolutions. You may find it hard to believe that there was a time when products weren't mass-produced and available on command. If a person wanted something, she had to make it or persuade someone to make it for her. In this chapter we highlight ten human developments that shaped operations management into what it is today and credit the people behind these developments.

Logistics

Beginning before the Roman legions, armies have always "marched on their stomachs" and developed increasingly robust methods to quickly move large quantities of food and supplies where needed. Thanks to those military needs, civilizations throughout the world have what's known today as *logistics*. UPS, a wildly successful shipping service, even hangs its sales and marketing hat on its highly refined level of logistics. And one might say that logistics is the foundation of what has become known as *supply chain management* (covered in Chapter 10).

Today, the Council of Logistics Management defines logistics as "the process of planning, implementing, and controlling the efficient, cost-effective flow and storage of raw materials, in-process inventory, finished goods, and related information from the point of origin to the point of consumption for the purpose of conforming to customer requirements."

Now, that's quite the definition when you consider that all the Roman legions wanted to do was position their troops and supplies near enough to their enemies to kill them!

Division of Labor

In his book, *The Wealth of Nations,* published in 1776, Adam Smith expounded the virtues of the division of labor. Up to this point, a single craftsperson would execute all the steps to produce a finished item, from sawing a log into boards to applying the final coat of varnish on a cabinet — a slow and costly process. This movement away from craft production fueled the Industrial Revolution. Division of labor helped workers become highly specialized and led to increased productivity. This division of labor was the foundation upon which Henry Ford built his empire, and the increased productivity is what allows humankind access to the wide array of affordable products and services available today.

Interchangeable Parts

The idea of using interchangeable parts — that one part could be substituted for another — made the concept of the assembly line possible. Previously, you couldn't even repair a broken machine with a part from another (same) machine without filing and adjusting the part. Each machine and its components were slightly different. Now, companies could place bins of identical components near an assembly line and use any of them to make the end product as it moved by. Eli Whitney popularized this concept when he applied it to the manufacturing of muskets in the late 1700s and early 1800s for the United States military.

Scientific Management

Scientific management is the study and analysis of processes and workflows. Frederick Winslow Taylor is regarded as the father of scientific management because he focused on industrial efficiency by breaking work into well-defined tasks with specific assigned times. His efforts were complemented by the work of Frank and Lillian Gilbreth, who studied exactly how tasks should be completed to remove any waste in effort and motion. Now standards could be set for ideally efficient production. The concept of scientific management reached its peak influence in the early 1900s and laid the foundation for mass production, which would revolutionize manufacturing. To see how craft production evolved into mass manufacturing and eventually into lean production, take a look at Chapter 11.

Mass Production

Combining logistics, division of labor, and interchangeable parts into standardized output, Henry Ford started the mass-production revolution when he implemented the moving assembly line in his plant in Highland Park, Michigan, to produce the Model T automobile. Mass production was further advanced by interchangeable parts and the use of standardized gauges to quickly measure the dimensions and quality of those parts. For more on mass production, see Chapter 11.

Statistical Quality Control

After World War II, consumers were flooded with mass-produced goods that were incredibly affordable thanks to mass production. The goods were so affordable that consumers could forgive the often shoddy quality and short life of the finished product. American manufacturers were forced to embrace quality only because of international competition. The high quality that Western consumers have come to expect in nearly everything they buy is the result of *statistical quality control* (a method of quality control that uses statistics). Walter Shewhart, an American physicist, engineer, and statistician, was at the heart of the application of statistical quality control, developing the *process control chart* (a method for monitoring process performance) and the concepts of *common* and *special cause variation* (variation that occurs in a process) in the early 1900s. (For more on these concepts, see Chapter 12.)

Inspired by Shewhart, W. Edwards Deming, after being shunned by American industry, took these principles to Japan after World War II. He introduced these statistical methods to Japanese industries, teaching them to countless Japanese engineers. Statistical quality control methods were pivotal to the success of Japanese manufacturing after World War II.

Deming also created the *plan-do-check-act cycle* (often referred to as the *Deming cycle*), upon which most other quality initiatives (including Six Sigma) are built. Today, the prestigious Deming Prize is awarded to companies for significant contributions to quality. See Chapters 12 and 13 for more on these quality topics.

Lean Manufacturing

Henry Ford's low-cost, mass-production revolution also created a legacy of large manufacturing runs and difficult model changeovers, particularly in the automobile industry. Lean manufacturing started with the Toyota Motor

Company and is often referred to as the *Toyota Production System.* The revolution began when Kiichiro Toyoda was looking for a way to save his failing company after World War II. Taiichi Ohno, inspired by the American grocery store, took the idea of providing frequent replenishment of small lots of inventory to the production floor, thus creating *just-in-time manufacturing.* Shigeo Shingo further enhanced lean manufacturing in the 1950s by developing the idea of quick changeover, where equipment could rapidly be changed from producing one product to another. See Chapter 11 for more on lean manufacturing principles.

Scientific Project Planning

The modern project-planning tools that operations managers use to plan and manage projects originally developed out of the work of several men:

- ✔ **Frederick Winslow Taylor**, in the early 1900s, produced the *work breakdown structure,* which separates a project into discrete tasks.

- ✔ **Henry Gantt**, in the 1910s, created what has come to be known as the *Gantt chart,* a bar chart that shows a project's schedule and helps identify where resource constraints exist.

- ✔ **Morgan Walker** and **James Kelley Jr.** identified the concept of the *critical path,* or those activities in a project that determine the project's overall timing for completion, in the 1950s.

The major impact of these tools was to introduce a far greater measure of control over the progress of complex projects, greatly enhancing the project manager's ability to anticipate and plan for future developments rather than having to react to a crisis when it occurred.

See Chapters 14, 15, and 16 for details on project management and how these tools improve scientific project planning.

Electronic Data Interchange

Electronic data interchange (EDI) is responsible for the transmission of data from one computer to another, allowing people to communicate digitally and enabling e-commerce. Perhaps the first known use of e-commerce was in 1910 by a group of florists who started the Florists' Telegraph Delivery Association to transmit flower orders throughout the country. The group, FTD, Inc., still brightens the days of many as it sends flowers throughout the world using modern EDI.

The standards of EDI in use today originated with the Berlin Airlift. Tracking the supplies sent into West Berlin by air was nearly impossible because of the lack of standardized documents and a common language. U.S. Army Master Sergeant Edward Guilbert, along with other logistics officers, invented a standard system that could be transmitted by several methods that reliably tracked the movement of supplies. Guilbert took this knowledge to DuPont after the war and developed a method to effectively communicate with suppliers. This evolved into the system that's used today to stock shelves and enable people to place an order with Amazon for the latest *For Dummies* book.

Supply Chain Management

The elements that make up what today is called *supply chain management* were started at Ford and Toyota. At his assembly plants, Henry Ford integrated an array of vertically integrated suppliers, and Toyota extended the management principles to include independent suppliers.

However, the term *supply chain management* wasn't coined until 1982 by Keith Oliver. The term didn't catch on until the 1990s, as companies really began in earnest to recognize the importance of the supply chain for success, something that Toyota had known for some time.

Supply chain management has become a management buzzword, but its importance to profitable business can't be underestimated. The complexity of managing a supply chain has increased significantly over the last few decades, as the number of suppliers to an individual company has increased and as these suppliers have become globally dispersed. Check out Chapter 10 for much more information on supply chains.

Chapter 20

Ten Mistakes That New Operations Managers Make

*E*veryone makes mistakes, especially when just starting out in a new job or activity. In this chapter we highlight the top ten mistakes that rookie operations managers tend to make. Don't feel too bad if you've made all of them; even experienced operations managers sometimes make them, too. But if you haven't yet slipped up on these missteps, just knowing about them increases your chances of avoiding them.

Beginning an Improvement Journey without a Map

Perhaps the most frequent mistake that even experienced operations managers make is not documenting their existing processes. In any process-improvement project, knowing where you start from is essential. How do you know whether you made any improvement if you don't know where you started? Although this initial documentation is often considered a waste of time because you end up changing it anyway, documenting the current process uncovers where in the process trouble spots exist — believe us when we say that what's wrong isn't always obvious — and is well-worth the time and effort.

If you have existing process documentation, by all means use it. However, your task in this case becomes to check that the actual work and workers follow the documented process. It's not unusual to find that workers aren't following a documented process. These discrepancies can also point you to process trouble spots.

Running without Metrics

Make sure that you measure the performance of the operations in the process. These metrics must be quantitative, relevant, and fairly easy to obtain. You want to take several different measurements, including these basics:

- ✔ How long each operation takes to complete its task
- ✔ Time needed for one product to get through the process from start to finish
- ✔ How much work each operation can complete in any given time period
- ✔ Quantity of inventory in the process
- ✔ An operation's level of consistency
- ✔ How well a product conforms to standards

Avoid measuring too many things, though, because you can get lost in data, which means you may get distracted from the most vital metrics. For more on performance metrics, take a look at Chapter 2.

Creating Overly Complex Processes

Simple is always better when it comes to designing processes, so avoid the temptation to develop overly complex processes. A common thing that happens in established processes is that steps and activities are added, often as a work-around for a broken operation, and those steps become a permanent part of the process, adding to the complexity.

When documenting and analyzing a process, be on the lookout for the statement, "Well, we've just always done it this way." Chances are good that you can greatly simplify a process that's related to such a statement. Also watch for processes that no one can fully describe. These processes are often too complex for the task they're supposed to accomplish. For tips on how to simplify processes, see Chapters 3, 4, and 5.

Missing the Real Bottleneck

If you don't properly analyze a process, you'll probably misidentify the bottleneck. The *bottleneck* is that resource that limits the process's production and is the resource with the smallest capacity. If you misidentify the bottleneck (or, worse, don't identify it at all), you'll waste time and money adding capacity to something that isn't actually limiting your production in the first place.

People often assume that the bottleneck is the most expensive or biggest piece of equipment in the system and mistakenly add capacity to it. Make sure you carefully analyze the process so you don't succumb to this faulty assumption. Find details about bottlenecks in Chapters 2 and 3.

Managing Based on Utilization

Many managers mistakenly think that their resources must be continuously working. Nothing is further from the truth, and this mentality only adds to the quantity of work-in-process inventory. The only resource that needs to be working 100 percent of the time is the bottleneck, and that's only if demand for it exists.

A big problem is that, unfortunately, operations managers are often evaluated on the utilization of resources. In this situation, keep in mind that the utilization metric is probably the worst one to use if you're concerned with the financial health of the company. Focusing on the utilization of the bottleneck is important, but for other steps in a process, you want to focus on eliminating waste and improving quality to improve operations overall. For more on utilization, flip to Chapters 2 and 3.

Not Standardizing

Standardizing processes — or designing processes that follow the same standards — is important to reduce complexity, and simple is always better. Standardization is especially important when more than one facility is producing the same product. Can you imagine what the impact on quality might be if every McDonald's franchise used a different process to assemble a cheeseburger and prepare French fries? Standardization allows a company to produce consistent quality in both products, and services.

Automating Bad Processes

If a process isn't performing as desired, you may assume that automating it can lead to improvement. But an automated bad process is still a bad process, no matter how much automation you implement.

W. Edwards Deming, an American quality guru who revolutionized Japanese manufacturing after World War II, once stated, "Workers are responsible for only 15 percent of the problems; the process, for the other 85 percent."

Many companies use enterprise management systems (covered in Chapter 9) to integrate and manage their processes. But these systems are expensive and time-consuming to implement and maintain, and they're only as good as the underlying processes. Until a company can fix its faulty processes, these expensive systems can't provide much help.

Misdefining Quality

No matter what you may think about a process or what you may be measuring, quality is what the customer says it is! When operation managers and company leaders forget this fact, they waste time and money on improving aspects of the product or service that may not be important in terms of profitability or customer satisfaction.

In other words, just because an output meets corporate target quality measurements doesn't mean that customers perceive it as a quality product. Creating quality products requires a company to know exactly what customers define as quality. Knowing what the customer wants makes it possible to develop a process to deliver it.

Another mistake to avoid is assuming that the definition of quality stays the same over time. Customer desires and tastes change constantly, and companies must adjust to meet these shifting requirements.

Don't compromise quality to meet schedule or cost pressures because this may lead to dissatisfied customers and product defects that in turn can lead to recalls, litigation, and a damaged reputation. Quality failures can put companies out of business. See Chapter 12 to find more on quality.

Not Doing Enough Project Planning Upfront

Here are some major rookie mistakes related to project management:

- ✔ Inadequate upfront planning
- ✔ Using one estimate for timing and cost rather than range estimates that recognize variability
- ✔ Not properly identifying the critical path

The *critical path,* much like a bottleneck (see Chapter 3), is that path of activities that determines the project's timing (details on finding the critical path are in Chapter 15). Failing to identify the critical path leads project managers to focus on the wrong activities at the wrong points in time. Proper upfront planning can help eliminate this mistake.

Find details on how to plan projects in Chapter 14.

Not Focusing on the Customer

Never forget that the customer is always right. Operations managers often forget the end customer — the person who ultimately buys the product or service. Instead, some OMs focus on internal performance metrics that have no consequence to the customer. Staying focused on what the customer actually wants requires a close link between operations and other departments, such as product development and marketing.

Chapter 21

Ten Traits of World-Class Operations

In This Chapter

▶ Being aware of your customers' changing wants and needs

▶ Improving your products and processes continuously

▶ Keeping things simple

*W*hat makes a company *world class,* or the best at what it does? Consumers can say why they like a certain product or service — and why they don't. But a firm's operations are a pivotal element in what customers experience. Operations spend company money, interface with customers, and make achieving business goals possible.

So what makes the operations behind a product or service world class? How do the operations produce the products and services that customers demand in a way that makes it profitable to their stakeholders? In this chapter, we point out common characteristics of companies that are generally considered to be world class.

Knowing Thyself

Successful companies have an intimate understanding of what they do well and what they don't do so well. They know their competencies and exploit them to get ahead of their competitors. This objective self-assessment is particularly critical for operations. They also realize what they don't know and outsource those items. For example, Apple knows how to design consumer electronics and they excel at it; they also know that they don't have the manufacturing expertise to cost effectively manufacture the products. That's why they outsource this part of the business. Find information on strategic outsourcing and core competencies in Chapter 17.

Companies that have well-documented processes and procedures in place to measure performance and control their processes are a giant step ahead of competitors that don't. Just keep in mind that knowing one's own processes doesn't mean that said processes are flawless; it just means that the company is aware of the status quo. You know where the blemishes are, and you're potentially working to improve them.

Possessing Profound Knowledge of the Customer

Companies that fully and genuinely realize that their customers are the lifeblood of the business know that they must provide the product and services that customers want, when they want them, and at a price they're willing to pay. Successful companies know who their customers are and what those customers expect from their product or service. They aim all efforts at improving the customer experience and are rewarded with loyal customers willing to buy their products — in some cases, again and again and again.

Focusing Intensely on Quality

When companies know that quality is what their customers say it is and devote their efforts to ensuring that products and services meet customer requirements, then customers are happy.

World-class businesses realize that disappointed customers are more vocal about their displeasure than satisfied customers are about their satisfaction. One bad experience with a product can cause a company to lose a customer forever, and a tarnished reputation is difficult to repair. If you need proof, just take a look at customer product reviews on any website. The number and passion of customers who had a bad experience are greater than those who write about a positive experience.

Quality is built into the process of well-built products and carefully considered services. Quality is woven into world-class operations. Effort invested in improving quality is rewarded with increased customer satisfaction.

Adapting to Change

The only certainty in business is change. Everything changes, and world-class operations are ready to adjust to changes in the business environment that threaten their profitability. Companies face technology shifts that make current products obsolete; new competitors enter the marketplace; and evolving customer requirements require changes to product specs, timing, and other elements of the output. This requires that firms be innovative and evolve to adjust to changes. World-class companies are agile enough to adjust their processes to accommodate changes in the business environment.

Getting Better All the Time

Some companies know that they always have room for improvement, and they continuously strive to get better. These companies benchmark competitors and other businesses outside their industry to find better ways to do things, and they utilize some form of the plan-do-check-act cycle (find details on process improvement tools in Part III). These good habits of operations management enable firms to identify problems quickly and implement improvements.

Just keep in mind that process improvement isn't a one-time project with a distinct beginning and end; it's a process itself that's continuous and sincere.

Appreciating Employees

When a company is truly dedicated to the people who create and deliver its products and services — and demonstrates its appreciation — it is rewarded with a workforce dedicated to the success of the company. A highly motivated workforce that's properly compensated tends to produce the best quality products and provide the best service to customers.

Today's workforce seems to know that compensation isn't strictly the size of a paycheck; people also care about how they're treated on the job. Training, adequate resources, career advancement opportunities, and recognition for a job well done are important aspects of being appreciated as employees.

Paying Constant Attention to Product Offerings

Choosing the types of products and services to offer in the marketplace is a critical decision for most businesses. Realizing that customers are not alike, companies often offer a portfolio of products. You've probably encountered this when shopping for appliances or electronics. Individual companies offer a range of products — from DVD players to refrigerators to washing machines — and produce different models within these categories to hit various price points and appeal to various types of consumers. Successful firms realize that different market segments shop and buy according to different requirements.

For example, the new college graduate moving into her first apartment requires different features in a washing machine than a busy working mother of five. Successful companies know how to offer this variety while exploiting the similarities of the product portfolio to make manufacturing profitable. For techniques such as commonality that enable companies to offer the demanded product variety in a cost-effective manner, see Chapters 8 and 11.

Using Relevant Process Metrics

Companies that know the importance of measuring process performance and can identify the few core metrics that drive their success avoid the analysis paralysis that some firms experience when they collect too much unnecessary data. Focusing only on metrics that drive customer satisfaction and reduce costs enables companies to provide products that customers want at prices that generate profit. For more on operations performance metrics, check out Chapter 2.

Balancing Respect and Expectations for the Supply Chain

Making sure that suppliers are well trained and involved in company processes, even during process development, demonstrates a firm's appreciation for its supply chain. Long-term relationships with key suppliers are essential to assuring that suppliers are invested in the company's success. And it helps if the company shares its success with the supply chain businesses because this creates a win-win situation for everyone involved. In other words, a firm's relationship with a supplier should be more like a marriage than a one-night stand.

In exchange, operations should expect that suppliers will have the company's best interest at heart and make their best efforts to provide the quality, price, delivery, and responsiveness the business needs to succeed. See Chapter 10 for more on supply chain management.

Avoiding Unnecessary Complexity

Unnecessary complexity in operations generates confusion and adds more places where things can go wrong. It increases the difficulty of managing processes, even in the best of circumstances. Disruptions in the form of absentee workers, broken machines, missing raw material, weather delays, and more occur all the time in operations.

Adaptability and contingency planning are hallmarks of best-in-class operations. Design of robust processes that can handle disruptions well, and planning for contingencies like adequate spare parts or an on-call list of workers, can help mitigate disruptions.

See Chapters 3, 4, 5, and 11 for information on reducing complexity in operations.

Index

• *Q* •

About the Authors

Mary Ann Anderson is an operations consultant and an adjunct professor in operations management at the University of Texas McCombs School of Business. She has served as the faculty advisor for the Supply Chain Management and Engineering route to business majors and teaches numerous courses, ranging from manufacturing and service operations management to project management to supply chain strategy and logistics, as well as being an instructor in the Master of Science in Technology Commercialization program. She received a master's in engineering, concentrating in operations engineering, from the Massachusetts Institute of Technology. She received her bachelor's in electrical engineering from Kettering University (formerly the General Motors Institute), with a minor in business administration.

Ms. Anderson is also an active consultant. She specializes in operations management, business process analysis and improvement, supply chain management, and project management. She has developed integrated strategy-marketing-operations computer simulations using the system dynamics computer simulation methodology for multiple firms, and she has published articles in such journals as *The Systems Thinker*.

Ms. Anderson has served as a manufacturing strategist for a start-up firm, and her consulting clients include such firms as Ford Motor Company, Sony Entertainment, HP, and Shell, as well as the National Aeronautics and Space Administration (NASA) and the state of Texas. Prior to her teaching and consulting work, she held a variety of positions as an engineer for the General Motors Corporation.

Dr. Edward G. Anderson, Jr., is an associate professor of operations management at the University of Texas McCombs School of Business and an IC2 Institute Research Fellow. He is the faculty advisor for the BBA in the Science and Technology Management program and codirector for research for the McCombs Health Care Delivery Innovation Initiative. He received his doctorate from the Massachusetts Institute of Technology and his bachelor's degree, with majors in history and electrical engineering, from Stanford University.

Dr. Anderson's research interests include outsourced product development (distributed innovation) and project management, knowledge management, supply chain management, and computer simulation. He also has published research in national security, particularly counterinsurgency policy. He has published articles in *Management Science, Organization Science, Production and Operations Management, MIT Sloan Management Review,* and *System Dynamics Review*. He is also the coauthor of the book *The Innovation Butterfly: Managing Emergent Opportunities and Risks During Distributed Innovation,* which describes leadership metrics, planning, and organization in the complex adaptive system that is innovation management.

Dr. Anderson won the prestigious Wickham Skinner Early-Career Research Award from the Production and Operations Management Society. He has received research grants from the National Science Foundation (twice), SAP, and Hewlett-Packard. He is the department editor of *Production and Operations Management* for Industry Studies and Public Policy and president-elect of the System Dynamics Society for 2013. Professor Anderson has consulted with Ford, Shell, Dell, and multiple other corporations and holds six U.S. and E.U. patents from his prior career as a product design engineer at the Ford Motor Company.

Dr. Geoffrey Parker is professor of management science at Tulane University in the A. B. Freeman School of Business and serves as director of the Tulane Energy Institute. He is also a faculty fellow at the MIT Sloan School's Center for Digital Business. Parker received a bachelor's in electrical engineering and computer science from Princeton University, a master's in electrical engineering (technology and policy program) from MIT, and a PhD in management science from MIT. He has spent much of his career studying coordination in supply chains, especially when firms outsource complex work. Dr. Parker has also contributed to the field of network economics and strategy as codeveloper of the theory of "two-sided" markets. Dr. Parker's work appears in journals such as *Harvard Business Review, MIT Sloan Management Review, Energy Economics, Journal of Economics and Management Strategy, Management Science, Production and Operations Management, Strategic Management Journal,* and *System Dynamics Review.*

Dr. Parker has worked on projects with multiple firms, including AT&T, Cellular South, Chrysler, ExxonMobil, Hewlett Packard, IBM, International Postal Corporation, Microsoft, PJM, SAP, Thomson Reuters, and the United States Postal Service. Current research includes studies of distributed innovation, business platform strategy, and the design and performance of energy markets. His research is funded by grants from the National Science Foundation, the U.S. Department of Energy, and multiple corporations. He serves or has served as a National Science Foundation panelist and associate editor at multiple journals and is currently president-elect of the Industry Studies Association. Dr. Parker grew up in Oxford, Ohio, where he worked as an electronics technician and machinist in the Instrumentation Laboratory at Miami University. Before graduate school, he held multiple positions in engineering and finance at General Electric in North Carolina and Wisconsin.

Dedication

To the faculty at the MIT Sloan School of Management, who shared with us their profound knowledge of operations management. Specifically, we'd like to thank Dmitris Bertsimas, Gabriel Bitran, Steve Eppinger, Charlie Fine, Steve Graves, John Sterman, Karl Ulrich, Larry Wein, and Dan Whitney.

Authors' Acknowledgments

We'd like to acknowledge all the people who've influenced our thinking in operations management. In addition to the MIT faculty mentioned above, this includes the professionals we've worked for throughout our careers, especially Bill Colwell, who introduced one of the authors to the wonderful world of operations early in his career. We'd also like to thank the many industrial leaders and clients that we've had the pleasure to work with. They provided many of the examples that are used in this book.

In addition, we'd like to thank the many students that we've taught throughout our years at the University of Texas and Tulane University. They've taught us the best ways to communicate the information contained in this book. A special thank-you goes to the spring 2013 Operations Management and Master's in Science and Technology Commercialization students at the University of Texas, who provided feedback on the chapter contents. Edward Anderson would also like to thank John Butler and the IC2 Institute for all their support during his writing efforts.

Finally, we would like to acknowledge the staff at Wiley, especially Erin Calligan Mooney, Jenny Brown, Chrissy Guthrie, and Todd Lothery for all the hard work and dedication they put into this book.

Publisher's Acknowledgments

Acquisitions Editor: Erin Calligan Mooney

Senior Project Editor: Christina Guthrie

Project Editor: Jenny Larner Brown

Copy Editor: Todd Lothery

Technical Editors: Byron Finch, PhD;
  Karl E. Lyon; Gene Thornhill, MBA

Project Coordinator: Katherine Crocker

Cover Image: ©iStockphoto.com/Palto

Apple & Mac

iPad For Dummies,
5th Edition
978-1-118-49823-1

iPhone 5 For Dummies,
6th Edition
978-1-118-35201-4

MacBook For Dummies,
4th Edition
978-1-118-20920-2

OS X Mountain Lion
For Dummies
978-1-118-39418-2

Blogging & Social Media

Facebook For Dummies,
4th Edition
978-1-118-09562-1

Mom Blogging
For Dummies
978-1-118-03843-7

Pinterest For Dummies
978-1-118-32800-2

WordPress For Dummies,
5th Edition
978-1-118-38318-6

Business

Commodities For Dummies,
2nd Edition
978-1-118-01687-9

Investing For Dummies,
6th Edition
978-0-470-90545-6

Personal Finance
For Dummies,
7th Edition
978-1-118-11785-9

QuickBooks 2013
For Dummies
978-1-118-35641-8

Small Business Marketing Kit
For Dummies,
3rd Edition
978-1-118-31183-7

Careers

Job Interviews
For Dummies,
4th Edition
978-1-118-11290-8

Job Searching with
Social Media
For Dummies
978-0-470-93072-4

Personal Branding
For Dummies
978-1-118-11792-7

Resumes For Dummies,
6th Edition
978-0-470-87361-8

Success as a Mediator
For Dummies
978-1-118-07862-4

Diet & Nutrition

Belly Fat Diet For Dummies
978-1-118-34585-6

Eating Clean For Dummies
978-1-118-00013-7

Nutrition For Dummies,
5th Edition
978-0-470-93231-5

Digital Photography

Digital Photography
For Dummies,
7th Edition
978-1-118-09203-3

Digital SLR Cameras &
Photography For Dummies,
4th Edition
978-1-118-14489-3

Photoshop Elements 11
For Dummies
978-1-118-40821-6

Gardening

Herb Gardening
For Dummies,
2nd Edition
978-0-470-61778-6

Vegetable Gardening
For Dummies,
2nd Edition
978-0-470-49870-5

Health

Anti-Inflammation Diet
For Dummies
978-1-118-02381-5

Diabetes For Dummies,
3rd Edition
978-0-470-27086-8

Living Paleo For Dummies
978-1-118-29405-5

Hobbies

Beekeeping
For Dummies
978-0-470-43065-1

eBay For Dummies,
7th Edition
978-1-118-09806-6

Raising Chickens
For Dummies
978-0-470-46544-8

Wine For Dummies,
5th Edition
978-1-118-28872-6

Writing Young Adult Fiction
For Dummies
978-0-470-94954-2

Language &
Foreign Language

500 Spanish Verbs
For Dummies
978-1-118-02382-2

English Grammar
For Dummies,
2nd Edition
978-0-470-54664-2

French All-in One
For Dummies
978-1-118-22815-9

German Essentials
For Dummies
978-1-118-18422-6

Italian For Dummies
2nd Edition
978-1-118-00465-4

Available in print and e-book formats.

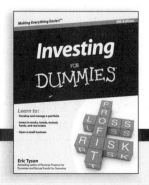
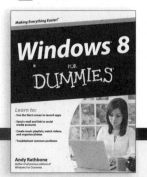

Math & Science

Algebra I For Dummies,
2nd Edition
978-0-470-55964-2

Anatomy and Physiology
For Dummies,
2nd Edition
978-0-470-92326-9

Astronomy For Dummies,
3rd Edition
978-1-118-37697-3

Biology For Dummies,
2nd Edition
978-0-470-59875-7

Chemistry For Dummies,
2nd Edition
978-1-1180-0730-3

Pre-Algebra Essentials
For Dummies
978-0-470-61838-7

Microsoft Office

Excel 2013 For Dummies
978-1-118-51012-4

Office 2013 All-in-One
For Dummies
978-1-118-51636-2

PowerPoint 2013
For Dummies
978-1-118-50253-2

Word 2013 For Dummies
978-1-118-49123-2

Music

Blues Harmonica
For Dummies
978-1-118-25269-7

Guitar For Dummies,
3rd Edition
978-1-118-11554-1

iPod & iTunes
For Dummies,
10th Edition
978-1-118-50864-0

Programming

Android Application
Development For
Dummies, 2nd Edition
978-1-118-38710-8

iOS 6 Application
Development For Dummies
978-1-118-50880-0

Java For Dummies,
5th Edition
978-0-470-37173-2

Religion & Inspiration

The Bible For Dummies
978-0-7645-5296-0

Buddhism For Dummies,
2nd Edition
978-1-118-02379-2

Catholicism For Dummies,
2nd Edition
978-1-118-07778-8

Self-Help & Relationships

Bipolar Disorder
For Dummies,
2nd Edition
978-1-118-33882-7

Meditation For Dummies,
3rd Edition
978-1-118-29144-3

Seniors

Computers For Seniors
For Dummies,
3rd Edition
978-1-118-11553-4

iPad For Seniors
For Dummies,
5th Edition
978-1-118-49708-1

Social Security
For Dummies
978-1-118-20573-0

Smartphones & Tablets

Android Phones
For Dummies
978-1-118-16952-0

Kindle Fire HD
For Dummies
978-1-118-42223-6

NOOK HD For Dummies,
Portable Edition
978-1-118-39498-4

Surface For Dummies
978-1-118-49634-3

Test Prep

ACT For Dummies,
5th Edition
978-1-118-01259-8

ASVAB For Dummies,
3rd Edition
978-0-470-63760-9

GRE For Dummies,
7th Edition
978-0-470-88921-8

Officer Candidate Tests,
For Dummies
978-0-470-59876-4

Physician's Assistant Exam
For Dummies
978-1-118-11556-5

Series 7 Exam
For Dummies
978-0-470-09932-2

Windows 8

Windows 8 For Dummies
978-1-118-13461-0

Windows 8 For Dummies,
Book + DVD Bundle
978-1-118-27167-4

Windows 8 All-in-One
For Dummies
978-1-118-11920-4

 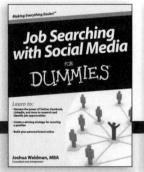  

e **Available in print and e-book formats.**